CAMEMBERT

CALIFORNIA STUDIES IN FOOD AND CULTURE

Darra Goldstein, Editor

CAMEMBERT

A National Myth

Pierre Boisard

Translated from the French by Richard Miller

University of California Press   Berkeley   Los Angeles   London

Le Camembert, Mythe National
Pierre Boisard
© Calmann-Lévy, 1992

University of California Press
Berkeley and Los Angeles, California

University of California Press, Ltd.
London, England

© 2003 by
The Regents of the University of California

Library of Congress Cataloging-
in-Publication Data

Boisard, Pierre.
  [Camembert. English]
  Camembert : a national myth / Pierre
Boisard ; translated from the French by
Richard Miller.
        p.   cm.—(California studies in food
and culture ; 4)
Includes bibliographical references (p.   ).
ISBN 0-520-22550-3 (cloth : alk. paper)
  1. Camembert cheese—History. 2. Cheese
industry—France—History. I. Title. II.
Series.
SF272.C33 B6513 2003
637'.353—dc21   2002154217
Manufactured in the United States of America

10 09 08 07 06 05 04 03 02 01
10 9 8 7 6 5 4 3 2 1

The paper used in this publication is both
acid-free and totally chlorine-free (TCF).
It meets the minimum requirements of
ANSI/NISO Z39.48–1992 (R 1997) ∞

*The publisher gratefully acknowledges
the generous contribution to this book
provided by the French Ministry of Culture.*

To Danièle

CONTENTS

Camembert, the odorous emblem of France, is the most popular cheese in a country known for its multitude of cheeses. Charles de Gaulle made a well-known reference to his country's great variety of cheeses when explaining to Winston Churchill the difficulties facing anyone attempting to govern France. Far from being some arcane witticism, de Gaulle's quip perfectly reflected the astonishing diversity of an overcentralized modern nation striving to be indivisible. The general might have added, "Fortunately, Camembert appeared and became a national symbol."

Chosen by the French virtually by acclamation (as the general would be), Camembert became France's most popular cheese in the 1920s, and it has maintained that position ever since. Abroad, it is automatically associated with its country of origin. Its popularity goes far beyond mere gastronomy; it appears almost everywhere, from comic strips—beginning with the well-known *Sapeur Camember* of Georges Colomb (known as Christophe[1])—to colloquial expressions.

Such a strong identification cannot be put down to mere chance, nor can it be without some greater significance. But what might that be? Will dissecting the cheese itself help us to grasp intimate aspects of the French nation? Do the present-day inhabitants of Gaul view Camembert in the same way that certain Amazonian tribes are said to view the yam, both as their favorite food and as a mythical object onto which they have projected their history, something that provides them with a concrete symbol of their origins? As a long-time devotee of the cheese, I set out to trace

Camembert back to its origins, guided only by these few vague and intuitive notions. Little did I suspect the problems I would encounter.

In the beginning, the project seemed quite simple. I had a few lines of inquiry in mind and a fairly straightforward plan of attack. I thought that I would only need to make a systematic investigation, both spatial and temporal. I was hardly embarking on the unknown given that the history of Camembert seemed solidly documented. The date and circumstances of its creation were well known. The familiar round shape of my subject was reassuring. Yet, although I had believed that my quest would be fairly easy going, I soon discovered that nothing that had been said about the cheese could be fully substantiated in fact. What had been accepted as the true story of Camembert did not hold up under investigation. The clear historical narrative turned out to be a legend filled with contradictions. I found that I would have to check everything and to question what had seemed most certain. Rather than attempt to establish the true story of Camembert, therefore, I chose to write the story of its myth, to try to situate it in its time and place, and to understand the context in which it had emerged, the better to understand its message.

It may seem questionable and even inaccurate to use the term "myth" with regard to Camembert, and especially the term "national myth." It is one thing to see "La République" on the label of a box of Camembert, but quite another to try to interweave their histories and turn a cheese into a national emblem on the pretext that its legendary creation coincided almost exactly with that of the creation of the République itself. Such an approach to writing history can quite rightly be qualified as cavalier. But I hope to be forgiven the incongruity, for I am indeed going to attempt to draw a parallel between the history of France and the history of Camembert cheese.

The myth of Camembert and its many versions and forms, all multifaceted, have fascinated me because its naive legend includes some of the better-known historical figures of the past two centuries and embodies some of the principal concerns of the French as a people and as a nation. Napoleon III, Louis Pasteur, Maréchal Joffre, Alexandre Millerand, and many others have crossed paths with Camembert cheese. Each stage of Camembert's history reflects some crucial juncture in the history of

France and its societal problems. In recounting the story of Camembert, and in analyzing the changes the story has undergone, one is constantly brought back to the evolution of the nation itself. In recounting Camembert's picturesque adventures, I intend to examine, from a different angle, some of the great moments in France's history and some of the characteristic traits of its national identity.

Chapter 1 | A MYTH IS BORN

THE AMERICAN AND CAMEMBERT

Sunday, 11 April 1928: Vimoutiers, a small village in Normandy, is having a celebration. The streets are thronged with a lively crowd made up of the local population and others who have flocked into town from the surrounding countryside. The Eastertide fair with its carnival attractions is not the only reason for the festive atmosphere, for the people have gathered to witness a unique event. They are awaiting the arrival of Alexandre Millerand, former president of the Republic and senator from the Orne. The well-known statesman is to unveil a monument to the memory of Marie Harel, the local heroine who did so much for Normandy and for France.

It is a cloudy day, presaging the showers that will soon, if today's mild weather continues, water the abundant grassy fields for which the region is famous. The excitement builds as President Millerand emerges from the largest building in the village, Sauraire's garage, where a banquet for three hundred invited guests has just come to an end. He is accompanied by all of the region's notables, including Dr. Dentu, the mayor of Vimoutiers, and Joseph Saffrey, the chairman of the Syndicat des Fabricants du Véritable Camembert de Normandie (Associated Producers of Authentic Norman Camembert, or SFVCN). The official party proceeds ceremoniously to the covered marketplace, where the monument dedicated to Marie Harel has been erected. In silence, President Millerand moves toward the statue, which depicts a farm woman in traditional Norman dress: bodice, apron, wooden shoes, and the local lace headgear with its descending panels down the back of the neck. Around her neck hangs a cross. On her right hip, she holds a copper milk jug, known in the local patois as a "cane." Behind her is a bas-relief panel depicting a farmyard, at the top of which a few words trumpet the heroine's claim to fame: "To Marie Harel, Creator of Camembert Cheese." Below, the words "To the Norman Farm-Woman" include those humble laborers in this tribute being paid to the most famous among them.

Thus, in that republican ceremony on 11 April 1928, was Camembert elevated to the status of national symbol. At the time, the event had few repercussions outside the region known as the Auge, and it was soon forgotten. Yet the cheese's official celebration by a former president of the Republic gave birth to a modern national myth in which Camembert was to become intricately associated with France itself. Since that day, Camembert has become France's foremost cheese, and France has become the country of Camembert. This stereotype, which is sometimes annoying but which cannot be denied, is thus revealed to be of fairly recent origin, whereas it is generally thought to have existed forever. And what is even more surprising is that the initiative behind it did not come from a Frenchman but from an American. It is a tale worth telling.

The Emissary from the New World

At around 3 P.M. on 15 March 1926, an unknown man knocked on the door of the pharmacy in Vimoutiers. The man, his dark hair flecked with white, wore an elegant checked suit and spoke French with some difficulty. Auguste Gavin, the pharmacist, was also the deputy mayor.[1] With a M. David, a friend and local engineer, he had been making plans for the forthcoming Easter fair. His surprise at the arrival of his unexpected visitor increased when he learned the stranger's purpose. The man, Dr. Joseph Knirim, claimed to be American and had come not to have a prescription filled, but rather to find out the schedule of trains to Camembert. He expressed a desire to go to that village to pay homage to the inventor of the eponymous cheese, whom he presumed was buried there. Gavin could not believe his ears. Camembert was a village with a population of three hundred, perched high on a hill and difficult to get to, and everyone knew that it had no train service. A foreigner might think that Camembert would be accessible by train, but only a madman would cross the Atlantic with the sole aim of honoring an almost-unknown Norman farmer's wife! Stupefied, and disconcerted by Knirim's weird French, Gavin was unable to understand why the American was so set on seeing Mme Harel's tomb. In an attempt to make himself better understood, Knirim took from his cardboard suitcase a document printed in French. Astounded, Gavin read the following:

> Savarin, the famous epicure, said that it was more worthwhile to invent a new dish than to discover a new star. How much more precious, therefore, must be the invention of a new dish of equal benefit to both the sick and to those who enjoy good health. This is the great merit of the late Madame Harel's discovery. I have traveled thousands of miles to come to honor her at the monument erected in her memory, and had I known the history of Camembert cheese earlier, I would have made this pilgrimage long ago.
>
> France possesses many cheeses, all of which are excellent, but when it comes to digestibility, Madame Harel's cheese, the "véritable Norman Camembert," is surely the best. Years ago, I suffered for several months from indigestion, and Camembert was practically the sole nourishment that my stomach and intestines were able to tolerate. Since then, I have sung the praises of Camembert, I have introduced it to thousands of gourmets, and I myself eat it two or three times a day. I shall never tire of describing the value of this wonderful product of your town, and in my efforts to convince the doubters, I have asked them to engage in an impartial trial. May Camembert's popularity increase the world over and may your town produce other benefactors of mankind to equal Madame Harel. In humble expression of my great admiration for Camembert cheese, which is shared by thousands of friends in the United States, I have brought with me across the waters this wreath of flowers to lay on the monument of our common benefactress. May the French and American flags be forever united in the service of mankind.
>
> JOSEPH KNIRIM, March 1926

Gavin and David were impressed by their visitor's determination, but somewhat abashed by having to admit to a foreigner their ignorance as to the exact site of Marie Harel's grave; nonetheless, they were flattered by this boost to their pride as Normans and they offered to help Knirim. First, they must find Mme Harel's burial site. Although the pair had of course heard of Camembert's inventor, they were unaware of the location of her resting place. Alert to the implications that this surprising American fondness for the cheese could have for the reputation of his region, Dentu set his office and all his acquaintances to work to glean information about Marie Harel. Upon questioning the inhabitants of Camembert, it was discovered that the Harels were supposed to have lived at a farm called Beaumoncel at the time of the French Revolution. Some even maintained that the family had given refuge to a recusant priest who was said to have passed on to them the secret of making a certain kind of cheese, supposedly the one now known as Camembert. The father-in-law of the mayor of Vimoutiers recalled having been told by a well-to-do farmer named Paynel, while they were hunting together, that Paynel had served a Camembert to Emperor Napoleon III on the occasion of his visit to the region. Paynel had also told him that he made his own Camembert according to the recipe handed down to him by his mother, Marie Harel. Since Paynel had come from Champosoult, the village adjacent to Camembert, Dentu believed that both he and his parents might be buried there.

And indeed, there was an impressive Paynel family tomb near the entrance to the tiny cemetery in Champosoult. On the stone was engraved the name of Marie Harel followed by two dates: 8 April 1781–14 May 1855. On 17 March 1926, therefore, Knirim laid a wreath of gilt laurel leaves adorned with the French and American flags at the Paynel family tomb, a tribute to Normandy from the United States of America.

His mission accomplished, Knirim then intended to set out for Plzeň in Czechoslovakia, in order to pay homage to that region, where they produced a beer that, along with Normandy's Camembert, he believed had cured him of his stomach ailment. However, on 18 May, prior to his departure, he was entertained by the inhabitants of Vimoutiers. The owners of the Point de France hotel held a sumptuous lunch in his honor to which they also invited the mayor and his deputies. When dessert arrived, Knirim rose to thank his hosts and, in his shaky French, said:

Gentlemen, there are many statues throughout the world, but there are few great benefactors of mankind like Madame Harel. I beseech you to raise a memorial to her. I am not wealthy, but I shall subscribe ten dollars to that end, and I shall add the contributions of three friends whom I treated and who were also cured with this same medicine, the "véritable Norman Camembert."

After making his statement, Knirim handed Gavin a twenty-dollar bill. Before leaving Vimoutiers for Plzeň, Knirim also visited Émile Courtonne's Camembert plant at Saint-Germain-de-Montgommery, near the village of Camembert itself. Then he departed and was never to be seen again. The inauguration of the statue eventually took place in the absence of the man initially responsible for its erection, for shortly before the ceremony, Dentu received word from the French embassy in New York that Knirim had passed away.

Camembert was well-known long before Knirim made the figure of Marie Harel known to the French. The dedication of a monument to the presumed inventor of Camembert did not increase consumption of the cheese; at the most, it added to the reputation of Norman produce. However, the Knirim effect is not to be measured in kilograms of Camembert sold but rather by its impact on the sphere of the imagination, in the realm of symbolism. The celebration of Marie Harel, the inventor who was reinvented after 130 years of obscurity, was to change the image of her cheese. Although by the 1920s Camembert was already the most widely consumed cheese in France, it was still but one among many. It may have been the most familiar, but it was also one of the least prestigious, a plebeian cheese in comparison to Roquefort, which could boast of a two-thousand-year lineage. The glorification of its creator gave Camembert a unique status that set it apart from other cheeses and made it stand out. From that time on, it acquired a personality all its own. Now, everyone knew that the cheese was Norman and that it had been created by a clever woman toward the end of the eighteenth century, and both of those merits raised it from the somewhat banal status to which it had been relegated ever since it had begun to be produced in large quantities in regions outside Normandy. Its popularity piqued the interest of the French, who wanted to know about Marie Harel and the circumstances surrounding her invention.

But although Marie Harel now had a statue, almost nothing was known about her. Such ignorance was unconscionable. The woman's background had to be made known, and because there were no facts, facts had to be created. In becoming famous, Marie Harel was to find herself endowed with not only a past but also a host of tales recounting various versions of her invention of Camembert and its apotheosis. None of these anecdotes created to support the "facts" were ever recounted in the conditional tense. Each version purports to be historically correct. Should we deal with this body of tales, almost all of which include the same characters, with the critical eye of a historian and therefore brush them aside? Such an attitude might well seem justified for at least two reasons. First, these little tales are not worthy of being taken as serious history; second, a knowledge of the exact circumstances surrounding the invention of Camembert may not really be all that important. After all, the stakes involved in such an investigation seem very small. If we adopt this somewhat high-handed attitude, why waste time trying to make sense of the tangled versions about the invention of Camembert? Yet, all the same, the legendary account of the cheese's invention does deserve further attention because it is one of the basic myths of the French nation. It may seem somewhat eccentric to find elements of a national identity in a box of Camembert. However, no one will deny that Camembert has indeed become a national symbol. We may smile at this, but we must also—while continuing to smile—give serious attention to the fact. Furthermore, the fact that the legend tells us that Camembert was invented in 1791, at the very moment that the French nation was also being born, raises questions about that very opportune coincidence.

The raising of the statue to the memory of Marie Harel was the consecration of Camembert's renown. It was also the moment when the myth began to take shape. Regional oral tradition, family veneration, and the imagination of local historiographers came together to concoct the tale of the invention of Camembert. Eager to show originality, each new narrator, seizing on locally available materials, constructed his or her own version. By superimposing the various versions of the myth, and by setting aside the less frequently mentioned events, retaining only those that are part of the common fund of knowledge, a story begins to take shape, one that I shall relate in my own way, thus becoming a part of the narrative chain.

Camembert, the flower of French cheeses, is said to have been created at a time of revolutionary turmoil, thanks to the clandestine combination of a Norman farmer's wife and the arts of a priest from the Brie region. During the great upheaval that produced the French nation, the fortuitous coming together of two regional traditions is said to have brought forth a new cheese in a country already possessed of several hundreds. The inaugural scene occurred in 1791 at the manor of Beaumoncel in Camembert, a small Norman village in the Auge, where Marie Fontaine met her husband, Jacques Harel. Although the couple had resided in the village of Roiville since their marriage, they were often found at the manor house, where Marie's father and his second wife lived. In those troubled times, the farm family of Beaumoncel offered refuge to a recusant priest. This clandestine priest, observing Marie Harel in the process of making cheese in the traditional Auge manner, suggested that she try the method used in his native region to produce the cheese known as Brie. Thus it came to pass that, making Brie in a mold used to produce Livarot, Marie Harel chanced to invent Camembert. Of course, the secret then had to be handed down to subsequent generations. Marie Harel's daughter Marie and her son-in-law Thomas Paynel took up the torch and carried it further by setting out to market the new cheese, which became increasingly popular, in the nearby towns of Argentan and Caen. The years passed, generation succeeded generation, and Camembert's realm continued to expand. In 1863, at the train station at Surdon in the Orne, Marie Harel's grandson, Victor Paynel, served one of his Camemberts to Emperor Napoleon III. The emperor found the cheese much to his liking; congratulated its producer; invited him to his palace, the Tuilieries; and requested that he deliver the product to him on a regular basis.

Before separating the truth from the fiction in this narrative, I should like to note what it reveals. It would be a mistake to take it literally, to read it as fact, and to accept it or reject it. It introduces us to four characters: Marie Harel, a recusant priest, Marie Harel's grandson Victor Paynel, and Emperor Napoleon III. The play is in two acts: act 1, "Origin," and act 2, "Consecration."

Act 1, scene 1, involves the clandestine. It creates an atmosphere of mystery. It takes place against a background of great historical change. The character of the priest produces several associations in the audience—with the church, with tradition, and with the sacred—in addition to invoking an atmosphere of antagonism toward the Revolution. In the popular representation, the priest is a kind of go-between. As part of the old order, his proximity to the people makes him the representative of a desire for change. A handful of priests did play a prominent role in setting off the Revolution and went on to join the Third Estate. When the Revolution entered its radical phase, and when the countryside, which had been pleased by the dismantling of feudal privileges, began to be affected by the unrest in the cities, some priests were caught up in the great turmoil they had helped bring about. The persecution of the clergy was to create the first great breach in national unity and was to increase, especially in western France, the oppositional contrast between city and rural area, between Paris and the provinces. As the bearer of tradition, the priest, if he had access to contemporary writings, was often the agent of modernity as well. A sacrosanct figure, he had near-supernatural powers that, in the collective mind, were allied as much to sorcery as they were to the Christian mysteries. In the farming regions of the western part of the country, peasants believed that priests possessed powers that were far greater than those of sorcerers merely because they owned more books. However, the imagined difference between Catholic priest and sorcerer was one of degree, not one of nature. After the Revolution, rumors spread that the books owned by emigrant priests had fallen into the hands of laymen, who were using them for their own benefit and handing them on to their descendants. This deep-rooted and widespread belief continues to enjoy some credence even today. An elderly Camembert maker who had managed a cheese factory in the 1930s gave me her version of Camembert's origins:

I have looked into the matter. In Normandy, when the Revolution began, they were killing priests, sending them all off somewhere. They pillaged the libraries in the priests' houses. That explains why there are so many healers of both sexes in small Norman villages; it's because all sorts of people got hold of such things. And why there are so many formulas for burns, for this, against that. And then you had people who practiced the laying on of hands.

I've known some myself. Well, I think that it was out of some book like that that Marie Harel or someone around her found the way to make this cheese.

By bringing a priest into the story, the history of Camembert is merely going along with a familiar platitude. Think of all the culinary innovations attributed to members of a religious order, beginning with Dom Pérignon and his champagne. However, our tale differs in two essential ways: it links the priest with a woman, an association that even the bowdlerized version does not entirely defuse, and it provides a precise historical setting. This adherence of the mythical narrative to history is a characteristic of the Camembert myth. As a narrative of origins or innovations, myth has no single meaning but is rather a construction made up of multiple and reversible meanings, one capable of generating new significations and of being reinterpreted to suit circumstances and needs. The fact that the birth of Camembert coincides with the birth of the Republic allows this myth to explicate the tensions that existed within the nation and to put forward solutions toward achieving a new unity. The scene of the cheese's creation at a crucial moment allows it to stand for the re-creation of national unity and to signify that it is also the heir to the old order. We can follow this operation of the myth through its various versions. One of the first, in 1927, was reported by Xavier Rousseau, a Norman scholar and the author of the first booklet known to have been published concerning Camembert's history.

> It was during the Terror, in the Auge region, and a recusant priest, pursued by troops, was about to fall into the hands of his pursuers. He was taken in by some peasants, who hid him. Although totally without funds, the fugitive managed to express his gratitude. He passed on the secret recipe for a cheese hitherto unknown in the area to the farmer's wife who had risked her life for him. Her name was Harel. She went on to make good use of the secret, and her cheeses were soon appreciated throughout the region around Vimoutiers.[2]

In this narrative, the origin of Camembert is a manufacturing secret imparted by a fleeing priest. The scene is reminiscent of others in which some god or messenger of the gods passes on an art or a gift to a mortal.

Thus Saturn, after having been deposed, taught humankind the art of agriculture. Here, we have revelation rather than invention, the transmission of some ancient lore or knowledge. As a rule, such myths do not reveal the origin of the secret being passed on. They merely stage it and tell of the circumstances of its transmittal, but never actually explain it. Thus, in keeping with the tradition, Marie Harel does not invent Camembert, she is merely given the secret of a tradition threatened with extinction. Thanks to her, a bit of old France, of pre-Revolutionary France, will survive.

Succeeding versions specify that the priest came from Brie, a cheese-producing region where the ladle-molding method was traditional. The secret imparted is thus nothing more than the recipe for Brie. With their greater detail, these versions led to the accepted one. An outside influence is added to the scene of creation. The priest passes on both the tradition of the old world and the know-how of another region. Thus, Camembert becomes the product of an old tradition made new and of a linkage between the knowledge of two different regions, of the secrets held by a priest and the know-how of a peasant woman. The myth integrates opposing elements, combining water and fire, in this instance the woman and the priest, the Ancien Régime and the Republic, the regions of Auge and Brie.

The creation narrative goes on to mention Marie Harel's commercial success in selling her cheeses in neighboring towns. The religious factor represented by the priest is balanced by Marie Harel's business sense. All of these meanings are not always explicitly present. Some of them tend to prevail according to the period or circumstances. However, they are all present and can all be brought into play when needed, causing this plethora of different versions to end up telling the same story.

The Imperial Seal

The creation myth is further enhanced by the encounter between Victor Paynel and Napoleon III. It makes little difference whether the anecdote is true or not, which is something I have been unable to verify. The essential thing about it is why the story has stuck in the popular memory, why it spread, and what it signifies. Marie Harel creates a line of cheese makers who carry on her work. The secret of Camembert's manufacture is handed down generation by generation through the family. As in the first act, the two characters, both by birth and by geography, are from two very separate worlds. In the normal course of events, their paths would never have crossed. Whereas in the first act the encounter between the farmer's wife and the priest took place because of Revolutionary events, the meeting between the emperor and Paynel occurs thanks to the railway. Like the former instance, the scene evokes French unity. However, between the two acts the factors underlying national unity have changed. Revolutionary violence in the former has given way to the peaceful construction of a network of railroads in the latter. Each encounter symbolizes a phase in the construction of that national unity. In the second act, Paynel, a peasant, finds himself in the presence of the emperor. This meeting is without, however, any hint of subjugation. Paynel acts independently, the relationship is commercial in nature, and its happy outcome will be the establishment of ongoing business dealings with the imperial palace. The process initiated by the priest's disclosure of the method of fabrication to Marie Harel continues with Marie's transmittal of the secret to her daughter, who herself then hands it on to her children. It culminates in the gift of the cheese to the emperor.

Marie Harel is also responsible for another development: the commerce of the new cheese. The meeting with the emperor marks the beginning of a new era, the progression from trade at the local level to national commerce made possible by the development of the railroad system and furthered by imperial approval. The first act showed a province, Normandy, benefiting from the national unification brought about by the Revolution; in the second act, Normandy bestows the fruit of that union on the entire nation. The figure of the emperor, like that of the priest, is fraught with many meanings. A president become emperor, Napoleon III united in his person ancient dynastic principle and elected legitimacy. He embodied the nation's authority and unity, notably via the railroad and its ever-expanding network, which he organized and endowed with a part of his majesty by traveling on it. The presence of the railroad, one of the peaceful fruits of the Revolution, gives the myth a mundane touch that marks the passage toward a new stage in the history of this cheese, which now achieves national consecration not only thanks to imperial recognition but also, and above all, thanks to its ability to be transported throughout France. The railroad, a powerful means of national unification that connected the provinces to Paris and emphasized the capital's preeminence, is what enabled Camembert to expand beyond its native Auge while other cheeses remained confined to their native regions.

The emperor, in inviting Paynel to the Tuileries Palace, was honoring not only Paynel, but all of Marie Harel's descendants for the patrimony they had passed on. Family connections are what forge the link between our acts 1 and 2. Relationships, by ensuring the continuity of the dynasty founded by Camembert's inventor, also guarantee the cheese's durability. On the other hand, the historical continuity of the nation, brought to birth by the forceps of the Revolution and strengthened by the establishment of the railroad, is somehow lacking. Napoleon III is not really a legitimate heir, but merely someone who happens to be the incarnation of state authority. Dynastic legitimacy, which was destroyed at the top in 1791, persists in civil society as a method of transmitting patrimony and serves as evidence of its economic fertility. The nation's prosperity is the result of the transmission of working-class know-how via family ties.

From this point of view, the erection of the monument at Vimoutiers in 1928 would seem to represent the myth's apotheosis. The Republic consecrated a cheese born of the Revolution and thereby recognized its own heritage, both its heritage from the Ancien Régime and the heritage that is the fruit of republican ideals. It coincided with the (temporary) achievement of domestic peace by transcending the contradictions between tradition and progress by means of a product that was at once provincial and national, rural and industrial. Camembert's republican consecration, performed by a former president, occurred when it had demonstrated its universal success, especially in the United States, a country linked with the French Republic since its birth. Millerand's political background made him the person most suited to preside at the event. A former president of the Republic, he was now a mere senator from a rural département. Having begun his political career as a socialist deputy from Paris' 12th arrondissement, the first socialist to become a member of the government, he had moved slowly from the far left to the moderate right, from a defender of the working class to a representative of vested rural interests.

The Flowering of the Myth

The myth as we have presented it did not spring up all at once. It was built up layer by layer over time and successively reworked, and it continued to develop over the years. Most of its elements had always been there, ready either to be used or to be forgotten. Knirim's visit and the erection of the Harel monument brought them to life. Some of them had long been familiar, although such familiarity had been confined to the restricted circle of the cheese makers themselves. Other elements were borrowed from local oral tradition. The myth's astonishing vitality, which allowed for its continual renewal, is due to one basic reason: the close intermingling of legend with actual historical events. For, in fact, the myth does borrow from both history, in which it attempts to situate itself, and from local stories. It presents itself as both historical truth and as a tale. It also contains a further strength created by the tension between Norman provincial demands and national claims. Because it is an attempt to resolve such tension, the myth's form is unstable. As a legendary tale, it lays itself open to challenge by historical investigation. It would continue to be called into question by various groups, but its magnetism and its force are such that even while some of its elements have been disputed, others have come to be accepted as historically true. The myth has developed out of a combination of skepticism and credulity. This astonishing mixture of established historical facts and legend has made it enormously attractive.

Doubts Begin to Stir

Even as the story's heroine was being consecrated in stone, the edifying legend around her was beginning to be questioned. As early as 1927—that is, in the period between Joseph Knirim's appearance and the erection of the monument—a small fifteen-page brochure made its appearance. The brochure recounted the myth, but also challenged certain of its elements. However, in the end, this investigation of the story merely served to strengthen it and even led to the development of new versions. Certain of the myth's elements, in particular the unverifiable presence of the dissenting priest, were called into question, but the image of Marie Harel was preserved. And that, with very few exceptions, was to be the attitude of all succeeding criticism. Although historians contested and upheld the story and either tore it apart or enriched it, they all ended by accepting it as the basis of their scholarly lucubrations.

The legend of Marie Harel, scarcely credible historically and a source of real discomfort to those in competition with the makers of Camembert, could not help but give rise to criticism. However, whenever it was contested, the only effect was the creation of additional versions of the cheese's birth. Of this plethora of tales—I have found at least twenty versions, all of them different—we can distinguish three principal categories. The first consolidates the different versions of the classic and legendary tale, and in answering the criticisms directed against them, attempts to establish the historical truth by pruning the narrative of its more questionable elements. Another category consists of the scholarly versions of Camembert's creation, which have nothing but contempt for the legend. These rationalizations of the mythic tale are in fact based on no historical investigation whatsoever, and their pretensions to "science" are based on their distancing themselves from the legend and on their authors' own reputations. In the end, all they do is to create other, apparently more logical legends that are bereft of charm, such as the one put forward by Professor Roger Veisseyre, a well-known specialist in dairy technology:

> The historical truth would appear to be as follows: Marie Harel was born on a farm in the Brie region where Brie cheese had long been made. Following her marriage, she moved to Camembert, a village already famous for its Livarot cheese. Marie Harel can take credit for making a Brie-type cheese in a Livarot mold. This is the cheese that has come to be known as Camembert.[3]

That no facts are produced in support of this theory is apparently unimportant. The person presenting it need only be a scientist for his entire thesis to be given the imprimatur of science. Still in the guise of historical truth, the geographer Jean-Robert Pitte set forth a similar version.[4]

The third category of the myth's development is the one in which the imagination has been given free rein. The narrators, no longer feeling themselves bound by a widely questioned tale, have taken it upon themselves to invent their own versions. I will cite but one, somewhat more unusual than the others, to give some notion of the nature of these descendants of the original myth. I came upon it in an English encyclopedia of food. In this work, we read that it was Napoleon—Napoleon I, obviously—who gave the name "Camembert" to a hitherto nameless cheese offered him by a young farm girl, whom he, in his gastronomical enthusiasm, had embraced on the spot.[5]

Piously handed down, embellished with new variants, or contested, the legend of Camembert's invention has been hugely successful. Marie Harel does not, of course, enjoy the popular audience granted Jeanne d'Arc, who was rediscovered and taken up by the Republic in this same period. Outside the Auge, she is unknown to all but a few of the initiated. At the same time, however, she reappears in articles by journalists or authors who are both charmed and amazed by her story, so redolent of the Norman countryside. Hundreds of thousands of French readers must once have heard the story of the origins of their favorite cheese and then, for the most part, forgotten it. Yet they will have retained a greater familiarity with that cheese and its linkage with the nation's history.

Joseph Knirim, convinced that he had cured his stomach ailment by the daily ingestion of Camembert "made in Normandy," certainly did not imagine when he went to Vimoutiers that he would be presenting France with a new heroine. The success of the steps he took on behalf of the modest Augeron dairymaid cannot fail to astound us. How can that sudden interest be explained?

Contrary to some subsequent statements, Marie Harel's name and the role attributed to her were not totally unknown at the time. Most of the existing treatises on cheese technology made mention of her as the creator of Camembert cheese. Furthermore, the directors of the SFVCN, some of whose founding members were descended from Marie Harel, knew of the role she had played. Yet, for the majority of the inhabitants of the Auge region where the village of Camembert is located, the circumstances surrounding the invention of Camembert were of no more than anecdotal interest. Knirim could easily have been regarded as a crank and his arrival in Vimoutiers could easily have left no traces. However, his initiative was immediately taken seriously and exploited. How are we to explain the fact that, in a region whose inhabitants are noted for being nothing if not frugal and down-to-earth, a decision was made to band together to erect a statue in honor of an unpretentious and nearly forgotten female cheese maker?

If Knirim's enthusiasm triggered and continued to be the impetus behind the enterprise, it is because he came along at the right moment and served various local preoccupations. For the town of Vimoutiers, his initiative was seen as a good way to add to its renown. For the producers of Norman Camembert, especially those who were members of the SFVCN, it represented an unhoped-for opportunity after a series of demoralizing setbacks. They quickly understood the advantage to be gained by honoring Marie Harel and the Norman origins of the cheese. Knirim's pilgrimage to Normandy made them aware of the publicity to be gained from Marie Harel's story, which they had not yet thought of exploiting. They soon realized that in Marie Harel they had a trump card in their contest with those whom they viewed as unfair competitors, namely the cheese makers from other regions who were being so bold as to affix the label "Camembert" to their counterfeit products.

The Defense of Norman Camembert

The year 1926 was a dark year for Normandy's cheese makers. Camembert's renown had never been greater, but Normandy was not the principal beneficiary of the increased demand for the cheese. In fact, the Norman producers, along with many others, had been greatly weakened by the First World War. In addition, they were now subject to a regulation that favored the provision of milk to city dwellers and restricted the quantity available for cheese production. They also complained of the barriers erected against exportation. The increase in demand principally benefited the new factories that had been set up in other regions. In addition, the English market had been invaded by Danish cheese makers. In 1909, the largest Norman producers had overcome their rivalries and created the aforementioned SFVCN—a confederation or association of Norman Camembert makers. The principal goal of that organization had been to achieve official recognition of Camembert's exclusively Norman character and to prevent the use of the designation "Camembert" by non-Norman producers. For a long while, the Norman cheese makers had worked for the issuance of a decree designating an *appellation d'origine* or "label of quality" for their Camembert cheese similar to that commonly granted for wines. In working toward that goal, they had mobilized all their local elected officials to bring pressure to bear upon the government. But their efforts were in vain; the legislature had remained deaf to all their appeals.

After considerable shilly-shallying, and after repeatedly having their hopes raised only to be dashed, the members of the SFVCN understood that they were not going to be granted a label of quality for their Camembert. Only one recourse remained: legal action. On the advice of its lawyer, an attorney named de Resbecq, the syndicate brought a suit for counterfeiting against a dairy cooperative at Ligueil. The trial ended in failure.

On 20 January 1926, the appellate court at Orléans dismissed the suit and ruled that "Camembert" had become a generic term and was not truly indicative of geographical origin. Normandy had no exclusive claim over Camembert.

Barely three months after that ruling was handed down, the Norman cheese makers learned of Knirim's arrival on the scene. They viewed it as a godsend. In April 1926, they were among the first to subscribe to the fund for erecting a monument to the memory of Marie Harel. M. Henri Lepetit, one of the larger Camembert makers and the creator of the well-known Lepetit brand, donated 500 francs and urged his colleagues to follow suit. Thanks to this early contribution, a stele was erected in Camembert itself. In 1927, a second subscription was opened to erect a statue. The syndicate contributed heavily, to the tune of 10,000 francs, while many of its members also made personal donations. At the conclusion of the syndicate's meeting of 22 February 1927, 3,800 additional francs had been collected. The sum needed to erect the monument to Marie Harel's memory had been amassed in under two years.

The commemoration of Marie Harel meant a great deal of publicity for Camembert. First of all, it was an assertion of the cheese's Norman origin and character. It meant that all of France could now be made aware that Camembert was a real Norman local community and village and that the cheese that bore its name was the result of the clever inventiveness of a local Norman dairywoman. Thus, the Norman cheese makers hoped that consumers would begin to remember that true and *véritable* Camembert had to be made in Normandy, as noted on the syndicate label affixed to the cheeses produced by its members. It is easy to understand why they would so eagerly seize this magnificent opportunity to boost their product.

This, however, does not explain why the event came to have such national importance. Had recognition of Marie Harel's role concerned only Normandy and its cheese makers, it would not have had repercussions elsewhere. Yet, despite the fact that the event was not especially striking or in any way spectacular, the national press picked it up and it was widely reported.

In April 1928, newspapers were devoting space to the legislative electoral campaigns and to the brilliant exploits of the French aviators Dieudonné Costes and Joseph Le Brix, who had just completed their round-the-world flight. President Gaston Doumergue congratulated the two aviators, whose plane had logged 57,000 kilometers. An enthusiastic crowd welcomed them on the Champs-Elysées. As for the regional press in Normandy, it was filled with details of the execution at Caen, before a large audience, of a certain William Follain, who had murdered a taxi driver and a colonel. Given the competition offered by those events, as well as by disturbing news from overseas—bomb attacks in Italy, communist subversion in Japan and Germany—coverage of the ceremony at Vimoutiers did not take up a great deal of newspaper space. But neither did it pass unnoticed. *Le Temps* gave it a few lines; *L'Illustration,* with its taste for the pictorial, gave it a full page accompanied by a large photograph of the ceremony. *Le Gaulois,* a newspaper with a longstanding reputation for exalting national traditions, covered the event in its column devoted to gastronomy, "The Table and Us."

It was not only because of Camembert's renown that the newspapers covered the story of Marie Harel. Their interest was not happenstance. Contemporary concerns predisposed the French to seek comfort in stories that flattered national pride and exalted the virtues of rural life. Ten years after the hecatomb of the First World War, the French were profoundly uneasy about the way in which their country was changing, about the questioning of traditional values and about the bases of French power. The particular context of the period explains the interest created by the story of Camembert and the impression that it had made, if not on individual minds, then at least on the collective unconscious. If we are to gain an understanding of this, more than seventy-five years after the fact, we must go back to the unsettled atmosphere of that uncertain time.

A Restless France

In the 1920s, the French had many reasons to feel anxious. Signs of national weakness were increasing at both the international and the domestic levels. The franc rose and fell erratically, the government had been forced to give in to American and British demands, and the countryside seemed to be in a decline and wasting away.

In 1926, England and the United States began to call in the loans they had made to France to support its war effort, but at the same time the government found itself unable to obtain any guarantee that the Germans were prepared to pay the reparations that had been imposed upon them.

The ensuing decline in the value of the franc meant the end of illusions. Raymond Poincaré was returned to power in an attempt to restore confidence. For two years, from 1926 to 1928, the fate of the franc remained in suspense. Confidence finally returned, but problems remained, in particular an enormous budgetary imbalance. On 24 June 1928, after considerable hesitation, Poincaré finally moved to devalue the currency. Although his prestige enabled him to proceed with the devaluation of the franc and thereby impoverish those with private means who had invested heavily in treasury bonds, he did so not on behalf of heavy industry, which such a policy actually favored, but under the pretext of protecting small family properties, both agricultural and artisanal. In fact, no French government at the time could have justified a policy designed to benefit large-scale modern industry. The only policy that could have found legitimacy with the population was one purportedly designed to strengthen the traditional pillars of French power: small landowners, artisans, family-owned light industries, and agriculture. The success of the Camemberts being produced in small rural dairies was a valuable counterpoint to large-scale industrial development.

In the face of the changes that were affecting the country's traditional equilibrium, concern continued to increase. The bloodbath of the Great War, in which 1,322,000 men had been killed, had considerably weakened the French population, occurring as it had at the end of a century of demographic stagnation. The return of men from the front had not had the hoped-for effect on the birth rate, notwithstanding the government's exhortations. In 1919, Georges Clemenceau had launched a moving appeal for civic-minded procreation from the rostrum of the Assemblée Nationale. "The [peace] treaty," he said, "does not provide that the French volunteer to produce numerous offspring, but that is the first thing that should have been included in it, for even though it may acquire every German cannon, France will still have lost the war because there will be no more Frenchmen."[6] Though his appeal received applause, it was to no effect, notwithstanding the repressive law of 31 July 1920 that banned contraceptives and birth control propaganda, including a heavy penalty for abortion. Nor was the law of 11 March 1932, which established a system of family allocations, any more effective; the birth rate fell below what it had been before the war.[7] Many regions saw an exodus to the cities, and their population fell dramatically. From 1911 to 1936, 85 percent of towns with one to two thousand inhabitants saw their population fall. Impoverished farmers and small artisans left for the big cities in droves. In 1931, the rural population represented no more than 49 percent of France's total population. Each year, the countryside lost some six hundred thousand inhabitants, eighty thousand of them farmers and agricultural workers. Poincaré's program of budgetary economy, which did away with 106 subprefectures and fifty-three local tax offices, brutally speeded up the decline of many medium-sized towns.

Far from being pleased by the growth of heavy industry, public opinion grew alarmed at the growing number of large working-class neighborhoods in the cities and at the emergence of a new proletariat with a high proportion of uprooted immigrants. The Renault factory at Billancourt, on the outskirts of Paris, took on forty thousand new workers. France, which produced 254,000 vehicles per annum, was the world's second-largest automobile manufacturer, although of course still far behind the United States.

Agriculture, sheltered by protectionist policies, stagnated. Small-scale agricultural units of 10 to 20 hectares (25 to 50 acres), exploited by a single family of five to ten persons, predominated. The very small output of such farms was not enough to make the country self-sufficient. The majority of the peasant class found itself unable to acquire industrial products and set money aside solely for the purpose of increasing property holdings and rarely for investment. Between rural France, stagnant and in decline, and industrial France, growing rapidly but underrepresented on the political scene and ignored by the media, the opposition was silenced by the apparent, albeit temporary, consensus that, thanks to Poincaré, prevailed for a time. However, there were in fact two French nations between which the gap was widening: a rural France of landowning notables and small farmers that the political class supported against all comers, and an urban and industrial France that enjoyed almost no public support. The fissure between them was growing, and no one could be completely blind to the country's weaknesses vis-à-vis the emerging new powers: the United States, with its industrial strength, and the USSR, a potent new force and hotbed of subversion.

France was changing, but the elite, as a group, along with the broad middle class, stubbornly continued to believe that the rural areas were still the country's center of gravity. As they began to be aware of signs of change, their concerns increased, and they feared unforeseeable consequences while deploring the rural loss of substance, the gradual disappearance of distinctive regional features, and the rising flood of standardized industrial products. This retrograde attitude virtually ignored industrial growth. For years, the majority of historians and economists were to continue to attribute the greater part of France's backward industrial position to the events of this period. Although the situation in rural areas tends to support this view, if we are to rely on contemporary discourse, large-scale industrial development would appear to contradict it.

The paradox rests in the fact that France was changing while its political discourse was managing to ignore the change—apart from a vague undercurrent of concern—and was continuing to exalt the virtues of savings and small industry at the country's endless agricultural fairs. The French dreamed of achieving industrial modernization without creating a working class, factories, or a rural exodus. The industry they wanted was to be a kind of rural manufacturing that would not upset the social balance and that would manage to combine agricultural, artisanal, and industrial activities. The majority of the French felt that the development of Normandy's cheese production, which was a combination of agriculture and small-scale rural industry, was exactly the kind of thing that was needed. In addition, the product was exportable. Ah, if only the broader economy could follow that peaceful example!

By chance, two contemporary events had occurred to encourage those French who were seeking signs of their country's return to its former greatness. A Norman dairywoman and a pair of aviators, each in their own way, served to reassure a worried France, which feared and resented continued decline as if it were somehow unfair. Like the Bréguet airplane with its Hispano engine flown by Costes and Le Brix, Marie Harel's Camembert in its little round box was destined to go around the world. Exported to every major country, it manifested in its own way France's universal presence and its industrial strength. On the one hand, the country possessed the advanced technologies that had enabled the daring deeds of its modern adventurers; on the other, it had its traditional regional products produced through the know-how of its modest but solid peasant women. With high-quality technology and excellence in gastronomy, France could continue to dream of triumphantly reconciling old and new, peasant and city dweller, agriculture and industry. The radical Republic had its feet planted firmly on the ground. While former President Millerand had praised peasant labor, current President Doumergue, his eyes lifted to the skies, congratulated Costes and Le Brix.

Although Costes and Le Brix flattered national pride, their exploit also had its unsettling aspects, promoting as it did the power of a new technology that was the fruit of modern industry. Aviation had of course played its part in battle during the Great War, but the nation felt that the debt was owed to the pilots who flew the planes and who were for the most part from the peasant class. Public opinion, nourished by the speeches of every French politician, believed that these men had once again upheld French grandeur and that it was also they who had paid the heaviest price. The war had left France with the belief that the country's strength and equilibrium came from its peasant class. The country was not against progress, but it rejected the achievement of progress at the expense of the rural population and the tranquil order of the countryside, which were the solid bases of the French empire.

A Monument to Peace

In the ten years that followed the end of the First World War, every French village had a monument to commemorate its dead. Following the mayor and the village curé, agnostic laymen and practicing Christians marched together in half-Republican, half-Catholic ceremony. However, the repeated extolling of the heroism of the *poilus* (the French soldiers), although it strengthened the fiber of Republican nationalism, was of no help to France in meeting the challenges of peace; in facing up to the combined power of its allies, Great Britain and the United States; or in dealing with Germany's resurgence. Other forces and other skills had to be brought into play. There was a growing realization that the victory over Germany was not going to yield any dividends. New myths were needed to reduce new tensions and to ensure that the notion of the permanence of French values prevailed.

The celebration of Marie Harel and of Camembert had its role to play in this regard. The fact that her name had been forgotten meant little, since Camembert, whose greatness and prestige were already known, was an omnipresent expression of the permanence of rural values. It may seem surprising today, especially to those who do not salivate when confronted with a Camembert, that consumption of the cheese had a role in alleviating the concerns of French people in the late 1920s. Joseph Knirim would never have imagined that his favorite cheese would end up assuaging the anxieties of an entire nation. Let us turn to the columns of *Le Gaulois*, a newspaper whose very name expresses the desire to proclaim the nation's ancient roots and the permanence of an identity aloof from the convulsions of mere politics. For this chauvinistic publication, the monument to Marie Harel embodied the reassuring values handed down by tradition: "The effigy exudes strength, balance, a sense of labor and frugality. This is obviously a rural Frenchwoman over whose eyes no one would dare attempt to pull the wool."[8]

Such was certainly the message that the sculptor had intended to transmit. It was why his proposal had been chosen over the seven others submitted to the selection committee made up of Camembert producers and local notables. In selecting Eugène L'Hoëst's statue, the members of the sponsoring group were choosing a peaceful evocation of female labor. The monument to Marie Harel was in sharp contrast to the veritable embarrassment of monuments exalting heroism in combat. Postwar sculptors were working in a bull market, and the tiniest hamlet paid homage to its dead by erecting a monument. The theme was a given, as were its figures. Over the years, hundreds of sculptors were to depict proud *poilus* with flags unfurled. From 1920 to 1925, no fewer than thirty thousand public funerary monuments were erected, an average of sixteen per day over five years. This devotion to a single subject imposed its own style and terms of reference.

In contrast, the monument to Marie Harel is obviously a contemporary work, but it is a monument to peace and to the glory of peaceful industry, and the theme and the symbolism of peace have replaced those of war. The sculptor, all too familiar with warlike themes, proceeded to invert those signs in magnifying Marie Harel's pastoral activity. The war has little place in L'Hoëst's work. The fifty-four-year-old sculptor had a predilection for rustic scenes. His own personality is reflected in the statue of Jeanne d'Arc he created in 1921, which is quite unlike the usual bellicose depictions of the national saint. Instead, in a statue notable for its curves, he portrays her as a shepherd lass. The only sharp and salient elements in the composition are the maid's lifted breasts and the distaff, an obvious symbol of the female universe, which she holds like a lance. In 1905, he had created a monument to three professors of agronomy. A haut-relief in white stone with three bronze medallions, it was erected in the park of the school of agronomics at Grignon. It, too, represents a young shepherdess gathering wild flowers amid her flock.

Warlike effigies are frozen in bronze, and the monuments to the fallen stand, sharp and menacing, in the center of town squares, near the city hall or the church. Sculpted in stone, the monument to the memory of Marie Harel was affixed to the wall by the portico of the public market. In the foreground, instead of a soldier, was a peaceful Norman dairywoman standing in front of a stele that depicted not a battlefield but a farm courtyard. The monument was not protecting a territory; it was welcoming commerce. There were no sharp edges, only rounded forms: the arch over the stele, the milk jug the woman supports on her hip. A Norman headdress replaced the soldier's helmet. The dairywoman, shod in wooden shoes, wore a fichu, an apron, a lace headdress, and a cross. The monument was not dedicated to those who had died for France but "TO THE FARMWOMEN OF NORMANDY." Just as the soldiers on the monuments were anonymous, the better to represent all who fought in the Great War, so the farmwoman sculpted by L'Hoëst was not offered as an exact portrait of Marie Harel but as the effigy of a Norman farmer's wife. Ten years after the Armistice, peace once again found representation in a public monument. The population's deep pacifism, evoked in some of the monuments to the fallen, was here given expression free from any reference to the war.

The vast majority of the French yearned for a future of peace, for the maintenance of their country's prestige, and for the preservation of a profoundly rural France. They regarded Camembert's success as testimony to the vigor and success of a reassuring form of technological modernity that was compatible with traditional order under the aegis of the Republic. The myth that was created, beginning in 1926, around the person of Marie Harel illustrates this synthesis between tradition and modernity, between rural activity and urban development.

Chapter 2 | MARIE HAREL AND HER DESCENDANTS

The First Century

THE HISTORY BENEATH THE LEGEND

The charming tale of Marie Harel served local Norman interests far too well and was much too far-fetched not to alert the skeptical. The Norman writer Jean de La Varende sensed that behind the cult lurked a clever publicity campaign that was all too typical of the sly opportunism of the inhabitants of the Auge. He recounted the following:

> One day in the interwar years, an American couple visited Vimoutiers. The husband was on a mission of gratitude. He came to thank Camembert for having, via its cheese, cured his stomach ulcer. . . . He wanted to erect a statue to its inventor. . . . Never look a gift horse . . . ! So they finally dug up Marie Harel, made a statue out of her, and the entire Auge region had a good surreptitious giggle.[1]

And indeed, the reasons for believing and for doubting were on quite different levels. It was possible to go along with the tales about the life and deeds of Marie Harel and Jeanne d'Arc for emotional reasons and because their charm or beauty attracted belief; the tales could also be questioned on the grounds of lack of proof and their various and obvious inconsistencies. However, the reservations expressed by one camp did nothing to weaken belief in the other. In her home territory, Marie Harel was regarded as a kind of saint. Did she not have her own statue, just like Jeanne d'Arc or the Virgin Mary? Of course, the Norman farmer's wife depicted in the statue was not intended to *be* Marie Harel, for there was no known portrait of her. Nevertheless, everyone believed that it was indeed Marie Harel herself who had been immortalized in stone. And since people came to pray before statues of the saints, why not pray before the statue of the Auge's heroine? This was obviously the reasoning of the peasant couple who were reported to have been seen kneeling before the statue one market day. However, for several decades, and notwithstanding this popular enthusiasm, Marie Harel's role, and even her very existence, were viewed with extreme skepticism by every historian and specialist who dealt with the dairy industry.

To counter the caustic incredulity of de La Varende and the skepticism of historians, local scholars banded together in an attempt to prove that the personage who had been commemorated in stone was fully deserving of her fame. Those attempting to check on the accuracy of the story of Camembert's invention were faced with three major questions. The first concerned Marie Harel herself. Had she actually lived in the village of Camembert? The second involved the precise role she had played in Camembert's invention. The third question revolved around the matter of the recusant priest. The earliest investigations undertaken by local historians eager to find proof that Marie Harel had indeed invented Camembert yielded some unexpected and contradictory results. Xavier Rousseau, the moving spirit behind the Argentan historical society and a specialist in local history, was the first to undertake a methodical investigation of the Augeron cheese maker. His work cleared the path somewhat and did confirm that Marie Harel had indeed been a native of Normandy. He managed to find the death and birth certificates of a Marie Harel born in 1781, the daughter of a Marie Harel née Fontaine, born in 1761. The latter could have invented Camembert in 1791, but at the time she was living in the community of Roiville and not in Camembert. Rousseau also uncovered a document dated 1778 that contained a reference to Camembert cheese. He was thus led to question the role attributed to Marie Harel, the mother, in the cheese's creation. According to him, she had invented nothing, and instead had merely taken credit for a local and traditional dairy process.

This hypothesis was later to be confirmed by the investigations of a Dr. Boulard, better known to the Normans by his pen name, Jean Bard. Although an ardent supporter of Marie Harel, Boulard's long and patient research caused him eventually to lose faith in his heroine. He demonstrated, in an apparently irrefutable manner, that Camembert had been in existence prior to its presumed creator. He quoted two texts written prior to 1791 that contained mention of the famous cheese.

The oldest was by Thomas Corneille, brother of the author of *Le Cid*, Pierre Corneille, whose geographical dictionary, published in 1708, contained the following passage under the article "Vimonstiers" *[sic]*:

> A sizeable town of Basse-Normandie, in the diocese of Lisieux and six leagues from that city and approximately two from Fervaques and Livarot, above Montgomery, on the river called "La Vie." It is a well-populated town and its parish church is served by 20 priests. There is a Benedictine monastery and a convent of Hospitalières, who care for the hospital. A large market is held each Monday, where excellent Livarot and Camembert cheeses can be found. There are many butchers and tanners, and there is a brisk trade in the livestock that grazes the rich local pastures. The town was formerly known as Vicus Monasterii (notes collected in situ in 1702).[2]

If Camembert did exist as early as 1702, it could not have been "invented" by Marie Harel in 1791.

The Camembert Enigma

In his history of Orbec, published in 1760, Charles Jobey, the syndic or mayor of Orbec, also made mention of Camembert cheese. With regard to the market at Pont l'Évêque, he wrote: "There, they sell many cheeses called 'Augelots,' which are not as large, nor as good, nor as rich as Livarot or Camembert cheese."[3] He also wrote of the market at Livarot: "The principal trade is in butter and cheese, which are sent to Paris and throughout France. It is said that the cheeses from Camembert, the neighboring parish, are even better."[4]

Although the mention of Livarot cheeses, which were already well known at that period, is not surprising, it is surprising to find the name Camembert in these documents. The local importance of Livarot, a large town whose market attracted the entire population of the canton as well as outside dealers, explains why its name was bestowed on many local cheeses. The same holds true for Pont l'Évêque. But why should Camembert, a tiny village off the main roads and without a market of its own, have given its name to a cheese that enjoyed a local notoriety as early as the beginning of the eighteenth century? I made a trip to Camembert, secretly hoping to find the key to unlock this enigma and I do not regret having done so. In the springtime, the green, hilly landscape dotted with flowering apple trees is superb, but the enigma refused to yield its solution.

Camembert is situated in the southern part of the Auge, five kilometers (some three miles) from Vimoutiers. Its irregular boundaries enclose an area of approximately 2,500 acres. It is traversed by the Viette, a small trout stream, and has many wooded valleys. The dwellings are scattered, and the village itself consists of no more than a small church surrounded by a cemetery, the town hall, a school, and three houses. Not far from the church, on a piece of higher ground, stands the manor house known as Beaumoncel, a handsome half-timbered building that served as the stage for Camembert's creation. Today, the community has approximately two hundred inhabitants. There are some forty farms devoted to raising livestock, taking advantage of the region's excellent natural pastureland. The well-known quality of its thick grass is undoubtedly the main reason for the village's renown and is, indeed, the source of the abundance and excellence of the milk produced by its cows. The farm produce, butter, and cheese, were formerly taken to be sold at the Monday market at Vimoutiers. On the surface, therefore, Camembert has nothing that especially attracts attention. There is practically no documentary mention of the village itself, aside from a brief article in *L'Annuaire de l'Orne* of 1889. From it, we learn that Camembert had 450 inhabitants, among whom were ninety indigents, some cloth merchants, and a handful of dairy farmers.[5] At the time, the main resource of the parish was its cheeses, augmented by trade in the local apple brandy. The inhabitants complained of the very bad condition of the roads, which hindered their trade with Vimoutiers, whose market was virtually their only outlet. During periods of heavy rain, the roads became impassable by horse-drawn conveyances, and all commerce came to a halt. The situation must not have been very different a century earlier, when Thomas Corneille was compiling his dictionary, and yet the name of this tiny village had already been attached to an esteemed variety of cheese.

At the beginning of the eighteenth century the market at Vimoutiers had been one of the most important in the region. Farm produce was sold there, as were the various locally manufactured fabrics. In addition to butter, cider, and poultry, the farmers brought in many varieties of cheese, designated either by the name of the maker, if he happened to be especially well known, or by the name of the principal market where the cheeses were sold. Cheeses of a lesser quality had no names at all. Those called "Livarot," because they were to be found at that town's market, were made from skimmed milk. The same type of cheese was also sold at Vimoutiers, which was only nine kilometers (approximately six miles) distant. There, they had competition from other types of cheese, especially those that were made from whole milk. We can surmise that the latter, the best of which came from the village of Camembert, were called by its name. Round like a Livarot, Camembert at this period was probably a whole-milk cheese. Why was it given the name of a tiny village like Camembert, rather than that of Vimoutiers? Probably because, unlike Livarot and Pont l'Évêque, it was totally farm-produced and did not leave Camembert until it had fully matured and was ready for consumption.

Today, there is a keen local rivalry—in the great French tradition—between Camembert and Vimoutiers over which village is to benefit from the glory shed by Camembert cheese. Hitherto, Camembert has had only the crumbs, with Vimoutiers grabbing the greater benefit. Vimoutiers has a Camembert museum, where visitors can examine a few dairy and cheese-making implements accompanied by photographs and explanatory cards. It is more a pious gesture than a real museum.

A handful of tourists, attracted by Camembert's fame, show up to satisfy their taste for the picturesque. Following their visit, they go off to take a look at Marie Harel's statue, which deserves little more attention, and then they go away again without bothering to make a trip to Camembert itself. This is a great mistake, for Camembert is a very pretty village. It is easy to understand the bitterness of its mayor and village council who, with the modest means at their disposal, do their utmost to attract visitors and attempt to fill the outsized shoes the legend has bequeathed them. A tourist brochure indicates any landmarks that could have a connection with Marie Harel. One can glimpse in the distance (it is private property, and visits are not allowed) the manor house where Marie Harel is supposed to have carried out her cheese-making experiments and where, purportedly, she hid the famous recusant priest who is said to have imparted to her the secrets of that soft-centered wonder with its savory crust. The manor's present-day owner is quite pleased to stand in for the famous cheese maker, and she takes the part of Marie Harel in the sound-and-light spectacles that are presented there. At the foot of the hill on which the church and manor sit stands a pyramid-shaped stone memorial to Marie Harel. Camembert also boasts two dairy farms that produce Camembert and a collector of Camembert labels who has managed to amass several thousand of them. However, the charm and interest of the village, which is actually no more than a few houses, reside in elements above and beyond these attempts to make itself a part of a legend. Camembert offers all of the beauties of the Auge, with its undulating fields and half-timbered farm buildings. Traveling the region's narrow lanes, one gets a real notion of the world in which Camembert was born, something that no museum can impart.

Looking for Marie Harel

Boulard proved that not only did Marie Harel have nothing to do with the invention of Camembert cheese, she never lived in the manor named Beaumoncel. Indeed, there is no trace of her ever having set foot in Camembert. In support of his argument, he quotes the formal notice given a certain Sieur Perrier, the farm tenant of a M. de Calmesnil, which is contained in the minutes of a meeting of the General Communal Council of Camembert held on 13 August 1792:

> In the name of the Nation and the Law, the township informs Monsieur Perrier that he is to render an exact accounting of the tithes owing on the overall receipts owed by him to Monsieur de Calmesnil, the proprietor of the Beaumoussel Farm of which he is a tenant.[6]

Thus, at the time when Camembert was supposedly being invented, the manor of Beaumoncel—*Beaumoussel,* according to the spelling of the day—was inhabited by a man named Perrier. In addition, no one named Harel appears on a contemporary list of the farmers resident in the community. Between 1792 and 1804, no births, marriages, or deaths are registered in Camembert under the Harel name. Nevertheless, Marie Harel's supporters have refused to admit defeat and in spite of everything have continued their efforts to give the legend a basis in historical truth. The last attempt of this kind was made by the Vimoutiers historical society, whose chairman, Gérard Roger, undertook to reply to the questions about Marie Harel's precise role:

> Did Marie Harel invent Camembert cheese? In fact, no one can answer that question because, although we know the manner in which she went about it, we do not know the practice employed by the dairymaids who preceded her. Therefore, she could well have created a new method of production.[7]

However, he is unable to draw the logical conclusion of his statements. Moving from doubt to affirmation, he concludes with a resounding expression of faith: "What is certain is that Marie Harel refined and perfected the process for making Camembert cheese."

Thus, the town of Vimoutiers, which has in a sense annexed Camembert, has attempted to back up its heroine's reputation. Did she really need this somewhat rash zeal? There was no need to continue to maintain, counter to all evidence, that she had invented Camembert, when such a stand risked discrediting her completely. It would have been enough to emphasize her real merits. For, if she did not actually invent our national cheese, Marie Harel née Fontaine did play an important part in its history. Again, one must attempt to arrive at the facts as best one can. In an attempt to clear up the whole matter, which does have some elements that cannot be determined, I shall attempt to indicate those that are actual fact, those that are likely to be true, and those that are possible but must be taken on faith.

We now know that, apparently, Marie Fontaine never lived in Camembert. A parish registry reveals that she was born at Crouttes on 28 April 1761. Her mother, Marguerite Legendre, died on 12 October 1782. Her father, Jacques Fontaine, took as his second wife Charlotte Perrier, the daughter of Jean Perrier, a farmer tenant of the property called Beaumoncel in Camembert. It was through her father's second marriage and his move to Beaumoncel with his wife that Marie Fontaine met Jacques Harel, who was a farm worker employed by Jean Perrier. Marie and

Jacques met at Beaumoncel and were married at Camembert on 10 May 1785. The couple then went to live at Roiville, Jacques Harel's native village, where their daughter Marie was born on 29 December 1787. These facts, reflected in the official records, explain why no trace of Marie Fontaine is to be found in Camembert, even though she did in fact stay there at one point.

Based on those established facts, we come to the likely ones. There is almost no doubt that our Marie Harel née Fontaine did indeed produce cheeses after the Camembert fashion. Her descendants have stated so, and there is no reason to question them. However, she probably deserves more credit than that. Although we cannot be certain about it, we may reasonably assume that our heroine did become adept in the delicate process of creating the local cheese and that, as a result, she made a name for herself by commercializing it beyond its traditional orbit. According to Jules Morière, who probably got his information from Marie Fontaine's grandson, Cyrille Paynel, whom he visited on several occasions, she not only sold her cheeses at the Vimoutiers market, she also transported them to Argentan, where in 1798 she established a storage facility on the premises of a certain Dame Trouvé, "seller of foodstuffs, rue de l'Horloge." [8]

As for exactly what her innovative methods were, that remains a mystery. Some highly imaginative hypotheses have been put forward. According to Auguste Gavin, the Vimoutiers pharmacist who welcomed Joseph Knirim, Marie Fontaine, following the instructions of the recusant priest, developed an aging process for a local cheese that had previously been sold fresh at the Vimoutiers market. This purportedly made it more easily transportable and prolonged its shelf life, thus making it more marketable. Born as she was in Crouttes, whose name sounds like the French word for "crust," it is poetically fitting that her cheese should also have one. Others have maintained that she created a white cheese out of a cheese that had formerly been blue. None of these hypotheses is worthy of consideration.

The Annunciation

Did Marie Fontaine hide a recusant priest at Beaumoncel? On 12 July 1790, the Constituent Assembly reorganized the church with its adoption of the Civil Constitution of the Clergy, which set out to reconstruct that body to conform with a rational and uniform system and to bring it under governmental control. Many priests refused to take the clerical oath of loyalty and preferred to go into hiding or to flee the country. Many churchmen attempted to reach England from the Norman ports of Granville and Honfleur. Others traversed the Norman countryside on their way to exile. One of these latter, who happened to pass through Vimoutiers, was captured by the inhabitants, who attempted to force him to take the oath and, when they failed, lynched him: "A fanatical curé from Basse-Normandie refused to shout, 'Long live the Nation!' Notwithstanding the efforts of the public officials, he was massacred." [9]

Many similar misadventures caused recusant priests to avoid the towns and to hide out in the countryside, which was better disposed toward the clergy. According to Abbé Guibé, a curé at Camembert after the Second World War,

> Over the course of ten years, I found documents signed by twelve different priests. Among them are Charles-Jean Bonvoust, priest, Benedictine monk, prior of Rouxville. Could this be the monk who, according to legend, was hidden at Beaumoncel and, out of gratitude, imparted to Marie Harel the secret of his monastery's cheese? Could this oft-repeated tale have some basis in fact? According to the documents he signed, he was in hiding at Camembert from July 1796 to February 1797. [10]

According to another source, two recusant priests were in hiding at Camembert during the Terror: Abbé Bourdon, who hid from 1796 to 1801 with the Loutreuil family, and Abbé Deschamps, who was taken in by Pierre Parent. [11] If one of those priests played a role in the creation of Camembert cheese, that would have occurred not in 1791, but in 1796 or 1797. It is therefore not impossible that Marie Harel could have come across a fleeing priest and that she might even have hidden him at the Manoir de Beaumoncel, where she came to visit her father and help out at the farm. We can even speculate that the priest might have given her some advice, but there is no proof for any of this. In any event, the participation of a priest in improving the fabrication of a cheese that had already been produced in the region for at least fifty years would not seem to be of any special importance. Given the region's reputation for fearing witchcraft, the help may have been nothing more than a blessing to ward off evil.

Marie Harel's great merit, and the one for which she has become famous, does not lie in the improvement in the fabrication of a cheese or in having increased its sales. Others who are now forgotten probably did as much as she in those areas. Her merit was to have handed down to posterity her daughter, her knowledge, the good name of her house, her luck, and her other numerous and enterprising offspring who were able to make the most of their ancestress's recipe.

Marie Harel, the daughter of Marie and Jacques Harel, married Thomas Paynel and set up housekeeping with him at Champosoult on the farm attached to the château. Together, they manufactured excellent Camembert cheeses by scrupulously adhering to the secret methods of Marie Harel. Together they also produced five children, three boys and two girls. All were to become cheese makers, as did one of Thomas Paynel's godchildren, Marie-Louise Morice. The three girls, with the assistance of their husbands, also went into the cheese business. Each of them founded firms that were to last for several decades: the Jouanne, Serey, and Paynel dairies. Cyrille Paynel, born in 1817, moved to the community of Mesnil-Mauger in Calvados. Victor Paynel took over his father's cheese business. In the third generation, during the early years of the Third Republic, Camembert cheese, which was still the monopoly of Marie Harel's descendants, was to achieve even greater recognition. It was being manufactured on a dozen or so farms and was for sale at all of the region's markets, as well as in Caen and in Paris. The children faithfully followed the ancestral recipe, expanded production, and introduced certain innovations that facilitated the process. Mme Morice, Thomas Paynel's goddaughter, set up the first real Camembert factory in the Calvados region. Thomas Paynel introduced Camembert to Caen through a local cheese merchant, Mme Chalange. In 1813, Camembert was made "a citizen of the city of Caen." The family's ambitions did not stop at the capital of Basse-Normandie. The development of the railroads opened the Parisian market by bringing Paris closer to the Auge.

Had it not been for the remarkable success of her descendants, Marie Harel would never have achieved her posthumous fame. Her grandchildren and great-grandchildren sedulously kept her memory alive and sang her praises. Their zeal was not entirely the result of family piety. The ancestor cult owes a great deal to commercial interests. By proclaiming their kinship with the woman who had invented Camembert, Marie Harel's grandchildren were giving themselves the stamp of authenticity and tradition. The first printed matter crediting Marie Harel, née Fontaine, with the invention of Camembert appeared around 1850. It was the product of the grandchildren at the Norman farm, led by her grandson, Cyrille Paynel. He formed professional contacts with the Association Normande, and especially with Jules Morière, who paid several visits to his cheese factory, and Professor Armand-Florent Pouriau, the foremost specialist in the technology of cheese production at the time. He was also a member of the newly formed Association Laitière Française (French Dairy Association), created in 1878. If Cyrille Paynel played an essential role in his grandmother's fame—if he can be said to have in a way invented it—he did so in order to distinguish his cheeses from those of his competitors.

As the inventor's grandson, he had a considerable advantage over other manufacturers. At the time Camembert was becoming increasingly popular and making a place for itself in the Parisian market, Marie Harel's descendants lost their exclusive rights to its fabrication. By hailing their ancestress as the inventor of Camembert cheese, her descendants—Paynels, Sereys, Jouannes, Morices, and Lebrets—were laying claim to an exclusive right that was theirs by inheritance. They alone, by virtue of their blood relationship, were in a position to produce true Camembert cheese according to the correct recipe. Other makers, ignorant of the secrets, were producing counterfeits. In fabricating this story, Marie Harel's descendants were attempting to make Camembert their own. By fostering the legend, Cyrille Paynel was acknowledging his debt to his real mother, née Marie Harel, and to that other, legendary Marie, wife of Jacques Harel, whom he had never known. Thus, the man who modernized the production of Camembert, improving the process and inventing new techniques, also affirmed the basic role that tradition played in his cheese. In particular, it is by providing tradition with a face that Marie Fontaine Harel's memory has been perpetuated, not only by her own descendants, but by Norman Camembert manufacturers in general, in order to distinguish them from their competitors in other regions.

If today we have a better understanding of why and how the mythical tale of Camembert's origins came to be, there is still uncertainty with regard to the precise circumstances surrounding the invention of France's most famous cheese. I cannot claim to shed any new light on the subject, but my approach to the attempt will be different. There are two ways to seek out the origins of an event. The first, always elusive, relies on what actually took place at the precise moment when it occurred. The second attempts to discover the steps that led up to it and made it possible. The myth deals with the first, whereas the second falls to historical research. Pinning down the exact moment of creation is more an exercise in mythological imagining than a use of historical rigor. In dealing with the myth, I believe that I have shed light on its meaning and indicated the elements that correspond to some factual reality, and it is now my purpose to uncover the origins of the cheese—the true origins, quite apart from the myth—and to discuss the conditions under which its manufacture began.

And There Were Angels ...

Whatever Marie Harel's connection with the science of cheese making might have been, two things are certain: there was a well-known cheese known as Camembert long before she came along, and Normandy had for centuries been recognized for the excellence of its cheeses. Heir to a long tradition of cheese making, Camembert did not spring up out of nowhere; before gaining its preeminent position, it already had its place on a well-stocked cheese platter.

Normandy is not a region with natural boundaries, but a heterogeneous province that includes several very different areas. What common elements are shared by the plains around Caen, the Bessin region, and the marshes of Vernier? In fact, the cheese-making tradition attributed to Normandy prevails only in two regions, the Auge and the Bray, which have no common border. The Auge specializes in soft-centered, fermented cheeses, and the Bray specializes in soft-centered, cream-enriched cheeses. For centuries, the Bray cheeses, which have been in existence for at least a thousand years, were more highly regarded than those of the Auge, where most of the regional income was derived from other kinds of produce.

Located between Upper and Lower Normandy, the Auge, with its landscape of undulating hills, is an extension of Upper Normandy, of which geographers once considered it a part. However, it is administered by Lower Normandy and is divided into three départements: nine-tenths of it is in the département of Calvados, and the remainder is in the Orne and the Eure. It extends from the coast, between Cabourg and Honfleur, to Merlerault. Its varied topography contrasts with the plains that surround it, consisting as it does of narrow plateaus and large, deep valleys through which flow the Dives, Touques, Vie, and Orbiquet rivers and their various tributary streams, fed by the abundant rain that falls upon the Auge's fields in spring and autumn. The valleys and glens are often separated by steep ravines. This natural area, known since antiquity as Saltus Algiae, has undergone several important changes in recent centuries. It was not declared an area of *appellation d'origine* for Livarot and Pont l'Évêque cheeses and Calvados brandy until as recently as 1926.

It is believed that Camembert, Normandy's most famous product, must be the fruit of an age-old tradition going back well before the nineteenth century. Today, it is hard to believe that the cheese was not well known prior to the second half of the nineteenth century, at which time the railroad enabled it to be sold in Paris. Prior to 1860, it was known to only a few knowledgeable and wealthy gourmets. In the region itself, it was to be found for sale in only a few markets. The cheeses known as Livarot, Pont l'Évêque, Gournay, and Neufchâtel were far better known; indeed, they were the names on which Normandy had built its reputation, until Camembert came along and took over.

We know that Normandy's cheeses were already famous in the Middle Ages, but we have no real knowledge of the part they played in the province's economy. The first written mention of them is in connection with the payment of the tax known as the dîme, or tithe, a tax in kind levied by the clergy against peasants and farmers, which came to a tenth of their production. Several eleventh-century texts speak of a tithe on the cheeses produced on certain estates. Hugues de Gournai, circa 1050, paid a tithe of cheeses to the monks at Sigi. At around the same time, the Abbey at Saint-Sauveur d'Évreux received from Count Richard a tithe of his cheeses from Quittebeuf. At the end of the eleventh century, the dukes of Normandy, who owned several *vacheries* (the term used to designate farms that specialized in raising dairy cattle), derived from them huge quantities of butter and cheese. What were those cheeses like, and how were they produced? We have no idea; we do not even know their names. In the sixteenth century, Charles Estienne mentions a cheese known as an "Angelot," a cherub or little angel. It was produced in the region around Rouen and in the viscountcy of Auge, today the canton of Pont l'Évêque, then in the bailiwick of Rouen. This ancestor of Pont l'Évêque owed its name to its resemblance to the English coin of the same name. Some maintain that the true name was "Augelot" (i.e., from the Auge region), but the oldest texts use the term "Angelot." However, the area in which it was produced did indeed include Rouen and the Auge viscountcy, whose principal town, Pont l'Évêque, was dependent on Rouen. The name "Angelot" was so appealing that it came to be applied to various different cheeses. In the fifteenth century, street merchants in Paris could be heard crying, "Angelots from Brie, both large and small! I beg you, buy from me, they are delicious all!" Of the cheeses produced in the Auge that are mentioned prior to the eighteenth century, the most prominent are undoubtedly Pont l'Évêque and Livarot. The name "Livarot" appears officially for the first time in 1690 in a text relating to the bailiwick of Caen.

Jean Bruyèrin Champier, in his gastronomical treatise *De re Cibaria* of 1659, and Charles Estienne in a treatise on agriculture dated 1554, praise the refined quality of cheeses from the Auge. However, cheese making, while far from marginal, was not the region's most important activity. From all that we know, the economy of the Auge was highly diversified, and that diversity is borne out by its fairs, including the one held at Guibray, a village near Falaise, the birthplace of William the Conqueror. The Guibray Fair was one of Europe's largest. The Auge also derived its wealth from the diversity of its agricultural products as well as from fabrics, and the region had many mills that produced cloth and lace. In this overall picture, cheeses and other dairy products were of secondary importance except in a few southern cantons. Until the sixteenth century, the Auge produced cheeses primarily for local consumption. Normandy's main cheese-producing region was Bray, which exported its products to Paris. Norman cheeses were also up against stiff competition from English cheeses. King Henry II ordered English cheeses to be sent to Gisors. An inventory informs us that there were thirty-three English cheeses at the Château de Falaise. In the twelfth and thirteenth centuries, English cheese was more highly regarded than Norman cheese because the Normans, following their conquest of England, had taken over the best farmland in that country and had most likely brought their cheese-making knowledge with them.

Pastoral Bounty

There is something seemingly permanent and timeless about the Auge that we see depicted on postcards, with its green pastures and orchards of apple trees heavy with their red and yellow fruit. Yet, up until the eighteenth century, it was a region with many diverse crops. The cultivation of grain and flax was more important than livestock. Everything changed during the course of the eighteenth century. The hitherto flourishing textile industry entered a period of crisis and progressively faded from the scene, while fields were no longer planted with crops. Land devoted to cereal crops was left to lie fallow. The present-day image of the Auge—green fields planted with cider apple trees and dotted with herds of peaceful dairy cattle—emerged during the Second Empire.

In a report written during the year 1698, Pomereau de la Bretèche gave the following description of the Auge:

> A rich area in which are grazed and maintained large numbers of cattle, which the inhabitants of the region purchase in the Poitou or in Brittany to be resold in Paris. There are also many dairy cattle that yield large quantities of milk, which is used in the fabrication of cheeses known as Angelots and Livarots, also sent to Paris with a large amount of poultry. . . . The hillsides provide rich pastures, but little of the land is arable.[12]

At the time, this described only a few cantons that still followed the old pastoral tradition, as was noted in 1631 by a man named Dumoulin, who wrote, "In the area between the hedgerow at Hiesme[13] and Pont l'Évêque, the cattle yield so much milk that in the summer a pound of butter can be had for two sols, a dozen cheeses for five."[14] The Auge thus produced not only milk, which the farmwives transformed into butter and cheeses, but a great deal of meat as well. There were more beef cattle grazing in the fields than dairy cattle. The region's farmers and peasants far preferred producing meat. It called for less work and was more profitable than milk. The cattle of the Auge were celebrated in Paris and sold well there: 40 percent of the meat consumed in Paris came from the Auge.[15]

The grazier, the typical inhabitant of the Auge in the eighteenth century, left his farm in the early spring wearing his long blue smock and black coat and traveled from fair to fair buying grazing cattle. He wore a fur cap or beret and thick boots to protect himself from the chill morning air. He either took the money for his purchases from the supply carefully hidden beneath his mattress or he applied to his banker for the funds he required. With the banknotes stowed in the leather bag slung on a cord around his neck, he would tour regions less rich in pasture than his own. He carried with him a large pair of scissors with which to mark his initials on the animals he would purchase. In all of this, he was called upon to exercise all of his abilities as an informed speculator. He selected the thinnest—and therefore the least expensive—cattle, avoiding animals he considered sick or too fragile, culling the ones that he believed would fatten the most rapidly. When he had enough livestock to populate his pasturelands, he would return on foot, herding the animals before him and allowing them to feed off of the grass at the sides of the road. In the autumn, he would set off again with his herd of fattened cattle, this time toward Paris, hoping to sell them at a good price to the wholesale butchers in La Villette or Poissy.

It is from these prosperous days that our image of the Augeron peasant has been derived: clever—even crafty—and with a nose for a good bargain, preferring the animation of country fairs over work in the fields. There is even a saying that in that region men can earn money simply by watching the grass grow. The graziers certainly enjoyed a better life than crop farmers, and their work was a great deal easier. However, it is hardly fair to accuse them of doing nothing. Watching over a herd and maintaining pastureland required work, as did haymaking, which involves far more than merely "playing around with hay," as Mme de Sévigné described it to her daughter in one of her letters. Yet the affluence was real. The value of grazing land increased by a third, and sometimes even doubled. Visitors were struck by the region's prosperity. Arthur Young, a well-known English agronomist and traveler who visited the area two years before the Revolution, wrote the following:

> The whole has singular features, composed of orchard inclosures, with hedges so thick and excellent, though composed of willow, with but a sprinkling of thorns, that one can scarcely see through them. . . . Pont l'Eveque is situated in the Pay d'Auge, celebrated for the great fertility of its pastures.[16]

While the menfolk went from fair to fair or saw to fattening their cattle, the women were busy in the house and farm. They were responsible for the milking and the production of dairy products. The milk was made into butter and cheeses for use on the farm, and the surplus was sold in the local markets, especially the better-known ones at Vimoutiers, Livarot, and Saint-Pierre-sur-Dives.

While revenues from dairy products were a major portion of the local economy in the Bray, they were less so in the Auge. Closer to Paris, Bray could transport its butter and cheeses there for sale. In the eighteenth century, the region specialized in dairy products. Neufchâtel cheeses, Angelots, and cheeses known as Bondes and Bondons were all exported to Caux and Picardie, and some even to England.

Beginning in 1850, the development of rail transport enabled other meat-producing regions to gain access to the Parisian market and to compete with products from the Auge. The Auge graziers were good bookkeepers, and comparing the income from dairy products and from beef cattle, they soon understood that they could make more money raising dairy cattle than they could from fattening herds for beef. They had all they needed to effect the change: abundant pastureland and a first-rate indigenous breed of cattle, the Cotentine, a variety of the Norman stock. And it was only logical to use the milk to produce butter and cheese. The only question was, which cheese? Following the example of Gournay, Bessin, in the region of Isigny, began to specialize in butter. In the Auge, the traditional cheeses produced had been Livarot, Pont l'Évêque, and, of course, Camembert. Each farm had produced cheese according to its own recipe, and the grouping of cheeses into broad categories was not, at the time, subject to very strict rules of fabrication. Indeed, some cheeses had no generic name and were distinguished only by the name of their maker. In the first half of the nineteenth century, one Norman farm family even had a name that predestined it to widespread fame: Fromage, the French word for "cheese." This dynasty had been founded in 1792 by Pierre Fromage, a native of Montpinçon, near Livarot, who had moved to Saint-Cyr-la-Rosière. His son Lucien, who succeeded him, dispatched boxes of cheese on a weekly basis to the courts of Louis XVIII and Charles X. In 1820, their first cheese warehouse was established in Paris in the rue Richelieu. In 1839, they produced more than 100,000 cheeses. The house of Fromage was awarded a silver medal for the quality of its product.

At this date, Camembert was still fairly unknown outside the borders of the Auge. From 1791, when it had purportedly been invented, to 1863, the year that Victor Paynel is said to have offered the emperor a taste, its fame was still very local and its production remained in the hands of

Marie Harel's numerous descendants. The identification of the Auge with Camembert cheese did not occur until the end of the century, when the number of dairies and factories producing the cheese began to increase to satisfy the growing demands of the Parisian market.

The new cheese's rapid rise to fame and the sudden fortune of the Auge graziers who turned to cheese production in the last decades of the nineteenth century transformed the region and created for it a new image that quickly took hold. To contemporaries, this amazing change, the wealth that nature had showered upon the region whose green pastures had once been cultivated with such difficulty, must have seemed like a miracle. Preferring the virtues of ingenuity and female labor to heavenly intervention, however, the Norman farmers hailed Marie Harel as the one who had brought them to this new era of well-being.

THE BIRTH OF AN INDUSTRY

The year 1850 is crucial in the history of Camembert. Earlier, it had been consumed only in the Auge, whereas other Norman cheeses—Pont l'Évêque, Livarot, and especially Neufchâtel—had been sold in Paris and elsewhere. After this date, Camembert was to undergo a striking advance. It conquered the Parisian market and then those of the majority of the country's large cities, before crossing frontiers and oceans. This amazing leap forward was caused by a combination of several favorable factors, foremost among which was the construction of a railroad network between the Auge and Paris.

A Cheese Takes the Train

There can be no question that the railroad is the factor that played the greatest role in the rise in Camembert's popularity and renown. The construction of a substantial network of railways connecting Paris with the many small localities in Normandy made the capital accessible to the producers of Camembert. It took less than six hours (when it had taken a stagecoach three days) to transport that redolent product from the dairies where it was made to Paris's central market of Les Halles. Since Camembert owes its conquest of Paris to the railroad, it is only fitting that the cheese's myth should recognize its role. We recall that it was on the occasion of the inauguration of the Paris-Granville line, in the train station at Surdon,[17] that one of Marie Harel's grandsons, Victor Paynel, is said to have offered a Camembert to Emperor Napoleon III. The emperor was won over by the refinement and flavor of the new cheese and was responsible for its entry into the Parisian market.

What credit can we give this picturesque tale, which is not mentioned in any contemporary document? From *L'Annuaire Normand* we know that in 1864 the Emperor's provisioner, a M. Chirade, purchased Camembert cheeses from Paynel at a cost of 50 centimes per piece.[18] Thus, the picturesque episode in the train station at Surdon may indeed have some foundation in fact. However, several of the details connected to the railway aspect of the incident that is supposed to have set the imperial seal on Camembert's creamy crust are clearly incorrect. If Paynel did offer a Camembert cheese to Napoleon III in the station at Surdon, this could not have taken place at the inauguration of the Paris-Granville line unless the act occurred not in 1863, as the stories would have it,[19] but several years later. In fact, the line in question was not completed until July 1870, in the final days of the empire. Nor could the incident have taken place in connection with the branch line to Surdon, which was completed in 1867. When Napoleon III visited Normandy in 1863, it was not to open a new railway line but rather to attend the horse racing at Pin-au-Haras. *Le Moniteur Universel,* the newspaper that reported this visit in great detail and with its customary self-satisfied tone, made no mention of the Camembert incident. Having left the Château de Saint-Cloud on Saturday, 8 August, in the imperial railway coach, the emperor arrived at the station in Argentan at 5 P.M. He then transferred onto the Paris-Cherbourg line and traveled on to Mézidon, where he boarded a coach of the Mézidon-LeMans line to Argentan, which was not yet directly linked to Paris. On the evening of his arrival, he proceeded to Pin-au-Haras by carriage and spent the night there. On Sunday, he attended Mass before proceeding to the racetrack at 1 P.M. After the races, which ended at 4:30 P.M., he was present at 9 in the evening at a fireworks display that was witnessed, according to *Le Moniteur Universel,* by some one hundred thousand persons. He left Pin-au-Haras the following day, and his train reached Saint-Cloud at 4:55 P.M.[20] Yes, he could have returned via Surdon—that town, which is near to Pin-au-Haras, had been accessible from Argentan on the Mézidon-Le Mans line since 1858—but the newspaper makes no mention of it. And it makes little difference whether the emperor discovered

Camembert in a tiny Norman train station or through the intervention of his cook. The anecdote is of interest because it reveals the connection between Camembert and the railroad network. Through the emperor, the French capital discovered Camembert, and it is the railroad that made that event possible.

The development of the railway system was a godsend for the cheese makers of the Auge. Several stations saw an enormous traffic in cheeses, not only the larger ones like Mézidon and Lisieux, but also smaller stations like Mesnil-Mauger, which Cyrille Paynel used to dispatch his Camemberts.

Meat or Cheese?

The vast outlet of Paris' central market, Les Halles, was now accessible, and the Augeron dairy farmers needed only to seize the opportunity and turn their energies to the production of milk and Camembert cheese. As we have seen, the principal activity in the Auge, with the exception of a few cantons, had been grazing or the fattening of cattle. In order to convince the prosperous Augeron graziers to change their ways and turn to cheese production, they had to be shown that this would be profitable. Jules Morière and Pierre Durand, two prominent members of the Association Normande, set out to do just that.

Founded under the Restoration at the behest of Arcisse de Caumont, the Association Normande was quick to see Camembert's economic possibilities. The association's aim was to promote rural modernization by popularizing new farming and breeding methods and the use of farm machinery. Its surveys had shown that cheese making was more profitable than grazing. Through its farm-visiting commissions and its competitions, which awarded the best producers and encouraged the most inventive and devoted proponents of progress, the Association Normande played a major role in the growth of the cheese industry in the region.

Unlike most of the members of the Association Normande, Durand, born in 1814 at Montpinçon, came from a humble background. Apprenticed to a pharmacist at Lisieux at a very young age, he went on to study to become a dispensing chemist. His high placement in the pharmaceutical examination in 1840 revealed his intelligence, and he was awarded a scholarship to enable him to continue his studies. While working as a hospice pharmacist, he received a science degree and, in 1849, a doctorate. His field of interest included many aspects of agricultural science, dairy production in particular. He was able to demonstrate to the Association Normande that cheese making would be more profitable than grazing and that, of the various cheeses, the most remunerative was Camembert. From 1849 on, he worked to encourage farmers to devote themselves to cheese production rather than to cattle fattening. In 1851, he wrote that he considered "the question of cheese manufacture to be one of the most important in the Lisieux region" and that "the best use to which forage can be put is the feeding of dairy cows. . . . Camembert cheese is the form in which milk becomes the most remunerative. A double liter of milk yields 0.50 francs when converted into Camembert cheese."[21]

Men listened to Durand, but his premature death in 1853, at the age of thirty-nine, deprived him of the pleasure of seeing the successful results of his advice. Although he was a pioneer in the development of the Camembert industry, he was quickly forgotten and his name has never been linked with the cheese's success, despite his having been one of the first to believe in it.

After Durand's death, Morière picked up the torch and published two articles on the development of the cheese industry in Normandy. In 1859, he calculated that a cow whose milk production was turned solely to Camembert would earn approximately 250 francs a year. Such economic arguments, illustrated by the success of the Paynel brothers, finally won over the Augeron farmers. There are, of course, no precise records available; even Cyrille Paynel, a modern farmer, kept very few, relying—as he was to note in his logbook—on his son:

> Although I can calculate my expenses and income on a yearly basis, I must admit that my ignorance of the principles of bookkeeping has not allowed me to maintain regular records. Not until 1871, when my eldest son took charge of the books, were my various operations recorded in any orderly fashion.[22]

However, we do not need a detailed record to note the profit that cheese brought in, since the keen business sense of the Norman farmer, acquired from his long experience at cattle fairs, rarely failed him. The shrewdest of them soon went into cheese production.

However, the development of the cheese industry did encounter some obstacles that proved to be more difficult to surmount. Although financial logic was on the side of cheese, domestic equilibrium rested on a long-established division of labor that was based on cattle raising. Husband-wife relations on Auge farms were typified not by the husband's absolute authority, but by an accepted complementarity between the two. Domestic tasks—house, stable, dairy—were the province of the wife; outdoor labor, especially anything dealing with the cattle that were the principal source of income, fell to the husband. The switch to cheese production as the household's principal economic activity altered its balance by making the wife's role preeminent. Despite the financial argument in favor of the change, the Norman male was unable to accept this. The shift in activities in favor of women could not be allowed to bring into question the traditional separation of tasks and the equilibrium between men and women. Even when they recognized the superior financial advantages of cheese production, men were unable to resign themselves to dairy work or to abandon their tours of the regional fairs. If men were to consent to forgo cattle raising and turn exclusively to cheese manufacturing, they would have to become the masters in this new enterprise traditionally reserved for women. It took several decades for the Normans to work out a satisfying response to this question. Even those farms that turned to cheese production on a large scale continued to engage in cattle raising, thus assuring the male a noble activity in herd management and trading. This was to be the case until the male created a front-rank position for himself where cheese making was concerned, namely, the role of senior manager, which dispensed him from the dairy activities that were still carried out by women and under female supervision while affording him a new management function and a commercial role.

Cyrille Paynel, Maker of Camemberts

Morière makes frequent mention of the enterprise run by Cyrille Paynel, a man who had no qualms about making cheese. The house in which Paynel lived is inhabited today by one of his descendants and her husband. Now retired, they ran the farm known as L'Église, which Cyrille Paynel had rented in the nineteenth century. They showed me the remains of the former cheese-making factory and the mementoes handed down by their ancestors, especially a notebook written by Paynel himself. The dairy built by Paynel's son still stands alongside the superb half-timbered house. The earlier dairy, where Marie Harel's grandson made his Camemberts, is no longer a dairy, and instead has been attached to the house and made into another room. In 1874, Paynel was preparing to enter a cheese-making competition for a prize to be awarded the following year. The notebook contains an account of his activities and explains his methods to the members of the committee entrusted with visiting the competitors' farms.

Although he derived a considerable income from Camembert, its manufacture was far from Paynel's only activity. He was above all a farmer or, in today's jargon, an agricultural engineer. Despite the amount of money he was making, he did not own his farms but merely rented them. At a time and in a region where many farmers had but one goal—to be the owners of a piece of land, no matter how small—this fact alone made him stand out, yet it is a situation we find with other cheese manufacturers, Paynel's own brothers among them. The ownership of land was less important to them than its exploitation, and these pioneer Norman cheese makers were businessmen before they were landowners. Having gone into the business with little capital and free from any particular cultural heritage, they devoted themselves to cheese production with intensity and great initiative. Their attitude was in sharp contrast to that of most local landowners, who were devoted to traditional methods and concerned above all with increasing their patrimony.

Paynel worked a considerable acreage of eight farms totaling 196 hectares (485 acres) of pastureland, on which he grazed a large number of cattle. Although he was a cheese manufacturer, the larger part of his herd was not intended to produce milk for cheese, but rather to be fattened for consumption. Each year, he "fattened one hundred beef cattle and cows,"[23] whereas he kept only seventy milk cows. Cheese production was a seasonal activity that came to a halt in the summer months. Despite the increase in cheese production, grazing for fattening up remained the primary agricultural activity. In addition to raising cattle to be sold at La Villette, Paris' principal meat market, selling week-old calves as veal at fairs, and producing butter and Camembert cheese, Paynel also fattened pigs and produced huge quantities of cider and apple brandy, not to mention all the other products to be found on a Norman farm, such as poultry, fruits, vegetables, and so on.

Paynel was aware of all of the cultural innovations of his day and gave proof of amazing inventiveness. He developed new tools to facilitate agricultural labor and came up with a recipe for improving cider. He took great pains to fertilize his fields to increase their yield. He not only spread them with manure, he collected alluvium from the river Vie, which flowed through his land, and used it to fertilize the ungrazed portions of some of his pastures; collected road dust to fertilize others; spread plaster; and drained fields that required it. His notebook gives a detailed account of all this:

I drained 22 hectares [54 acres] of land in three pastures on my farm, L'Église. Prior to doing so, some areas of the land were so marshy that it was nearly impossible to walk there, some areas were even fenced off to keep the cattle out and grew only poor quality grass. Good results were obtained in less than two weeks after drainage, the surface water disappeared, the ground firmed up and you could walk across the drained land without being afraid to lose your shoes. Since then, the drainage has continued to yield good results and the land today is covered with good grass that proves the effectiveness of the drier soil. Some drains were created crosswise to the slant of the land, some obliquely and others parallel. The latter two methods have yielded the best results. The mouths of the collectors are lead pipes of a shape devised by me and all empty into the river. In the small farm, the eastern part of the pasture called the little park was drained. Prior to that operation the water remained on the surface and some of it drained into the ditch alongside the road. I had 1,163 meters [3,814 feet] of trench dug out, which improved the drainage of the pasture. To drain approximately 2.5 hectares [6 acres] I spent 566.55 francs. That sum was repaid me by the landowner in 1872 upon expiration of my last lease. However, the various improvements meant that my new lease went up by 250 francs.

Paynel's inventiveness also found expression in the layout of his cheese dairy, a large building adjoining his house, as noted in this notebook entry:

The house faces east; one of its rooms, on the north side, was extended, at my expense, by 8 meters [26 feet] for use as a dairy having an interior dimension of 14 meters [46 feet] long and 5.5 meters [18 feet] wide. There is also a laundry room, which I have set up at the end of the dairy. Slabs of

Portland cement have been installed around and in the center of the room, on which eight hundred cheeses can be poured per day. The whey flows over these inclined slabs into underground pipes that lead to earthenware recipients lined with Portland cement and located outside the building. A drain has also been provided for the quick and complete evacuation of the water used to wash the slabs and the dairy floor. I have devised a small cart to facilitate the transport of the milk containers to any part of the dairy. Lastly, stoves have been placed at either end, their pipes extending the length of the room and ensuring heat in the winter. A portable stove is placed in the laundry room to which two pipes can be connected, one of which can be opened by means of a key to contribute to heating the dairy when necessary; with a minimum fuel expenditure, this stove enables the milk to be heated in a bain-marie, after which the hot water can be used to wash the boilers and other utensils. This apparatus, which cost only 67 francs, has produced a savings of 75 percent compared to the method hitherto employed. I have installed four of these devices in other dairies in the region and the results have been equally satisfactory. In the washroom, which is separated by a single wall, there is a brick tank with a capacity of almost 400 liters [106 gallons] that is filled by means of a pump in the same room. This tank feeds five faucets installed in the dairy for washing the slabs, three of which are affixed to hoses that can also be used to wash the dairy's paved floor. Lastly, a sixth faucet set beneath one of the slabs serves for cleaning various utensils. Another tin-plated copper tank with a 98-liter [26-gallon] capacity is set into the chimney of the fireplace and provides hot water via a faucet. On the north side is the drying room where the cheeses are taken after leaving the dairy; prior to 1857 this was merely a shed. I had this shed plastered and floored and turned into four rooms: first, the drying room, where I replaced straw with wooden racks with openings covered with fine metal screening to allow for ventilation; second, the curing cellar; third, the finishing cellar; and fourth, the packaging cellar. On the other side of the drying shed are wine and fruit cellars. There was another shed that in 1866, also at my own expense, I converted into an additional drying room and cellar. In toto, this wing measures 18 meters [59 feet] by 5.8 meters [19 feet], and it cost 600 francs. To the west, facing the main building, there are two cider cellars, one of which has been turned into a cheese cellar.

In 1865, Paynel's fifty-seven dairy cows yielded him an average of 7.13 liters (1.88 gallons) of milk per day, a very respectable amount for the period. Over the course of that year, he produced 1,292 kilograms (2,849 pounds) of butter, 3,215 Livarot cheeses, and 59,146 Camemberts. Camembert production was seasonal; it is a cheese that is sensitive to hot and stormy weather, and Paynel noted that he adapted his herd accordingly: "I kept a larger herd during the autumn because of the Camembert production, which begins in September and ends around the middle of April."

Thanks to the railway, he was able to ship a large part of his abundant produce to the Parisian market. On every working day throughout the season, he brought his cheeses in their wicker baskets to the train station at Mesnil-Mauger. Camembert was the only cheese then being shipped to Paris; the butter and Livarot cheeses were sold locally at the market in Saint-Pierre-sur-Dives.

A trustworthy middleman was a necessity when selling a product as delicate as Camembert. The problem was how to be sure that trust was not misplaced. Paynel had a clever answer to this difficult question, as he described in his notebook:

> Desirous of increasing my production and acquiring a speedier dispatch of my produce, upon my arrival in Mesnil-Mauger I contacted a Monsieur Trouvé in Paris and agreed to supply him with fifty dozen cheeses per week from 10 December to Holy Week. The next year, I made the same agreement, but beginning on 1 November. Monsieur Trouvé had made me a verbal promise to do his best to sell an even greater quantity, but he did not live up to his word, and hoping to learn the reason, I went to Paris myself the following month, where, working in disguise, I discovered that Trouvé, after having sold my cheeses, was offering a reduction of from 25 to 50 centimes to keep the paper wrappers with my name printed on them—I even saw him offer 75 centimes. He then used those papers to wrap other cheeses of a far inferior quality that he was getting from markets in and around Argentan. This fraud was making my cheeses less appreciated and drastically reducing demand for them. I immediately abrogated my agreement, and Trouvé, aware that I was onto his guilty maneuvers, did not even ask me why. However, convinced that Paris was the place where I had to create a clientele, I immediately set up a gentleman named Goubin d'Aubry le Panthou, to whom I guaranteed a fairly high revenue. This man was entrusted with the sale of my products exclusively. It is to his intelligent and devoted support that I attribute a large part of the success that I have enjoyed over the past fourteen years. That is how I endeavored to demonstrate to the consumer that we were able to provide high-quality Camemberts.[24]

The Parisian market was not enough; in order to keep abreast of his competitors, who were sending the majority of their production to Paris, he turned to still wider markets. Paynel noted:

Today, I am attempting to introduce our products in the city of Lille, in Flanders, just as I did in Paris in 1858, Camemberts hitherto having been ignored by the restaurants and food merchants of that large city. This attempt will this year cost me from 4,000 to 5,000 francs, but I am determined to prove to Lille's consumers that they can rely on me to furnish them with good-quality Camembert in Lille just as I do in Paris. And since they will not be able to resist them once they have tasted them, I am hoping to foster the spread of this product to my own advantage as well as to that of my fellow producers.[25]

Commercialization was to remain the Achilles' heel of the Norman cheese producers. From the moment their cheeses left their factories, they were obliged to have trustworthy middlemen—market brokers and specialty grocers—to ensure their distribution and sale. However, like Paynel, no one was safe from fraud. Dedication to cheese making in the Auge was not, therefore, the result of an age-old tradition, but rather the result of a contemporary choice based on economic calculations and abetted by a few innovative farmers with the backing of the Association Normande.

Lightning Growth

The spread of Camembert production was especially rapid. Tempted by the potential profits, cheese manufacturers sprang up all over the Auge and throughout Normandy, and then began spilling over to other dairy regions. Whereas the cheese had barely been known in 1850, less than thirty years later it was being produced throughout Normandy and in many other parts of the country as well.

The first Camembert producers had been located in the Orne sector of the Auge. Following in the footsteps of Julie Paynel Lebret, Cyrille's sister, several dairies were set up in Calvados. In 1859, there were some thirty establishments in that département and an even larger number in the Orne. However, the total Orne production was not even half that of Calvados. In 1878, Morière listed fifty Camembert producers in Calvados. He estimates the annual income from the production of Camemberts in that region at 2 million francs, which is ten times greater than it had been in 1859, while during the same period the production and sale of Livarot had merely doubled. In 1903, the Eure département had twenty-five cheese-making dairies, and there were around forty in the Orne and forty-eight in Calvados, not counting home production.[26]

Most of the dairies had a limited output, and their life expectancy was haphazard; many of them went out of business after a few years while others appeared to replace them. Up until the end of the century there were few large cheese factories, but many small enterprises had sprung up. Thus, in the tiny community of Boissey, with a population of barely four hundred, there were in 1880 three Camembert factories, "one of which produced seventeen hundred to eighteen hundred cheeses per day."[27]

From 1886 to 1894, the sale of Camembert at Les Halles nearly doubled, from 1,241 to 2,330 tons.[28] Despite this growth, however, it had still not attained the level of sales of Brie.

Technological Progress

In 1859, the two largest cheese-producing dairies were owned by two of the younger Paynel brothers, one at Coupesarte and the other at Champosoult, each producing forty thousand Camemberts per year, while Cyrille Paynel was turning out thirty-five thousand at Mesnil-Mauger. Over a twenty-year period, their output increased fourfold. By 1879, Léon Serey was producing 160,000 Camemberts per year and Cyrille Paynel 150,000. That rapid growth reflects the success of this new, developing commerce, fed by growing demand but without having experienced any notable technological change. The increase in the scale of production was made possible largely by the creation of special locales adapted to fabrication and maturing. The cheese-making factory was no longer merely an annex to the dairy, but a specific building connected either to the dwelling or to one of the farm outbuildings. However, the scale of production was limited by the size of the dairy farmers who provided the milk. Large farms were needed to supply a cheese factory. In 1872, Cyrille Paynel was working almost 200 hectares (495 acres) spread over the eight farms he was renting, the largest area at that time.

The only precise descriptions we have of cheese factories at this period concern the large producers. What do we know of the smaller ones, which were far more numerous? In these establishments there was no specific building or equipment for the purpose, apart from the essential implements: pans, ladles, and molds. Cheese making took place in the dairy, where the women skimmed the milk and made butter, and the aging process was carried out in the cellar. If one were to have a specially equipped area set aside for cheese making, one had to be able to count on producing several hundred cheeses per day. Without the technical setup necessary to ensure mass production, the small cheese makers had a hard time turning out quality cheeses. Further, they did not all have that indispensable knowledge that can be gained only through experience. However, some small or medium-sized producers, cleverer than others, did manage to win prizes at agricultural fairs. These were often awarded to "housewives," which was not surprising, given the fact that they were usually the ones who knew the manufacturing secrets.

This growth was of unequal advantage to the three principal cheeses of Lower Normandy. When it came to transforming milk into cheese, the fabrication of Camembert was in competition with that of Pont l'Évêque and Livarot. Both of the older cheeses retained their preeminence up until the end of the century, after which Camembert finally surpassed them. In the canton of Livarot, nevertheless, many farms continued to turn out Livarot cheeses, which was better adapted to their needs. In those farms, the cream, after having been skimmed from the milk, was churned into butter, and the milk was used to make raw cheeses that were then sold to refiners for aging. In Boissey, where there were three Camembert producers, there were "eighteen or twenty producers of Livarot cheese."[29]

Why did such farms continue to produce Livarot rather than Camembert? A study in 1881 by the Association Normande had this to report:

> There is little difference in income between the products. The Camembert
> industry, however, requires greater care, special buildings, and runs the
> risk of losses involving greater amounts of cheese.

This problem proper to Camembert explains the greater number of small producers of Livarot and the tendency to concentrate Camembert production, a situation that prevailed from the very beginning. The technical problems involved in producing Camembert, while limiting its small-scale farm production and favoring large, specialized factories, would later work in favor of its growth to the disadvantage of Livarot and Pont l'Évêque, which continued to be produced in the traditional way.

The End of a Monopoly

Beginning in 1870, the continued growth of the Camembert industry ran into problems created by the very people who had been its pioneers, namely, Marie Harel's descendants. They exercised a jealous control over a field of endeavor that they regarded as a family monopoly. In their view, the ability to make Camembert and the right to sell a cheese bearing that name were part and parcel of the family's patrimony that could only be passed on by inheritance. Until around 1850, those families had a virtual monopoly on the manufacture of Camembert, considered the heritage of the mistress of the house. For although financial patrimony was passed on to the male members of the family, the secret of manufacturing the cheese was handed down orally and through apprenticeship from mother to daughter.

Nevertheless, the Harel clan's claims to exclusive rights were not supported by any legal patent or registered trademark. The family's only protection was the relative ignorance and inexperience of the new producers, who, lacking expertise and ignorant of the jealously guarded secrets of the cheese's manufacture, were unable to compete with Marie Harel's heirs. However, the lure of the profits to be realized impelled the more enterprising to persevere despite their ignorance and to go into Camembert production, even if it meant improvising.

The only truly effective protection against competition is expertise, the reputation of the producers, and the bonds of trust they have established with their clients. Such protection is fragile when there is a sudden and large-scale increase in demand. It can ensure the fidelity of gourmets and wealthy cheese fanciers, but it cannot prevent new consumers from turning to other producers. At that period, anyone was free to commercialize any kind of cheese and to sell it as Camembert. In the absence of any precise definition or legal protection, the market became the ultimate judge in any dispute between rival producers. Even though in those days anything was allowed, if one wanted to make a decent profit it was preferable to produce the best possible Camembert and to strive to match the quality of the cheeses sold by the Paynel family, who won most of the medals at agricultural fairs.

Competitors attempted to get hold of the secrets of fabrication, the carefully guarded tricks and special techniques, by any means available. Some managed to do so by hiring away a subordinate who might, after the mistress of the household, have knowledge of production methods. At the agricultural fair held at Lisieux in 1851, a Mme Montier, from the community of Glos, was awarded the silver medal by the jury for her cheese production. She manufactured Mignot and Pont l'Évêque, but her principal business was said to be the manufacture of Camembert, which she sold in Lisieux and in Paris.[30] How had she managed to master the delicate process of Camembert production?

> Madame Montier made great financial sacrifices when she undertook this type of production. For a year, and at a very high salary, she had hired a servant from the Camembert community who had learned the secret of making the best cheese; after having learned the method from this woman, she began to produce it herself, and her efforts were crowned with success.[31]

A glimpse into how industrial espionage was carried out in those days! Marie Harel's secret, divulged by a female employee for a few gold coins, could well be part of the legend. Luring away the best professionals is an age-old and widespread practice that even highly placed government authorities have not hesitated to employ. But can we really speak of a secret, in the sense of some precise formula, the knowledge of which would ensure an excellent product? Here we are not dealing with that, but rather with a body of professional skills learned from recognized and experienced teachers and refined through long practice. Where Camembert is concerned, it was even less of a secret in the region itself, where many farms transformed their surplus milk into a soft-centered cheese similar to the one produced by Marie Harel. Each farm had its own recipe and could have aspired to the name "Camembert." Yet, to sell at a good price one had to have a quality product and a well-known producer. What better renown could there be than the one attached to two or three generations of cheese makers, all claiming to carry on the work of the woman who had invented Camembert? In successfully reproducing the quality of such a delicate cheese, the experience handed down over decades of practice was an enormous advantage. Competitors were forced to content themselves with selling for lower prices than did the heirs, unless they could truly rival them in quality. Thus, it was not so much a secret that they were hoping to discover by hiring women who had worked with the Paynels or the Morices, but rather experienced artisans who knew the tricks of the trade and who would enable them to produce the best cheeses on a regular basis.

Whether real or imagined, production secrets continue to be a part of Camembert production. Each brand claims to possess its secret or secrets of fabrication and strives to protect them, forbidding its competitors access to its production facilities and warning its employees against going to work for one of them. At the same time, the owners strive to discover their competitors' secrets and resort to all sorts of tactics to do so. A retired cheese manufacturer who had been one of the most prominent in the Auge confessed to me that more than one fabrication secret had passed from one firm to another in the course of an intimate moment in the bedchamber or even in an apple orchard or haystack. Cheese manufacturers went out of their way to seduce the female employees of competing firms. My informer himself admitted to having pursued the female owners of cheese-making establishments, "floral offerings in hand."

The Quarrel over Legitimacy

One of the very first definitions of Camembert cheese was made by Armand-Florent Pouriau in a book published in 1872,[32] but it is purely indicative in nature. After leaving the family that had given it birth, Camembert quickly spread beyond the boundaries of the Auge and set out to conquer the rest of the country. The Marquis of Jucoville, who had established one cheese-making center in the Auge, went on to create another one in the Bessin region.[33] The spread of Camembert did not stop there, but overflowed beyond the borders of Normandy. In 1870 it began to be produced in Brittany, and then in the Loire Valley; in 1876 we find a M. Fould[34] at Liercy-Lévy, in the Allier, becoming a well-known producer. In 1888, Pouriau, who taught at the Institut National de Recherche Agronomique, records six cheese factories producing Camembert in Ille-et-Vilaine, one of which, at Noyal, was making between fifteen hundred and two thousand cheeses per day.[35] He also mentions the same output in "the large industrial dairies of the Nord, Eure, and Charentes départements, etc."[36] Camembert production was to spread to other regions as well, without the Norman creators being able to do anything about it. Each new site gave rise to the same accusation.

Product definition was the crux of a dispute that arose between farmers and producers. The Harel-Paynel dynasty had appropriated the "Camembert" label, which had existed in the region for decades, and used it as a pretext to exclude other makers. Only cheese produced in the family-owned establishments had a right to the name. As for others who made similar products, they were eventually allowed to use a label reading *façon Camembert*, tantamount to "imitation Camembert." The earliest manufacturers of the cheese who were not connected to the Harel-Paynel dynasty found themselves deprived of access to the term "Camembert." Mme Barel-Lanos, of Mesnil-Simon, won a bronze medal at the regional fair at Caen in 1854 for her "cheeses *façon Camembert.*" In fact, the "imitation Camembert" cheeses were Camemberts in all but name, since lacking any written description of the cheese, no one knew the precise criteria necessary for a cheese to be accepted as Camembert.

As the demand grew, other makers finally managed to win recognition in the marketplace and access to the "Camembert" name, notwithstanding the indignant protests of the Paynels. Gradually, dozens of farmers began to produce the cheese. It would appear that the modes of production varied greatly from farm to farm. Although the influence of the Paynels enabled them to retain de facto exclusivity over the "Camembert" label for a while, the time came when it slipped out of their control.

As early as 1894, other regions had made marked inroads in the Parisian market, accounting for 27.5 percent of sales.[37] At century's end, Camembert was being produced in many regions outside Normandy, but cheese aficionados were already beginning to single out true Camembert, which, according to the geographer Victor-Eugène Ardouin-Dumazet, "came from the relatively narrow zone of pastureland around Mézidon, Saint-Pierre-sur-Dives, Livarot, and Vimoutiers,"[38] and to distinguish it from the imitation Camembert produced elsewhere. It was at this period that the notion of a "vintage" or exclusive area for Camembert, outside which it would not have its specific characteristics, began to take shape.

The same author denounced both the spread of the cheese beyond its region of origin and the growth of industrial production, which, at that period, was hardly what we would call "artisanal" or homemade:

> In fact, this extraordinary growth has led to a large number of counterfeits in regions totally lacking in both the traditions of Vimoutiers and in pasturelands with the outstanding savor of those deep Norman valleys. Further, production facilities where the cheese is made in large quantities create, of necessity, an industrial product; the milk must be brought in from a considerable distance. Milk from different sources cannot yield the same quality cheese as milk derived from a single source.[39]

The End of a Dynasty

As we have seen, cheese, and Camembert cheese in particular, is a family affair. During the first half of the nineteenth century, the many descendants of Marie Harel had little difficulty in preserving exclusive rights over the production of Camembert, or at least over its commercialization beyond Vimoutiers. At the time, Camembert was even known as "Madame Harel's cheese."

The exclusive reign of the first Camembert dynasty came to an end around the beginning of the second half of the nineteenth century. Some farmers who did not belong to the founding clan had always produced and sold, albeit on a small scale, cheeses called Camembert, just as they had before Marie Harel's day. However, their production was extremely small and never represented any real competition. Things began to change in 1850, when several small cheese makers went into production on a larger scale and took steps to enter the Parisian market.

The preeminence of the dynasty of the Harels, Paynels, Jouannes, Morices, Lebrets, and so on rested on their mastery of large-scale production, with the ability to turn out several hundred Camembert cheeses per day. The family's experience, essential in a field with so many risks, was much greater than that of their competitors. As succeeding generations possessed of such expertise began to grow in size, continued contact between the different branches of the family represented great advantages to them all, enabling them to retain superiority in production, while the family's renown enabled it to retain a first-class clientele. For more than a century,

Marie Harel's descendants alone benefited from this continuity, while other cheese makers found themselves unable even to establish a foothold. Competing cheese makers would go into business, begin to grow, and then disappear for lack of heirs or be taken over by outsiders who were forced to start learning to make cheese all over again. So long as the body of knowledge remained oral, and often even unspoken, and was handed down basically by imitation, no competing firm proved able to stand up to them. Two important factors were to breach this unquestioned superiority. One was the early attempts in 1870 to put the cheese-making technique involved into print; the other was the creation of large competing firms with powerful backing who were able to call upon scientific experts, if needed.

Not until the end of the century do we find such rival dynasties as the Lanquetots, Lepetits, Bissons, and Buquets. Despite their competition, the firms of Marie Harel's descendants continued in operation. Some remained in the fore until the beginning of the twentieth century, and many of the 1909 founding members of the Syndicat des Fabricants du Véritable Camembert de Normandie were descendants of Marie Harel. Yet none of those firms were to survive beyond the 1930s.

SECRETS OF FABRICATION

I will spare the reader a boring account of cheese making in general and of Camembert production in particular, from the earliest times up to the present day. Yet it would be impossible to comprehend the originality of Camembert and the changes it has undergone without some minimum information regarding its production. Since, therefore, it cannot be avoided, I shall try to make it as diverting as possible. I trust that it will become clear that the personality of Camembert cheese and a part of its success depend on the subtle alchemy of its fabrication, which requires a keen sense of observation and a huge amount of initiative in dealing with the unpredictable behavior of milk curd.

At the risk of disappointing cheese lovers, it should be made clear from the very start that Camembert cannot be made at home. It is one thing to make a batch of yogurt in one's own kitchen, but maturing cheese is something else altogether. One must bear in mind that the fabrication of

Camembert is an art that requires great experience and one that entails production on a scale that not even the most voracious household could possibly ingest.

Although today a relative uniformity in the methods of production of both traditional and pasteurized Camembert cheese has been achieved, in the nineteenth century, each manufacturer relied on its own recipe. There was no one method of fabrication; there were only general principles and an infinite number of variations. Over the past 150 years, the methods of producing Camembert have changed considerably, including the methods of producing the so-called traditional version of the cheese. It is not easy, therefore, to talk about Camembert manufacture without referring to a specific era and a specific method. Of course, some general principles can be established, but we must not lose sight of the fact that actual production methods have always differed greatly from one maker to another.

Like every cheese, Camembert is the result of the fermentation of curdled milk. Prior to aging, the curd goes through the following processes: after it is formed, it is cut or shaped, drained, molded, unmolded, and salted. On the basis of that universal process, each individual dairy will have its own secret methods of fabricating its particular cheese. Here, I shall describe Camembert manufacture by drawing upon the oldest detailed descriptions, to discuss the principal changes that have taken place in the process and the differences in the methodology of various producers. Morière and Pouriau were the first to describe the creation of Camembert on the basis of their own direct observation of the work of experienced cheese makers. Morière wrote his description in 1856, giving an account of what he had observed at Cyrille Paynel's establishment at Garnetot. In 1878, having returned to Paynel's factory, which had moved from Garnetot to Mesnil-Mauger, he published a new and more complete account of how Camembert was made in *L'Annuaire Normand*. In 1872, Pouriau also explained how "Camembert cheese" was made. In his book on the dairy industry, he emphasized the special problems involved in producing the cheese:

> [Camembert] is one whose production, which is extremely tricky, demands special temperature conditions and, in a word, presents infinitely more problems than does any other cheese.[40]

Pouriau bases his description on observations he made on the premises of a M. Quiquemelle, a cheese maker located at Chaumont in the Orne, where he himself had participated in the process.

The creation of a cheese begins with milking. Nature does not give milk away. The milk's quality depends on the expertise of the dairy farmer and the care with which the cow is milked. Pouriau emphasizes the need for clean premises, noting that the cow's udder should be washed prior to milking. The warm, foaming milk should immediately be strained. At Paynel's dairy, the milk was passed through a cloth known as a *couleux* into Noron stoneware vessels with a 70-liter (18.5-gallon) capacity called *serènes*. After the milk has rested for two or three hours, the thin layer of cream that has risen to the top is carefully lifted off with an *écremette,* or creamer, a utensil resembling a small pierced scoop. In the vividly descriptive language of the Auge, this operation is known as *essévage,* roughly, de-sapping, or sap removal, the cream being regarded as the sap of the milk. This cream is especially rich and yields a much-prized butter. The milk collected at the evening milking is set in a cool place. The next morning, it is lightly skimmed and then mixed with the unskimmed milk from the morning milking. This method yields milk with a fat content of approximately 30 percent. The evening milk has been acidified by lactic fermentation, but the acidity must be controlled, and overly acid milk should be set aside. In the cheese-making establishment of M. Paul Vignioboul, at Jort,

> The milk is collected in wide-mouthed milk cans. The cans brought in in the evening are left open and set in cement troughs filled with cool running water, where they stand all night. On the following morning, the contents are tasted and the acidity checked with an acidometer and, in case of doubt, a cremometer, after which the two milkings are combined and put into a multitubular warmer. In this method, if a can happens to contain bad milk, it can be set aside and will not have an adverse effect on the production.[41]

After this preparatory phase comes the rennet phase, during which a small amount of rennet, an enzyme distilled from the lining of a calf's fourth stomach that serves to enhance the curdling process, is added to the milk cans. There is no set amount of rennet or exact length of time involved in the process; the cheese maker relies on his experience, taking into account weather conditions and milk quality. The amount of rennet used depends on its concentration, which, since it is homemade, is not constant. At Paynel's dairy, one spoonful of rennet was added for every 20 liters (5.3 gallons). The operation was carried out at the same temperature as the new milk, or approximately 38°C (100°F), a temperature achieved by "heating some of the morning milk in a bain-marie and then adding the evening milk to it."[42] In order that the rennet should be evenly distributed throughout the milk, the mixture was stirred for about two minutes with a large spoon. A wooden cover was then placed over each container. At Paynel's dairy, the curdling process required five or six hours; at that of Quiquemelle, it took some five hours at 26°C (78.8°F). At other dairies, the length of curdling time was between two and three hours, much less than the time taken by Paynel and Quiquemelle.[43] The variations in curdling time were due to the lesser or greater amount of rennet used. The more rennet added, the faster the curdling process.

In deciding whether the curd was sufficiently firm, the Augeron cheese makers performed a *boutonnière,* or "buttonhole test": "The curd is ready when it no longer sticks to the finger; when it is pressed, a kind of buttonhole is formed that contains pure whey, and then closes up again on its own."[44]

When the cheese maker estimates that the curdling has reached the proper stage, the molding process immediately begins. It is of the utmost importance that the precise moment be determined. If molding is begun too early, the curd will be too fragile and will break apart in the mold. However, if it is delayed too long, the draining process will be slowed down by overly clotted curds. Ladle-molding therefore takes place as soon as the curdling process is complete. Using "an ordinary soup spoon," the curd is removed from the containers where it has formed and put into "*éclisses,* or cheese trays, in this case cylindrical rounds of ash wood."[45] The bottomless molds are set out side by side on tables covered with rush or rattan matting or on wire stands covered with fir mats. The draining tables have sloping surfaces that allow the whey to be collected for feed for the pigs. The dairywoman doing the molding uses a special tool to lift the curd gently from the container and into the mold without breaking it. The operation calls for speed and skill, for the curd must not sit too long in its tank and it must not be broken up. The molder starts at the outer edge of the container and works around its circumference, continuing in a spiral path until she reaches the center. She then does the same with the succeeding layers. Some cheese makers reserve the final layer of curd, which is not used in the fabrication of first-quality Camembert. A mold will contain four or five spoonfuls of curd. It takes from forty-five minutes to an hour between each addition for the curd to drain without pressure. The temperature in the molding room should be approximately 18°C (64.4°F). A day after it has been molded, or the same evening if it was molded in the early morning, the cheese is carefully turned: "In turning the cheese, the left hand is slowly slipped under the mold and the right placed across the top opening; the cheese is then adroitly reversed and slid back onto the matting."[46] On the following day, the mold is removed and the cheese is salted: "The mistress of the farm takes each cheese in her left hand and rotates it on her fingers, distributing the salt evenly around the perimeter."[47]

The salted cheeses are then set on wooden shelves above draining tables. They will stay there for one to four days before being taken into the *hâloir,* or drying chamber, where they will sit on straw-covered racks for twenty to twenty-five days. Throughout that period, they will be turned, first on a daily basis and then every other day. In order for the cheeses to age properly, the drying chamber must have sufficient air circulation. To achieve this, narrow vertical slits are pierced in the room's whitewashed walls, like the vents in the walls of medieval castles through which arrows and other projectiles were fired. The openings are covered with screening to prevent birds and mice from entering. Small sliding shutters are affixed to them, so that the size of the opening can be varied according to the force and direction of the wind, thereby ensuring that all of the racks will be touched by the fresh air: "The placement of the openings in the walls of the drying chamber is the most important element in obtaining a good end product; it is here that the know-how of the cheese maker can be most clearly discerned."[48]

On the third day, the cheeses will begin to form small brown spots, and then a white coating that takes on a bluish tinge. At the end of the aging process, some red spots appear. When the cheeses have become soft, they are removed from the chamber.

They are lightly pressed on the surface by the fingers to judge their degree of firmness, and when they have acquired a suitable softness, which can only be known by experience, when they no longer adhere to the fingertips, they are placed on planks and carried to the finishing cellar.[49]

Once placed in the cellar, the cheeses continue to age for twenty to thirty days at a temperature of 12–14°C (53.6–57.2°F). They are set on wooden slabs and arranged by age. They are turned every day or every other day. During this phase, additional red patches will form on the surface and take on an increasingly intense color as the interior becomes increasingly soft. All in all, the fabrication of a Camembert, aging included, takes seven to nine weeks.

Once aged, Camembert is fragile and must be transported with great care. Some makers avoid this problem by shipping their cheeses before aging has been fully completed, relying on the cheese merchant to complete the process. However, this system has several drawbacks. First, it deprives the maker of control over the final phase, which is the one on which the cheese's quality truly depends. By entrusting aging to a vendor, the cheese maker runs the risk of seeing all his work come to naught. Further, by delivering an unfinished product, he also cuts into his profit margin. Both his reputation and his financial interests are involved, therefore, and demand that he complete the aging process himself. On the other hand, of course, the shipment of large quantities of soft cheeses presents a real challenge. Many Camemberts that have left the factory in good shape have come to a bad end, their creamy innards oozing out through large cracks, victims of the unthinking brutality of some overhasty shipper: "For shipping, the cheeses are stacked by the half-dozen and separated by rounds of paper; this package is enclosed in straw, whence the term *paillots* [pallets; *paille* = straw in French]." As an additional protection against shock, the cheeses are then packed in rattan baskets or in slatted wood crates. On the shelves of his cheese merchant, the consumer will find soft and aromatic Camemberts whose color will vary from bluish-gray to orange-pink. Their nakedness is sometimes covered by a waxed paper bearing the maker's name.

Thus was Camembert prepared at the establishments of Paynel and Quiquemelle around 1870. Other firms employed other methods. If there were so many different methods of making the cheese and so many variations in those methods over the years, is there any sense to the term "Camembert," or is the name nothing but an illusion maintained for commercial reasons? Is there any "truth" where Camembert is concerned, and if so, what is it? All of these variations in process may make us shake our heads, but they also enable us to discern a few fixed rules. Above and beyond the diverse methods of production, and despite the absence of a precise definition or written recipe for the cheese, the cheese makers in the Auge all observe minimal rules that tend to make Camembert different from all of the region's other cheeses. Unlike Livarot, Camembert is usually made of unskimmed milk, although some makers do skim slightly. This accepted practice is not without its abuses, and some makers, greedy to have their Camembert and eat it too, so to speak, have been known to skim their milk thoroughly before adding rennet, thereby producing low-fat Camemberts that are, unfortunately, dry. The originality of Camembert cheese, what gives it its delicate consistency and makes its fabrication so difficult, resides in the way in which the milk is turned to curd.

All cheeses, of course, are made from curdled milk. Their differences begin with the manner in which the curdling process is carried out. A few technical details involved in this process are needed to help us to understand what makes Camembert a cheese unlike any other. There are two principal ways to curdle milk: one is spontaneous and occurs through the action of lactic acid bacilli when milk is allowed to stand at room temperature; the other is achieved with the help of various substances such as rennet or the carbohydrate juices of plants like artichoke, thistle, or fig. Curds can be produced in various ways, but the apparent uniformity of the result conceals important differences. After twenty-four or thirty-six hours, milk curd will have the fragile and fluid consistency of yogurt. It must then be kept in an airtight container. Curdling with rennet is faster (it takes from thirty to forty-five minutes) and yields a compact and highly cohesive curd. Many cheeses are the result of mixed curdling, in which both lactic fermentation and rennet play a role. For some, like Livarot, Pont l'Évêque, Munster, and Maroilles, the principal action is due to rennet; for other cheeses, like Camembert, Neufchâtel, and most goat cheeses, lactic fermentation plays the principal role. The curd of these latter cheeses is especially fragile and its handling is a delicate matter.

In practice, mixed curdling requires aging. Time must be allowed for the lactic bacilli present in the milk to act prior to the addition of rennet.

This is the most common method, but the details of its implementation are left to the discretion of the maker. It is in this early stage of production that the cheese maker has a real opportunity to demonstrate his artistry. The quality of the cheese depends on the balance between the action of the lactic bacilli and the action of the rennet, and thus on the duration of each stage, temperature, monitoring of the milk's acid content, and the amount of rennet. On each of those elements, individual makers will differ. To shorten the time required for curdling, the maker need only increase the amount of rennet or work at a higher temperature, but in so doing, he alters the nature of the curd, which becomes less lactic and thus firmer and easier to work with. From the point of view of yield, increasing the rennet dosage has nothing but advantages: the process is much faster and handling is much easier. Thus, over time, cheese makers have been increasing the amount of rennet used in order to improve their yield. As a result, the curdling time, which took over five hours some 150 years ago, takes only an hour today.

The creation of traditional Camembert is a subtle joust with nature. Transforming the curd into a delicious, creamy-centered cheese requires its maker to possess a keen eye, to exert near-constant attention, and to have a delicate touch. The majority of cheeses call for considerable physical manipulation. The curd is generally cut into small pieces and is ultimately pressed in order to facilitate draining. By contrast, in the case of Camembert, the curd must be neither cut up nor pressed, but allowed to drain naturally in the molds. The rind is neither brushed nor washed; after the fermentation process has begun, mold must be allowed to form naturally. Nature must be allowed to take its course with only such interference as is required to nudge it in the right direction, which explains why the making of Camembert is the most delicate of operations, since natural phenomena are unpredictable and capricious.

Over the course of time, Camembert has preserved its uniqueness despite all of the innovations introduced to produce it on a large scale and to improve the cheese maker's control over refractory natural phenomena. Comparison between Morière's two descriptions of Camembert production at Cyrille Paynel's establishment, separated as they are by an interval of twenty years, gives us a fairly detailed notion of the changes that occurred between 1850 and 1870, the period during which the Camembert industry took off.

The most important innovation was in the highly delicate *hâlage,* or drying, phase. This calls for special premises, the expense of which made the exercise prohibitive for many small producers. Paynel came up with a workable technical solution by devising an ingenious system of adjustable openings. The majority of cheese makers were to adopt his system, which enabled them to vary the air circulation according to the direction and intensity of the wind. Aside from the drying chambers, the major improvements involved such relatively minor elements as the molds and the draining tables. The earliest molds had been *éclisses,* or cheese trays made of ash. In 1856, tin-plate molds began to be used, which were more expensive (they cost 8 francs per dozen), but which lasted longer than the wooden ones. By 1878, the wooden molds had disappeared and metal molds were being used exclusively; the price had fallen to 5.50 francs per dozen, the decrease reflecting the move from manual to industrial production. As demand grew, industrial firms specializing in dairy equipment also stepped up their production.

In the first cheese factories, the cheeses were set in the drying chambers on *glui,* or straw. By 1878, the straw had been replaced by wooden racks made of poplar. Improvements were also made in the draining tables. Cyrille Paynel, who was never short of ideas, set the 100-liter (26.5-gallon) receptacles in which the milk curdled on little carts to facilitate their transport to the long tables on which the molds were set out. At Champsoult, his brother Victor adopted the same system. Thus, each cheese maker, with varying degrees of effectiveness, worked to improve manufacturing conditions and final product.

In the early days, the rennet, also called the *tournure* (turning element), was produced at the dairy by using calf abomasum, or rennet stomach, dried and kept cool. The dairymaid would macerate a small amount of dried abomasum in a mixture of weak vinegar water until it became a *tournure,* which she would then add to the milk to cause it to clot, or curdle. That method, however, did not yield rennet with a consistent concentration, which, in turn, led to irregularities in the speed and firmness of the curd produced. Morière notes that "many farmwives, instead of preparing this mixture themselves, prefer to purchase it from Monsieur Delauney."[50] This gentleman, a pharmacist at Lisieux, had been honored in 1861 by the Association Normande, which had awarded him a bronze medal for his creation of a "most usefully recognized" rennet. In 1874, in

Denmark, Hansen succeeded in extracting and stabilizing rennet that could be kept and whose curdling power remained unchanged, thereby eliminating one of the elements of chance in the process. The Boll firm began to commercialize this rennet in France in 1876.

Over the years, the spread of the methods being used by the large cheese producers and the development of a small industrial sector producing material and products for their use had brought about a uniformity and stability in such basic stages of the process as molding. However, although the makers all used broadly similar methods, each had his own personal recipes and tricks of the trade.

Chapter 3 | CAMEMBERT GOES NATIONAL

At the end of the nineteenth century, Camembert entered a new era. The reign of the first dynasty, that of Marie Harel, was drawing to a close, and a new power was emerging. For seventy years, from 1880 to 1950, a handful of prominent families took over the Camembert industry and raised it to a new plateau. Marie Harel's cheese was to undergo several changes and a considerable growth in its production.

CAMEMBERT'S METAMORPHOSES

Freed from the control of Marie Harel's descendants, the fabrication of Camembert was no longer exclusively guided by respect for tradition. In order to increase production, the leading families introduced several important changes that would markedly alter the cheese-making process and the product's final appearance. In 1880, Camembert was still a farm product, a fragile cheese that did not travel well over long distances. Its rind was most often a grayish-blue and not the pristine white that we see today. Three crucial innovations were to bring about a vast increase in its production and sales and provide the new dynasties with the wherewithal to expand. These were first, the box that allowed for its safe travel; second the *Penicillium candidum* that gave the cheese its white color; and last, the process of supplementary milk collection from other, nonaffiliated dairies in the region, which ensured that cheese makers had a greater supply available to them.

Boxing

In the nineteenth century, precious Camembert cheeses, carefully tended, often arrived on the retailer's shelves in pitiable condition. There was nothing the merchants could do about it, for the cheeses were not girded for battle. They traveled almost naked, set out on a fragile bed of straw. The thin sheet of paper in which they were wrapped was hardly sufficient protection against the jolts of the journey and the often rough handling to which they were subjected, and they required some more solid protection. This was to come in the form of a wooden box. Today, it is hard to imagine Camembert without its round wooden box, so wedded have they become in our minds. And yet, they have been together for little more than a century. The union of Camembert and its box is but one additional mystery in the cheese's history. Unfortunately, there is no record of the great event, for such indeed it was. When and how did it occur? We do not know. There are several accounts, which bestow credit for the idea on at least three different persons. The name that comes up most often is that of a man named Ridel, an engineer by profession. Mention is also made of an exporter named Rousset and of Auguste Lepetit, the owner of the cheese factories that bear his name. Everyone does, however, agree that it was around 1890 when the first Camembert was put into the first round box. The event most certainly occurred prior to 1896, since a volume published that year informs us that

> The perfect cheeses are wrapped in waxed or albuminous paper and put into a wooden box whose cover bears a label noting the factory and the name of the maker.[1]

However, which man—Rousset, Ridel, or Lepetit—was the first to have thought of putting Camemberts into boxes? My own research has not enabled me to identify the clever food-packaging specialist with any certainty. Without purporting to deliver the truth, let me put forward the version that I find the most plausible.

Around 1890, Rousset, an exporter at Le Havre whose name could be found on many labels toward the end of the nineteenth century, was looking for a way to protect the cheeses he was shipping to the United States. He had an additional reason for finding such a method, since he was also the director of a Camembert-producing firm known as Les Fermiers Normands. Perhaps inspired by the packaging of other items he exported, perhaps even by other cheeses, he had the idea of putting Camemberts into round wooden boxes "like the Tyrolese pharmaceutical boxes." [2] The term "Tyrolese boxes" or, as some catalogs listed them, "Parisian boxes known as 'Tyrol,'" was used to designate the boxes used for pharmaceutical products. The earliest versions were made of discs and slats of spruce and were fabricated in the Jura at Bois-d'Amont, a small town known for the production of small boxes of all kinds. Several small establishments there were working for cheese makers, one of which, Lamy Curey Flavien, advertised itself as a "maker of boxes of all kinds, especially pharmaceutical and post boxes." The letterhead of a bill dated 1894 reads: "Specialist in round, square, or triangular cheese boxes: Mont d'Or, Brie, Camembert, Pont l'Évêque, Munster, etc." By that date, therefore, wooden boxes were also being used for cheeses other than Camembert.

Perhaps it is Ridel's background—born at Vimoutiers, his father a cabinetmaker—that has led some to attribute the creation of the box to him, but in fact, his contribution was of a different nature. It was his invention of a machine for making cheese boxes that enabled Georges Leroy to industrialize its fabrication. [3] As for the Lepetit hypothesis, all we have to go on is a publicity leaflet put out by that firm. It is thus likely that it was Rousset, the exporter, who should be given credit for having first put Camembert into its box. Whoever invented the box, he rapidly found himself copied. At first, the Norman cheese makers were supplied from the Jura region in eastern France, but they soon began to look for a closer source of supply in order to reduce transport costs and shipping delays. The "Fromagerie du Château" at Bourg-Saint-Léonard first contacted a Parisian producer, Lucien Henry, and then the L. Roger establishment at Caen. Local sawmill owners were recruited, notably M. Ledru at Sainte-Marguerite-de-Viette in Calvados. At the time, Leroy was working in the sawmill owned by M. Leveau at Breuil-en-Auge, very near the Breuil cheese factory. M. Blondel, proprietor of the latter, had spoken about his packaging problems with his neighbors and asked them to help him to find a practical and simple solution. Leroy suggested a box made of poplar,[4] a wood abundant in Normandy and very inexpensive. The boxes were made of two thin disks and strips of wood planed from a block. They were assembled by domestic labor: the workers would take the wood shavings home with them and nail them to the disks with tiny nails that they held in place with a magnet, using a serrated mold as support. The small Breuil workshop was soon flooded with orders, and Leroy expanded. His first factory opened at Livarot in 1907; another opened at Saint-Pierre-sur-Dives in 1928. In order to be more independent, Léonce Abaye, the manager of the Tremblay cheese factory, opened his own box-making works. A contemporary observer described one of these as "an organizational marvel": "It turns out extremely thin sheets of poplar and beech that inventive machines, mostly operated by women, transform into Camembert boxes. It produces up to fifty thousand boxes a day."[5] Abaye also owned another factory at Saint-Pierre-sur-Dives that was later taken over by Leroy.

Safe and protected in its box, Camembert was thus able to travel risk-free over considerable distances and to withstand longer pre-sale delays. Thanks to the box, the label—which had become an essential element—had something to which it could be affixed. One might even surmise that the box could well have been created solely for the purpose of displaying the label.

The Pasteur Institute Turns Camembert White

Can we imagine Camembert other than white? Yet before acquiring the snowy cover we know today, its rind was closer to blue. In the nineteenth century, the color of Camembert varied, and although it occasionally approached white, it was most often somewhere between blue and gray, with brownish-red spots. In the early twentieth century, there were increasing quantities of white cheeses, but that color—or lack of color—did not become the norm until the 1920s and 1930s. Even then, the term "white" was relative, since the rind continued to be more or less covered with brown spots. It was only in the latter part of the century, sometime after 1975, that the cheese began to flaunt the pale hue that had once been viewed with a certain suspicion.

We may be sure that this was not the result of some spontaneous transformation. It happened through actions that took place far from the world of the cheese makers and through the appearance of a new player, one who had not been invited but who had in a way forced his way onto the stage, namely, the scientist. Everyone boasting any knowledge of Normandy's best-known cheese, whether it be distant or firsthand, whether they be makers, experts, or merely Camembert aficionados, seems to suffer from a strange form of amnesia. Almost all of them appear to have forgotten Camembert's original color. As for the rare ones who do mention it, they appear to know nothing of the precise circumstances that caused the cheese to turn white. Camembert's blue period is brushed aside as though it had been some abnormality, the stigma of something disgraceful in its background. Are contemporary cheese makers trying to erase some of the less appetizing aspects inherent in the cheese's rural origins, of which otherwise they seem so proud? In France, there has long been a problem involved in laying claim to roots that are totally peasant and rural. Wildflowers, fresh air, the song of birds, fresh milk—yes! But manure, mud—yekkhh! The rural life sells only when it has been properly sanitized. When countryfolk come to town, they are expected to dress up a bit and wear clean boots. As for Camembert, it has doffed its blue and donned an impeccable white.

It was not enough, however, for Camembert to turn white, and ever whiter, from its rind to its creamy center; it became necessary to maintain that it had been ever thus and to remove any suspicion that there had been any intervention from outside the realm of the cheese dairy. Some versions of the primal story give credit to Marie Harel for having provided Camembert with a white rind. The cheese is said to have existed prior to her arrival on the scene, but in a crude version, one fit only for vulgar peasant appetites. In this unusual version of the Immaculate Conception myth, it is another woman, appropriately named Marie, who was inspired by her priest and produced a Camembert that was virginally white.

One understands the amnesia of the Norman cheese makers caused by their desire to be faithful to Marie Harel and her story. However, why have scientists and technologists kept silent about their role in making Camembert white? For them, the change of the cheese's color is unimportant, nothing but the symbolic sign of their having entered the world of cheese manufacture. Their concern has been focused elsewhere, on pasteurization. Pasteurized milk, cream, butter, and cheese, pasteurized un-til the last undesirable bacterium has been eliminated—that is the only battle that interests them.

Thus, given the indifference of the scientists and the makers' denial that they have altered the cheese's color, how can we get to the true facts? I searched through the various treatises on cheese production looking for the earliest mention of the change. To my surprise, I was unable to find anything precise about it. Camembert's whitening is barely mentioned, as though the circumstances surrounding it and those responsible for it were being kept hidden. Not only is the person responsible for turning the cheese white never clearly designated, the greatest confusion seems to pre-vail, even in scientific literature, with regard to the microorganisms re-sponsible for the color of the rind. However, by consulting and combin-ing various sources, I managed to identify the principal actors involved in this important step in Camembert's history and to fix the approximate time and circumstances. Before revisiting this purposely forgotten epi-sode, however, and because this question is an integral part of the myth, I should say something about its context and origins.

If we wish to identify the concealed personality behind the whitening of Camembert cheese, the man the myth ignores (although he himself has become a kind of mythic figure), it is not the priest we should seek, but rather the scientist, the benefactor of humankind, one of the Republic's most outstanding citizens. In order for Camembert to become a national myth, it had to be touched by one of the most famous of all French sci-entists, Louis Pasteur, whose picture might very fittingly be reproduced on the cheese's label. For in fact, it is his work, his teachings, and his dis-ciples who have left their mark on the cheese, which was one of their ba-sic experimental tools in the dairy field.

In 1847, Pasteur abandoned crystallography to investigate the phenom-enon of fermentation. His interest in the industrial applications of his work was a constant throughout his career. During his time at Lille, the local brewers asked his help in improving beer production. After study-ing beer fermentation, he turned to wine and then to vinegar, but he left the study of dairy products to his disciples. Strong bonds sprang up be-tween the Pasteur Institute and the cheese industry. Scientists acted as advisers to cheese makers who, in turn, financed their laboratory work.

Émile Duclaux, who was born at Aurillac in 1840 and who served as Pasteur's successor as head of the institute, established an experimental dairy laboratory at Le Fau in the Cantal region. There he made a special study of the fabrication methods employed in producing Cantal cheese. In 1877, he submitted to the Academy of Sciences a paper on the fabrication of that cheese. In 1892, he published a work titled *Principes de Laiterie (Dairy Principles)*. According to Dr. Émile Roux, another of Pasteur's pupils, "Duclaux's work represents the beginning of the scientific era in the dairy industry."[6] Pierre Mazé, who was a section head at the institute, developed lactic fermenting agents and molds for cheese factories. Antoine-Marie Guérault, the son of a cheese maker who was himself engaged in the activity, divided his time between his work at the Pasteur Institute, his teaching, and his own cheese factory. Professor Guittoneau presided over a laboratory of ten scientists at the Gervais factory in Gournay-en-Bray. In the 1920s, the Pasteur Institute and the National Institute of Agronomy collaborated on a large-scale program of practical and theoretical research into cheese fermentation.[7] This scientific interest in cheese making had a widespread effect. Science, by playing a role in cheese manufacture, laid the groundwork for its industrialization. However, it took nearly a half-century for that process to be completed.

Before turning to pasteurization, the scientific community had long attempted to understand the mechanics of maturation and to identify the microorganisms involved. It was noted that soft-centered cheeses got their color from the microscopic molds that grew on their surface. This vegetation appeared spontaneously on fresh cheeses and was a product of the environment, either from objects that came into contact with the cheeses or from the ambient air. Various kinds of mold are to be found on cheeses, and depending on which ones are most prevalent, the color of the crust can vary as the cheese matures from the original white to blue, green, or gray, or it can remain white. In Normandy, the dominant mold tends to produce a grayish-green hue. Maurice Desfleurs, a member of the Faculté des Sciences at Caen, reported the following:

We recall having witnessed in the first decade of this century the manufacture of Camemberts: the cheese maker took care not to overclean the racks on which the drained, salted, and molded curd was set, thus ensuring that it would be seeded and become moldy. Soon, the *Penicillium camemberti* would cover it with its white mycelium. Subsequently, the cheese would turn a pale gray-green and finally a pale gray with a greenish tinge.[8]

When Pasteur's students set out to rationalize cheese making, they immediately ran into the problem of mold. We know that Pasteur's theories concerning microorganisms arose out of a pitched battle against the notion of spontaneous generation advanced by Archimède Pouchet. For Pasteur's followers, nothing was more untenable than the cheese makers' belief that maturing occurred spontaneously. They expended great efforts in demonstrating that the whole process was caused by the action of various microorganisms, bacteria, and molds. Having succeeded in doing that, they then set out to replace chance with a planned and logical intervention, introducing into the milk the germ necessary to its transformation. They waged this battle against ignorance and empiricism in the name of science and technology. They wished to set up rational procedures that would normalize the manufacturing process, but at the same time they retained a certain respect for the traditional cheese makers, admiring their gifts of observation and their know-how. They wanted not to take their place, but rather to enable the cheese makers to benefit from their own knowledge.

The scientists succeeded in isolating and cultivating the lactic agents of fermentation that act in the acidification of milk prior to the addition of rennet and lead to the formation of mold. After much trial and error, they managed to identify several molds of the *Penicillium* family, notably *P. album, P. glaucum,* and *P. candidum.* Of these, *P. album* begins white and usually turns gray-blue as it develops. *P. candidum* has the quality of remaining white and of producing an immaculate, snowy rind. Both the scientists and the cheese makers were agreed in thinking that it was best to prevent the development of patches of blue mold on Camembert, but opinions differed as to the ways to achieve this. Up until the beginning of the twentieth century, the art of the cheese maker consisted in his bringing his Camemberts to maturity without any—or with as few as possible—blue markings. A quality Camembert was recognized by this lack of blue, but the majority of cheeses still had traces of it. To avoid the blue altogether, one had to see to it that the red bacilli began to develop prior to the *P. album*'s beginning to blossom. By halting the development of the

Penicillium, the red bacilli would prevent the blue from appearing. However, this method demanded immense know-how and was still uncertain.

Three men, Georges Roger, Émile Louïse, and Professor Pierre Mazé, all connected to the Pasteur Institute in various capacities, played important roles in making Camembert white. Louïse was a veterinarian, Mazé a scientist at the Institute, and Roger the owner of a well-known millstone factory. Unlike Louïse and Mazé, Roger had had no scientific training, yet it was he who pioneered the study of the surface molds on soft-centered cheeses and who is the person most responsible for the whitening first of Brie and then of Camembert.

From his father, Roger had inherited a factory at La Ferté-sous-Jarre, in the Brie region, that produced millstones. In 1896, he retired from the business and began to study microbiology. The Agriculture Society at Meaux asked him to assist the region's Brie producers in controlling the fermentation of their cheese in order to stabilize its quality and appearance. Roger sought advice from Duclaux, then the director of the Pasteur Institute, and following his recommendations, began to cultivate microorganisms scraped from the rinds of Brie cheeses. By 1897, he had isolated *Penicillium candidum* and had worked out a rational method of seeding the cheeses with it. To protect the cheeses from undesirable molds, he advised the makers to swab down the interiors of their factories with an antiseptic solution and to seed their cheeses with the pure cultures he was producing in his laboratory. In 1906, the laboratory was handed over to his son-in-law, Bernard Boisseau, and his partner, Maurice Mesnil. In the Brie region, news of the success of the Roger laboratory had spread quickly, and most of the makers in the area were successfully using its bacilli. Many of them wrote to Roger to congratulate him; a letter from a cheese maker at Saint-Dizier-la-Tour, in the Creuse, is typical: "The bacilli you sent worked very well, the cheeses are snow-white, you couldn't ask for finer." Roger's establishment thus became the first private laboratory to "deliver to cheese manufacturers, not only in Brie but in every other region as well, culture media made up of several types of microbes acknowledged to be the best." [9]

While Brie cheese, thanks to Roger's ingenuity, had achieved a dependable and uniform whiteness, Camembert was still subject to the caprices of its molds and varied in color from white to gray-blue to gray-green. In 1901, Louïse, the director of the Agricultural Research Station at Caen, advised the Norman cheese makers to seed their Camemberts with *Penicillium candidum.* He described the superiority of the mold in a speech before the Association Normande:

> In order to obtain a fine white mold without blue, green, or black spotting, the cheese should be seeded with spores of *Penicillium candidum.* We have initiated this practice in Normandy, where it has had very successful results.[10]

Louïse had been a former colleague of Roger's prior to moving to Caen. Together in 1899 they had published a volume titled *Contribution à la Maturation des Fromages (Contribution to the Ripening of Cheeses).* He was thus well aware of the virtues of *Penicillium candidum.* However, despite all his advice, acceptance of the mold was far from unanimous. The cheese makers in the Auge still preferred to rely on the old way of doing things. Only a few of them ordered bacilli from La Ferté-sous-Jouarre; most of them were reluctant to change, especially since *Penicillium candidum* had still not convinced everyone, not even some experts. In 1905, Mazé, of the Pasteur Institute, published an article on the role of microorganisms in the dairy industry in the *Annales de l'Institut Pasteur,* and in 1910 the article was reprinted in serial form in the *Journal des Fromagers de Normandie,* a short-lived local publication with radical politics, which purported to reflect the interests of the small cheese makers. Mazé compared the respective merits of two molds, *P. album* and *P. candidum,* and pronounced in favor of the first:

> *P. album* is thus indispensable. However, although it should not be set aside, it can be replaced by *P. candidum,* which does not expose the manufacturer to the many disappointments that can result from the use of *Penicillium album.*
>
> Use of *[P. candidum]* is a temptation that has not yielded good results in practice. Cheeses with *P. candidum* mature with difficulty and do not have the finesse of true Brie and Camembert cheeses. They are covered with a thick layer of white spores that could be mistaken for a coat of plaster. Notwithstanding all of its shortcomings, the maker would be right to stick to *P. album.*[11]

Roger and Louïse carried the day against Mazé, however, and managed to impose the use of *Penicillium candidum*.[12] Yet Mazé's doubts were not unfounded. It is a fact that changing the strain also modified the cheese's maturation speed and its taste. According to Maurice Desfleurs, a well-known Camembert expert,

> The casein enzymes of *P. camemberti* (alternate term for *P. album*) appear to be more powerful than those of *P. caseicolum* (alternate term for *P. candidum*) and one can obtain, if not more rapidly, soft-centered cheese with greater solubility and maturity and hence a more distinctive taste.[13]

By changing the type of mold, Camembert thus changed not only its color but most probably its taste as well. It became less sharp, losing its peasant bite and thereby enlarging its circle of admirers. For several years, the Pasteur Institute provided both the *album* and *candidum* strains on request: "They were delivered in bottles containing suspensions of the elements and spores of the strains in distilled water."[14]

The change in color did not occur overnight. The first white Camemberts appeared at the beginning of the last century, but until 1930 blue Camemberts were still being produced. It would take another twenty-five to thirty years before white reigned supreme on every rind. Many cheese makers obviously continued to stand firm against the whitening process, since in 1927 two specialists noted that *P. album* still had its supporters:

> Either *P. album* or *P. candidum* is still being used, although there are those who accuse the spores of *P. album* of yielding a darker color and thus prefer *P. candidum*. On the other hand, the partisans of *P. album* believe that the rind it produces is less dense than that of *P. candidum* and that it is more likely to produce red bacilli.[15]

Eventually, the blue tint once deemed natural began to be seen as a defect and steps were taken to combat it. In the 1950s, cheese makers in Normandy were panicked by an epidemic of blue bacteria caused by *P. glaucum,* and scientists were called in to put a stop to the untimely reappearance of the suppressed blue.

The consumers' preference for white removed the cheese makers' last reservations. However, it was not easy to obtain the white color. The cheese-making facilities were impregnated with *P. album* and *P. glaucum*, both of which contaminated the cheeses. Frequently, the only solution was to build new factories. In order to ensure the proper development of surface flora, it was necessary to sprinkle a suspension of *Penicillium candidum* spores over the cheeses at the beginning of the ripening process in addition to seeding the milk. That practice also began in the 1920s. Earlier, seeding had occurred spontaneously via the air in the drying rooms and the shelves on which the cheeses were set. Despite precautions, however, accidents could always happen. There is very little difference between *P. album* and *P. candidum*. It is now known that, despite earlier theories, they are the same species, and their variations are due to ambient changes. To obtain stable varieties of *Penicillium candidum*, strains collected in place must be selected out under laboratory conditions. By culturing the selected species, a stable strain of *Penicillium candidum* can be obtained. The achievement of a white Camembert thus bears the stamp of science, and especially of the Pasteur laboratories. In imposing on Camembert its whiteness, evocative of hygiene and asepsis, Pasteur's disciples were telling the cheese makers that the era of empiricism had arrived and that the cheese, the product of peasant know-how, could become a product of mass consumption only if it were "cleansed" under laboratory control.

Although converted to whiteness, cheese makers did not necessarily give up the fight. They continued to try to bypass the laboratories in their search for the now-obligatory snowy surface, and it was easier for them to get their *Penicillium candidum* from other cheese makers. Some Bondons, a cheese produced in the Bray region, are naturally white, while some can be blue. Camembert producers ordered regular deliveries of white Bondons, which they crumbled into their milk to seed it with *P. candidum* and eradicate the *P. album*. Eventually, after years of such treatment, *P. album* disappeared altogether. In 1961, Desfleurs discovered a fugitive colony of it in a small cheese factory that had called him in to halt the appearance of a blue growth on the Camemberts. Since that time, there has been no recrudescence of the mold, which is also known as *Penicillium camemberti*. One of the key players in Camembert's history, one that was part of its very creation, has thus disappeared and, in light of the service it once rendered, been unjustly forgotten. Surely it deserves a place of honor in its own crystal Petri dish at the Institut National d'Agronomie!

Today, every cheese maker, even those most faithful to traditional methods, seed their milk with laboratory-produced *Penicillium candidum*. There is no question of allowing the ambient atmosphere the privilege of performing that task. In this sphere, the success of Pasteur's science has been total. However, its most significant victory has been the quasi-universal use of pasteurization itself, beginning in the 1950s. In that connection, the whitening of the cheese's rind represents a first step and can be viewed as a metaphor of the pasteurizing process.

Milk Collection

Up until 1870, cheese production in the Auge created domestic agricultural revenue. The dairy farmer's wife turned a part of the milk from her cows into cheese. Under those conditions, production was necessarily limited. In order to increase it, larger herds of cattle were needed, and that, in turn, required larger pastures. The Paynel brothers were able to increase their Camembert production by increasing the size of their farms. To procure the milk they needed, they rented several additional farms so that they could raise the maximum number of dairy cows. Instead of putting their limited financial resources into the purchase of land, they preferred to rent the land they needed to produce on a larger scale. However, this put them in a shaky position, for it made them dependent on the goodwill of the landowners, who set strict conditions for the use of their property and who were not shy about raising the rents when they learned what the sale of Camembert was bringing in. Despite the 200 hectares (approximately 500 acres) he was farming, Cyrille Paynel did not have the quantity of milk he required to satisfy his customers. Likewise, most of the cheese makers were short of milk, and this limited their production capacities. Increased production to meet the growing demand came up against the cheese makers' lack of sufficient milk supply, and the overall growth in Camembert production was to be achieved only through an increase in the number of small cheese makers.

This constraint was removed not by some technological change, but by the emergence of a new economic and social environment: cheese makers began to purchase milk directly from dairy farms in the region. As obvious as this solution seems today, there was nothing inevitable about it.

In the nineteenth century, the notion of either buying or selling milk to be made into cheese was difficult to conceive.

There was a further pressing reason for dealing in milk. In the Auge, milk was not some ordinary substance to be bought and sold in the usual way. It was an intimate material and closely linked to the place where it was produced. Dairy cows were cherished domestic animals, not anonymous producers. They were almost a part of the family, and their milk was not to be handed over to the first comer, even for money. A retired cheese maker spoke about this unique relationship between farmer and milk. For decades, M. Lebaron, let us call him, had presided over an establishment renowned for the excellence of its Camemberts. For him, milk was almost holy:

> I consider milk to be an element, not a sacred one—that would be going too far—but respectable, and I believe that when one has dealt with it, one has to have a certain respect for those who provide it. I would have no problem if I owned a spinning factory and bought my wool in Sydney, Australia. It would be foolish for me to concern myself with the Australian sheep owners. But when it comes to milk, you have to know its source, you have to know the region where it is produced. There is something emotional, respectable, about milk that makes it different from other products. First of all, because it is more unpredictable, you feel closer to it because for that reason, you have to treat it right, you have to know how to deal with it. I am generally very broad-minded, but when it comes to milk, there are certain obligations that I would not accept otherwise.

Milk collection implies a mutual trust between buyer and seller. In a region like the Auge, where farmers trust only what they produce themselves, this raises various problems.

For cheese makers, the origin of their milk is a real concern. They cannot produce a good cheese if they do not know where their milk comes from. Conversely, the milk provider will not sell his milk, the product of a dairy farm in which he has a heavy investment, to any concern that he does not respect and that he does not trust to put it to good use. Even after his milk has been sold, he continues to feel attached to it; the sale has not totally broken the bond between them. This very special bond that milk creates between producer and cheese maker was very well expressed by M. Lebaron:

> That milk [in the area where he collected it] is at once my milk and not my milk. I have only appropriated it. I collected milk from people whose grandparents had provided me with milk. I could have told each of them about his grandfather, how "your grandfather bought that pasture, that was not one he started out with," because we share each other's lives, we are neighbors.

Neighborliness; a common, shared history; a relationship lasting over several generations; a profound knowledge of the land, of animals, of conditions, and of the farmers who produce the milk, all give the cheese maker a stronger right to the milk than mere formal ownership of it because he has paid for it. However, the cheese maker who buys the milk is also responsible to the person who produced it for the use he makes of it. The money he has paid out does not absolve him of his moral responsibility. The bond created between neighbors cannot be anonymous. It represents a strong and lasting commitment on both sides in which their reputations are at stake, and it binds them closely together.

Thus, what the dairy farmer views as important is not so much the price he is offered, but his trust in the person who is proposing to buy his milk. As for the cheese maker, his main problem is to maintain the quality of the milk he buys as he begins to collect it over an ever-larger area. While his collection zone remains limited, he has no trouble in ensuring the quality of production. He knows the dairy farms where he buys and their owners' reputations; he knows their methods and the care with which they tend their herds.

Milk collection began under these conditions of closeness and trust. Purchases and sales of milk were business, of course, since the cheese maker was paying for the milk he collected from the supplier. However, neither party regarded this as a purely commercial transaction. The term "sale" was never used; indeed, it is not used today. When it comes to milk, one speaks of *cession*, or "transfer," and of the *retrocession*, or "retransfer," of whey products and cheeses.

The Morice couple, at Lessard-le-Chêne, were the first to purchase milk from their neighbors in order to make cheese. Up until around 1930, milk collection was carried out with a horse-drawn cart. Motorized vehicles began to be used in that decade: the collector would make his rounds of the dairy farms two or three times a day to collect cans containing the product of the most recent milking. In 1914, the Lepetit cheese factory at Saint-Maclou was absorbing, per day, 15,000 liters (3,963 gallons) of milk that was collected from sixteen hundred dairy farms, to which was added 1,600 liters (423 gallons) from its own: "A dozen vehicles equipped with tanks would make the rounds of the suppliers two or three times a day." [16] At that time, the cheese factory was producing seven thousand to eight thousand cheeses daily, whereas in 1880, the largest cheese producer had produced fewer than five thousand.

The wider collection zone made control more difficult and relations more tenuous. Trust was no longer enough, and some oversight became necessary. The dairy farm milk was tasted and sampled on arrival at the cheese factory by a trusted employee, the chief of the loading dock, whose job it was to detect any possible imperfection. [17]

The method of milk collection altered the relationship of the cheese factories with the environment. Cheese makers collected milk and were themselves producers on their own land. Their status as property owners, the size of their holdings, and the reputation of their establishments lent them respectability and justified their purchase of milk from their neighbors. A new form of suzerainty was created between the owner of the cheese factory and the dairy farmers in his collection zone. The factory owners were, in fact, without using the title, the new lords of the Norman countryside. They no longer owned the land itself, of course, nor did they have any formal rights over the dairy farmers, who were free to sell their milk or not, and to whomever they pleased, at least in principle. In reality, however, the dairy farmers sold their milk to the cheese factory nearest them, or possibly to another one if it happened to be larger. Once the relationship was established, nothing could alter it save some basic change of activity.

The growth in collection area rapidly led to conflicts among neighboring cheese makers, all of whom were after the same milk suppliers. This thorny problem, as we shall see, was to become one of the major concerns of the Norman cheese makers, torn between the growing need for milk and their desire to avoid ruinous competition amongst themselves.

What a change from Marie Harel's Camembert and the cheese that had delighted Parisian gourmets in the 1920s! The rustic original had been spruced up, its taste had been tamed, its rind had become white, and it had traded in its straw wrapping for a wooden box with a brightly colored label. Such was the price paid for access to nationwide and export markets, and such was the consequence of production on a larger scale. From the beginning of the twentieth century, in certain large cheese factories, the fabrication of Camembert has involved modern techniques and equipment, steam-run machinery, refrigerating facilities, and measuring apparatus. In tandem, a small and specialized industry of special suppliers emerged. Camembert, although still rural, fell in line with the times, benefiting from technological progress and scientific discoveries. Its claim to fidelity to tradition in no way prevented it from welcoming innovation. However, although the small, closed world of cheese makers went along with modernization, it closed ranks to reject any change in the social fabric.

THE FAMILIES: THE SYNDICATE SYSTEM

On the afternoon of 20 March 1909, a group of fifty cheese makers crowded into the largest room in the town hall at Lisieux. The subprefect himself was honoring the meeting with his presence. Given the size of the gathering, it was obvious that some serious threat must be hanging over the cheese industry in Normandy. It was, indeed, the first time that so many Camembert producers had agreed to set aside their differences and meet. All of the most important of them were present: Lapidate, Maurice Lanquetot, the Saffrey brothers, Alba, and even Marie Harel's descendants, the Sereys. The presence of two women of a formidable mien, the widows Seigneuret and Serey-Dutac, cast a certain damper on any attempt to engage in frivolities. It was a solemn moment, for Normandy's Camembert was in danger. Such was the conviction of the fifty-three producers present on that day, forty-seven of whom were from the Auge. They were determined to take action against their foes, which they considered the correct term for anyone daring to sell as "Camembert" a pale imitation cheese made outside of the borders of Normandy—and with skim milk! On that day, the historic decision was taken to create the Syndicat des Fabricants du Véritable Camembert de Normandie (SFVCN).

The Norman coalition was justified by the situation in which the small Camembert industry found itself at the turn of the last century. The problem was not with sales—far from it! Yet the repercussions of the cheese's commercial success were threatening the prosperity of the Norman producers. The cheese makers were especially concerned by two results of the Parisian consumers' demand for Camembert: new competition from cheese factories that had been set up in the center and eastern sections of the country, and the increase in local milk prices.

The cheese factories in the central and eastern regions of France were proving themselves tough competitors with Norman Camembert in Paris's central market, Les Halles. For some time, Camembert had ceased to be a uniquely Norman product. So long as demand had been greater than production capability, and so long as the Norman producers had been able to maintain their predominant position in the Parisian market, the situation had not been unduly worrisome. However, new factories, which were often more modern than the tradition-bound Norman establishments, were now selling Camemberts at far lower prices. The newcomers were exercising pressure to bring down the cost of the cheese and thus were cutting into profits. In Normandy, the increase in the number of producers and the resultant competition vis-à-vis the dairy farmers were driving up the price of milk and affecting the cost-price ratio. The combination of outside competition, which was lowering the sale price, and local competition, which was increasing production costs, was posing a threat to the success of Normandy's Camembert.

The principal goal of the syndicate created at Lisieux was to counter this pincer effect and ensure a profitable future. To combat the competition from cheaper cheeses, the syndicate extolled the superiority of Norman Camembert and was determined to guarantee its excellence. To eliminate damaging local competition, the Norman producers drew up and signed an agreement. The first of its broad goals, the protection and extolling of Norman Camembert, became the object of widespread publicity. The second goal of controlling competition at the local level was pursued much more discreetly, in secret meetings among the syndicate's members. Yet it, too, was to occupy an important place in the statutes adopted at the assembly.

Camembert production had emerged as a small industry with no specific regulatory framework or formal organization. In the early days, the designation, or *appellation,* "Camembert" did not need protecting, because the cheese did not exist apart from those who produced it. The name of the producer, indeed, was nearly as important—if not more so—than the name of the cheese itself. For dealers and consumers, Camembert was cheese from Mme Harel or from one of the farm's heirs to her tradition. In addition, there were cheeses that were designated as "*façon Camembert,*" or imitation or "school of" Camembert. And, in fact, there was no "plain" Camembert produced by any concern that wanted to do so. The maker's seal was a sufficient guarantee of authenticity, and the reputation of the cheese merchant combined with that of the producer was enough to win the trust of consumers. All of this was thrown into disarray with the appearance on the market of a large quantity of imitation cheeses. No longer was the Camembert *appellation* the property of a family or even of a region. This upheaval occurred at a time when the original family had already lost its predominant position in cheese production in the Auge. Once it had escaped the clutches of the family framework, Camembert was freed from the exclusive control of the Auge producers and became an ordinary marketable product subject to the rules of competition.

The region's cheese makers had already attempted to take some common action to protect their interests. In 1887, the producers in the region around Saint-Pierre-sur-Dives had protested a plan by the City of Paris to place a tariff on soft-centered cheeses. However, apart from a few scattered and local actions, they had never come together collectively.

The year 1909, therefore, marked the beginning of a new era. The declining original family was replaced by a board controlled by the families who owned the largest cheese factories. The Norman cheese makers were indeed breaking new ground by forming a professional syndicate, but their innovative action was aimed at preserving the essence of local tradition by establishing strict limits and reaching strict understandings. In addition, the family spirit that had marked their product's beginnings survived in the new structure, which affirmed the prime importance of the land, local ties among producers, and relationships among colleagues with regard to supply and demand.

True Norman Camembert

In order to preserve Normandy's preeminent position in the world of Camembert, the most radical step was to prohibit other regions from producing the cheese. To counter broad production, which was bringing down prices, the syndicate first demanded that Camembert be confined within precise limits; in other words, they insisted that Normandy be granted exclusive rights to the cheese. The Norman cheese makers hoped to have a rapid decision on an *appellation d'origine,* or official designation of origin, that would reserve for Normandy the exclusive right to produce Camembert. Preliminary contacts with the Ministry of Agriculture gave hope that such a decree would be issued. Those hopes were dashed, however, in 1910, when the minister of agriculture informed M. Lecherpy, the deputy from Calvados, that Normandy's Camembert was "no better than the kind produced elsewhere." In his opinion, and that of his palate, there was no justification for granting an *appellation d'origine.* One can imagine the indignation of the Normans at the minister's gustatory deficiencies. However, despite their persistent efforts, they were never able to get what they wanted. Their attempts to achieve their goal through the courts were to prove equally fruitless.[18]

This setback failed to discourage them. If they could not stop their competitors from using the term "Camembert," they would attempt to set up regulations that would prevent them from selling a product that was more cheaply produced. The syndicate therefore turned its attention to the cheese's fat content and succeeded in setting a minimum of 36 percent. Why did they decide on fat content? Their reasoning was as follows: most of the non-Norman producers (and even some of the Norman ones) were offering cheap Camemberts made from skimmed milk. The skimming process was linked to the production of butter, which sold at a fairly high price. The fixing of a 36 percent minimum fat content was one way to limit the practice of skimming to produce a cheaper cheese. In addition, both the amount of fat content and the amount of dry milk solids are easily verifiable. Commercially, the notion of "fat" had positive connotations, evoking something creamy, mellow, and rich. In those days, the masculine paunch was fashionable, a sign of opulence, and public opinion had not yet succumbed to the appeal of the thin and the svelte.

For the Norman producers, the obligation to respect a minimum fat-content requirement had additional advantages. The milk in their region was creamier than that available in most other regions. Most of them were used to producing Camemberts with a high fat content, since tradition called for light skimming, done naturally and by hand and not with a me-

chanical skimmer. The syndicate brought legal proceedings against anyone selling Camemberts with a fat content below the minimum 36 percent. In 1912, it managed to have two producers, the Braud brothers, fined
200 francs for selling Camemberts with a fat content of only 20 percent.
To prove the superiority of the Norman product, members of the syndicate began to go beyond the minimum and to market Camemberts with
a fat content of at least 45 percent. In the 1920s, Alba, the manager of a
dairy at Tremblay, even called for a minimum fat content of 50 percent,
but his proposal was rejected and the lipid inflation was brought to a halt.
At the syndicate's General Assembly of 13 May 1911, a motion was adopted
to exclude producers who did not adhere to the 45 percent standard:

> The Syndicate, while continuing to pursue its demand that the Camembert
> name be reserved to the cheese producers of Normandy, and while guaran-
> teeing to uphold the quality of products manufactured in Normandy, de-
> cides to exclude from its membership any producer whose product, as a
> result of any investigation carried out by the Board, is found not to corre-
> spond to the provisions set forth in the statutes.[19]

Although the Norman producers were guaranteeing 45 percent fat content, consumers were left without data or any means of comparison.
Printed notice of the percentage of fat content, which would have enabled
the purchaser to make an informed choice, did not become obligatory
until 1919, at which time labels were announcing fat contents that could
vary from 20 to 50 percent.

As the guarantor of quality, the syndicate supervised its members'
products and verified that their methods met its requirements. The right
to have the syndicate's seal on one's label was subject to a strict adherence
to the quality standards set by the board. Cheese makers who put poor-
quality cheese on the market were expelled from membership and forbidden the use of the seal, a distinction that ensured a higher price. In
March 1921, the chairman informed

> those members present that on his last visit to Les Halles in Paris his atten-
> tion was drawn to the substandard quality of cheeses dispatched by a mem-
> ber of our Syndicate and bearing, unfortunately, the Syndicate's seal. Based
> on the contents of his note dated 24 March of this year, the Committee de-

cided to send this colleague a first notice warning him of the possible sanctions that could be put into effect should there be a recurrence. Monsieur Maurice Lanquetot expressed the wish that a general inspection of cheeses be carried out so that energetic measures might be taken with dispatch against those members of the Syndicate delivering doubtful merchandise bearing the Syndicate's seal.[20]

In 1911, the principle of inspection was adopted, but no action followed. Although they agreed on the principle, the cheese makers refused to allow the inspectors into their establishments. In April 1921, the syndicate voted the creation of a "private committee to supervise the quality of all first-class cheeses bearing the Syndicate seal."[21] Two years later, however, the committee had still not been formed. The cost of such controls and the unwillingness of many cheese makers to have inspectors patrolling their premises were the underlying reasons for the delay. The syndicate's board returned to the charge, and in November 1922, it called for "implementation of this measure, which has become absolutely necessary for maintaining the authority that the Syndicate's seal of approval has won in the eyes of consumers."[22] Finally, a year later, in October 1923, a syndicate inspector was appointed. Selected cheeses were inspected in the Roger laboratories at Lisieux, which specialized in supplying cheese makers with bacilli. However, for several more years some producers continued to refuse entry to the inspector, fearing discovery of their manufacturing secrets . . . or their fraudulent practices.

There was a need for some kind of distinctive sign to make it easy for the consumer to recognize quality-controlled Norman Camembert cheeses on the displays set up in the markets. The syndicate seal on the label distinguished the best Camemberts. It depicted "a seated woman, in profile, her arm outstretched to the horizon and the steeple of the village church."[23] In addition, the customer needed to be made aware of the syndicate seal and of its significance, and this inevitably led the cheese makers into the realm of advertising. They entered this unknown world attempting to rely on long-familiar paths. Their first advertising effort, in 1921, consisted simply of tucking into each cheese box a slip of paper informing consumers of the excellence of its contents. They also paid to have slides of the syndicate seal flashed onto the curtains of theaters and music halls at intermission. In 1922, aware that this was not enough, the syndicate decided to launch a broad-based publicity campaign:

> As a body, we have hitherto ignored the powerful means at our disposal to help consumers to distinguish our good Norman product from the other clearly inferior products being offered them under the name "Camembert." We must use advertising to make the consumer more aware of what our seal represents.[24]

The first agency contacted, Havas, was not hired for the job because the syndicate regarded it as "far too administrative." Instead, the syndicate called in an "advertising engineer," who drew up a campaign:

> The goal of this advertising campaign is to reach the consumer and to set up a mental connection between the Syndicate seal and the origin and qualities of the Camembert on which it is placed. Three necessary and effective methods are suggested: 1. Notices in the press. 2. Posters. 3. Pamphlets. Newspaper articles will fix in the mind of the potential customer and consumer the elements of the Syndicate seal, what it looks like, and what it depicts; they will also be a way of emphasizing the virtues of the cheeses to which it is affixed and, finally, to inspire a taste for Camembert. The poster will be a more permanent way of bringing the seal to the consumer's attention and thus support the publicity contained in the newspaper notices. Pamphlets will put into the hands of the consumer all of the necessary information about the production of Norman Camembert, the care with which it is produced, the minimum quality requirements set by the Syndicate, the Syndicate's quality-control activities—in short, they will give the consumer a clear and precise idea of what the Syndicate seal means and what it stands for.[25]

The cost of the projected campaign was estimated at 175,000 francs. The syndicate called for a contribution of one franc for each Camembert produced on a certain day in October. To judge by the sales reports on Norman Camembert at Paris's Les Halles, its efforts had borne fruit. According to the syndicate, "Between a cheese bearing the seal and one without the seal, the difference in price is approximately 20 centimes."[26]

Having understood the advantages to be gained by advertising, the syndicate then went a step further. In 1927, the Havas Agency proposed placing advertisements in several newspapers, in particular the Communist-owned *L'Humanité*, "which has a large working-class readership." From that date on, campaigns began to be aimed at particular types of customers. Workers ate Camembert in the summer, when it was less expensive, so they were especially targeted during that season. In 1931, the praises of Norman Camembert began to be sung on various radio stations. Radio Paris broadcast forty publicity spots, Radio Toulouse forty-five. Between 8:30 and 11:00 P.M., listeners heard the following message:

> Creamy, tasty, delicious, expertly prepared, the only true Camembert can be recognized by its label. There, a young farm girl sits looking at her church. The best brands carry the seal of guarantee of the Syndicate of Producers of True Norman Camembert.[27]

That same year, Parisians could gaze up at a huge "lighted advertisement" some 100 meters square (119 square yards) at the Gare Saint-Lazare. Some publications aimed at women also printed special advertisements of a medical nature, praising the benefits of Norman Camembert and urging women to feed it to their families.

The Milk of Discord

United in promoting their product, the Norman cheese makers were constantly divided when it came to the question of equitable access to the milk supply. In the early days, these conflicts were easily settled locally, among neighbors, among fellow producers, and even at the family level. As milk began to be collected over an increasingly large region, frictions increased and the bonds uniting families and colleagues weakened. In the absence of any regulatory body, relations among cheese producers began to grow more strained. The largest dairies attempted to attract business away from their colleagues by offering to pay more, a competitive ploy that the syndicate dreaded, fearing that it would raise prices and be divisive for the profession. In 1924, the chairman, indignant at the milk suppliers' attempts to obtain higher prices by fomenting rivalry among the cheese makers and playing on their need for raw material, voiced a complaint: "We are the victims of the suppliers who are giving their milk to the highest bidders."[28]

Every effort went into nipping such destructive competition in the bud. For the most part, the syndicate avoided even using the word "competition" and spoke about "outbidding," thereby expressing the reprehensible character of the practices that were putting personal relations on a commercial basis. In an attempt to protect a procedure that had promoted relations based on mutual esteem, neighborliness, and the prestige of those in authority, the syndicate stepped into the breach created by the decline of the old family system and began to act as a superior kind of family council to arbitrate disputes. Article 7 of its statutes forbade competition among members. The price of milk was theoretically uncontrolled, but the cheese makers undertook not to poach on their colleagues' sources of supply. This understanding proved to be a fragile one. The syndicate's first chairman, Paul Vignioboul, frequently heard complaints from members who accused their colleagues of having stolen their suppliers. At each meeting, a new situation would be brought before the board, which was often called upon to appoint a committee of arbitrators to settle things. During a general assembly held in 1913, the chairman, speaking in the general interest, deplored the disputes that he feared could well destroy the syndicate:

> The internal battle being waged over milk is threatening the Syndicate's very existence. The foundation of any Syndicate is union, loyalty, the setting aside of special interests in the general interest—which may sometimes go against personal concerns even though the two are usually the same. But we are constantly at war, and that is most dangerous![29]

The milk shortage created by the First World War exacerbated the competition among cheese makers. Well aware of the situation, the suppliers acted in character. Some of them, seeking higher prices, claimed to have received higher bids from competing cheese makers. The syndicate's board warned its members not to fall for this: "Many of our colleagues are making the mistake of entering into the struggle without having taken the trouble to learn the facts." It advised the cheese makers to check on the reality of the supposedly higher offers.[30]

In any case, competition increased, and so did the disputes among the syndicate's members. Given the situation, why not just abolish article 7 of the statute and allow cheese factories to turn to new milk suppliers?

This seemed even more timely now that many of the newer cheese factories were not syndicate members and did not hesitate to poach on the syndicate's clients. In January 1921, Chairman Vignioboul spoke to the new situation:

> Notwithstanding noncompetition among Syndicate members, a milk supplier may, for various other reasons, decide to change his usual purchaser and spontaneously turn to another Syndicate colleague, who—under the very strict provisions of the statutes—must reject the offer. Since the vast majority of manufacturers are members of the Syndicate, this measure can have no other result than to anger the supplier, who feels that his freedom is being restricted. The war has produced many cheese makers who are not Syndicate members, and it is clear therefore that when a member categorically refuses an offer made to him, the supplier will then offer his milk to a dissident manufacturer who, in turn, will understandably accept it with alacrity and thereby cause the Syndicate to lose the supplier. A method must be found to protect us against this risk.[31]

A new wording was put forward for article 7. The principle of noncompetition was retained, but a supplier's switch from one cheese maker to another was accepted, subject to compensations.

> Syndicate members will refrain from soliciting milk supplies from among a colleague's suppliers. There will be no exception to this basic principle. Any member receiving an offer of a supply of milk must, prior to accepting the milk, make certain that the offer does not emanate from a supplier of one of his fellow Syndicate members. If it does, he must, and without delay, inform his colleagues of the offer made him in an effort to effect a reconciliation with the defecting supplier. The latter, upon receipt of this notice, will have forty-eight hours to contact his supplier and attempt to persuade him to alter his decision to redirect his milk supply. Once the forty-eight hours have elapsed, if the supplier persists in its first decision and the offer remains on the table, the colleague to whom it was made may then accept it, but only if he also turns over to his now-deprived colleague an equal quantity of milk or indemnifies him by a sum to be fixed beforehand by the committee.[32]

This reform was not adopted. The original version of article 7 remained in effect, despite the fact that it was continually being flouted.

Although the cheese makers continued to buy up farms to increase their milk supply, some purchasing one per year, they were always short of milk. The situation became even more acute when companies that collected milk to supply the Paris region moved into Basse-Normandie: Nestlé moved to Lisieux in 1924. In 1928, when the Lepetit brothers resigned from the syndicate, an even more serious problem arose. The minutes of the meeting held on 28 October 1928 give some idea of the tense atmosphere that prevailed at the time. There was a sharp dispute between Mme Renée Rendu, who managed a small cheese dairy, and Lanquetot. Joseph Saffrey, who had succeeded Vignioboul as syndicate chairman, tried in vain to effect a settlement. First, Lanquetot gave his version of events:

> With no provocation on my part whatsoever, Mme Rendu went to my suppliers and offered them excessive prices, varying between 2.40 to 3.25 francs. She even outbid me for Monsieur Palace from Mesnil-Guillaume, a big supplier whom I had lent to the Nestlé company for the summer and which was to return him to me. In self-defense, I was forced to inform my suppliers that I would meet whatever prices Mme Rendu offered them. Of course, unfortunately, things got out of hand, and we ended up paying exorbitant prices.

Mme Rendu counterattacked by complaining about Lanquetot's conduct. He was said to have seized not merely a supplier, but the produce of an entire farm when its ownership changed. As a matter of tradition, indeed, the cheese factories' collection rights were connected to the land, not to the person.

> I was assured that Palace had never sold his milk to the Lanquetot company; was that a lie? M. Lanquetot took milk from Leduc, at Firfol, some 230 liters [61 gallons] of it, and paid in excess of 3 francs for it. Now, the Leduc farm was formerly occupied by a Belgian, Touque, who had given us his milk for four years.

Lanquetot contradicted this, protesting that his relationship with the farm was even older:

The Bellemare farm at Firfol taken over by Leduc had given me milk prior to the Belgian's arrival. And last year, Leduc himself gave me milk from that farm, which makes him my supplier.

Rendu then turned over to Saffrey a list of the suppliers she claimed had been taken from her, as well as the quantity of milk still owing her, approximately 685 liters (180 gallons) from Fermiers Réunis, 770 liters (292 gallons) from the Nestlé company, and 480 liters (126 gallons) from Lanquetot. Lanquetot reverted to the Palace matter, which was at the root of the dispute, upon which Rendu, who could not deny that she had taken this supplier from Lanquetot, shouted: "You can't blame someone for trying to make a living! Besides, we were there long before Bienfaite!" Bienfaite, of course, was the name of Lanquetot's cheese factory at Saint-Martin-de-Bienfaite-la-Cressonnière. Rendu's claim of priority, while devoid of any legal validity, had immense moral force. In the world of the Augeron cheese makers, seniority always weighed most heavily. Lanquetot felt called upon to reply, and did so by stating that his cheese factory was actually older than Rocques, the factory owned by Rendu: "Wrong! Bienfaite was founded in 1890, and Rocques in 1896." Rendu, having run out of arguments and perhaps feeling herself a victim of male solidarity, thereupon rose and handed Saffrey a letter signed by her mother containing the latter's formal resignation from the syndicate.[33]

Article 7, having become unenforceable, was finally repealed in 1929. Competition among members continued. In order to avoid overbidding, the cheese makers were prompted to set up joint contracts to share collection zones. Although disputes among neighboring cheese factories were never-ending, the producers did nonetheless manage to see to it that prices did not go up, well aware that in the long run they would be the principal victims. Other means were found to lure suppliers away. The cheese maker who wanted to take over a supplier would pay him a visit and remind him of the long-standing relationship that existed between their families or would offer to do him certain small favors. There was great mutual distrust among cheese makers. In farm areas, everyone saw all and knew all. The syndicate's board was constantly peppered with complaints from cheese makers who accused colleagues of having called upon their suppliers and tried to take them over. The most innocent visit was viewed with suspicion. An employee at one cheese factory had only to drop by to say hello to a supplier connected to another cheese maker for doubts to arise. What was he doing there? Had he been instructed to get the client for a competing colleague?

In 1919, during a period of great shortage, the authorities imposed fixed milk prices, which were set on a monthly basis by departmental committees made of up suppliers and cheese makers. These committees were officially disbanded in April of 1921, but the cheese makers in Calvados and the Orne went on meeting with suppliers on a monthly basis until 1928 to set a mean price for milk and were thus able to avoid a price war. Even after the elimination of the interprofessional committees, mutually agreed prices remained the norm. This, however, did not mean that suppliers were not wooed away by other means.

The Order of Cheese Makers

The syndicate's obsessive combat against competition was not confined solely to the question of controlling the price of its principal raw material, milk. Avoiding competition also entailed an avoidance of broader commercial relationships. Norman cheese makers were loath to see the traditional bonds weakened by the laws of the marketplace. The SFVCN, therefore, was more than just a syndicate and more than a mere pressure group, it was also a kind of professional "order," almost in the monastic sense. Beyond protecting its own economic interests, it defended rules that governed relations among its own members and between itself and its various partners: dairy farmers, milk suppliers and contractors, sales agents at Les Halles, carriers, and public authorities. It saw itself as the exclusive and obligatory representative of everyone who made Norman Camemberts.

As the representative of the cheese makers, and possessing a large membership, the syndicate swung into action whenever their economic interests were at stake. When the container manufacturers moved to raise their prices in 1913, the syndicate did not merely protest, it threatened to take over the container business and turn out its own boxes. It ended up appointing itself sole purchasing agent, thereby obtaining reduced prices on its huge orders. When up against the carriers, both truck and railway, and with the agents at Les Halles, it brought pressure to bear to maintain costs or commissions at the lowest possible level. The syndicate was determined to ensure the best prices for its members' products, but it was also determined to control the material conditions of their transport and sale. It negotiated with the railroads to ensure that freight cars loaded with Camembert were not kept standing in stations for lengthy periods of time. It insisted that Camembert not be sold after it had been refrigerated.

Prepared as it was to exert pressure and bring its economic weight to bear, the syndicate was also active in other areas. It also strove to improve relations with its partners. The largest merchants at Les Halles were kept informed of the board's deliberations and often invited to its banquets. The syndicate did its best to be a trustworthy partner, the guarantor of the high quality of its members' products. It established relations of trust with the firms selling its cheeses.

Its collective authority was an adjunct to the patronal authority that already weighed heavily on those employed in the cheese factories. There, too, the goal was to prevent competition so as to keep salaries low and to reinforce the bond between the wage earners and their employers. This was aimed primarily at the best and most experienced workers. The syndicate attempted to prevent cheese makers from competing among themselves for the best workers and the latter from taking advantage of such competition to obtain higher salaries and weaken patronal authority. One of the very first measures adopted by the syndicate was a ban on persuading workers to move to another employer. It was set forth in one of the resolutions adopted at the General Assembly on 31 July 1909:

> Certain members have taken employees from their colleagues by corresponding with them directly. The action is considered disloyal, and to avoid its recurrence we are putting forward the following proposal: "Syndicate members undertake not to correspond in writing with the employee of a colleague if the employee has not given advance notice of leaving or has not been let go." Adopted unanimously.[34]

The following year, the syndicate prohibited the employees in cheese factories, under penalty of discharge, from seeking employment in another factory without having first informed their employer. The only competition to be tolerated was in the area of sale price. However, even this was subject to two important conditions: the market must be confined to Norman producers, and the de facto superiority of demand over supply must be maintained. As thus set up, the market created higher prices rather than lower. Although respectful of authority, the syndicate did not always recognize the authority of the state. In its view, legitimate authority was conferred solely through the success of a local initiative or through recognized merit. Elections, diplomas, high office—none of these was sufficient to legitimize authority. As a result, the syndicate's relations with the public authorities were often in a state of flux. They were good when the government went along with its demands and when the syndicate deemed that those with whom it was dealing were vested with a legitimate authority. On the other hand, relations deteriorated when the public authorities began to eat into the syndicate's prerogatives, turned a deaf ear to its grievances, and dealt with it through minor officials.

The syndicate had nothing against the principle of republican authority or universal suffrage, but it viewed local notables as being far more important than any central government representative or elected official. Many of its members were mayors of their communities,[35] but their elections were a well-earned recognition of their success and worth. The syndicate members usually enjoyed good relations with Normandy's senators and deputies. Henry Chéron, the deputy from Calvados, was named honorary chairman of the syndicate. On the other hand, relations with local prefects, who were appointed from Paris, varied according to the level of tension vis-à-vis the central government. At the time of its creation, the syndicate had received encouragement from the subprefect of Lisieux, but in the aftermath of the First World War he strongly opposed the prefect of Calvados during the milk shortage. When it came to government ministers, it was often a question of lack of understanding. To the syndicate, it was incomprehensible that the minister of agriculture should reject a request to protect the "Camembert" name, incomprehensible that a tax be set on profits, which was viewed as state interference in business management. Social legislation, and especially the laws limiting work hours, also angered the cheese makers, who inveighed against state interference in their affairs. The syndicate was opposed to government control over what it viewed as its members' private affairs, whether it involved employees, profits, the price of milk, or the control of trade. It was, however, quick to call for government action to protect it from what it regarded as unfair competition.

Above and beyond the personal relationships some cheese producers enjoyed with various deputies and senators, the syndicate had recourse to another very popular method of creating and maintaining good relations with men of authority and influence: the banquet. There was nothing like a sumptuous banquet for creating goodwill, cementing friendships, and getting in well with the authorities. The cheese makers, experts in the delicate art of appealing to the taste buds of important men, were well aware of what a successful banquet could accomplish. The syndicate's history is replete with such banquets, all held to bring the cause of Camembert to the attention of the guests. To celebrate the first anniversary of its creation, on Sunday, 22 May 1910, the syndicate invited twenty-three well-known figures as its guests. With the seventy-nine members present, a total of 102 persons sat down to the feast held in one of the rooms of the Lisieux nursery school. Chéron, the undersecretary of the Navy and honorary chairman of the syndicate, occupied the seat of honor. At his side were the prefect of Calvados, the subprefect of Lisieux, and the town's deputy mayor. Everyone expected to be served a succulent Camembert, but to the general surprise, there was no cheese to be seen. The syndicate's chairman explained its absence to his guests: "I saw no cheese on the table. I did not want there to be any, for had there been, it would have turned a pleading eye upon you, Monsieur le Ministre, as if to say: 'Ah, how I wish that you would let me have an *appellation.*'"

Yet although it never managed to "define" Camembert, the syndicate did invent Norman Camembert and secure its fame. Even today, the few surviving Norman cheese factories producing Camembert from ladle-molded, unpasteurized, whole milk still hold meetings to ensure its promotion. Over nearly a century, the syndicate has waged many battles, with varying results. At its founding, its membership consisted of fifty-three cheese makers. The following year, there were more than 100. Until the late 1930s, the general assemblies were very well attended, with more than fifty members regularly present. During the First World War, the syndicate succeeded in making itself the body on which the Army Quartermaster Corps relied to ensure the regular delivery of Camembert cheese to the troops. As I shall show, that one accomplishment enabled Camembert to gain national status, and the syndicate won official recognition of its place in local economic activity. Despite a continuing drop in its membership owing to the closing down of many small cheese factories, the syndicate had always brought together the great majority of the most important Norman producers. Its power remained virtually intact until the Second World War. Up until 1940, it had played a prominent role in the way the profession operated. The German occupation, however, totally disrupted cheese production in the western part of the country. Restrictions reduced the production of Camembert to practically nothing. Many cheese makers were bankrupt and unable to resume activities after the Liberation. From 1950 on, the acceleration of concentration and the shutting down of small cheese factories further reduced the number of syndicate members, but its activities continued. Nevertheless, since the end of the Second World War, its goals and activities have changed. No longer is it bent on maintaining intact the former social order, protected from competition and from social legislation. It has been forced to accept large-scale industry's invasion of its peaceful rural universe and to tolerate the rule of the marketplace and the laws governing labor. Its sole remaining cause is the defense of the trademarked Camembert cheese of Normandy.

THE *POILUS'* CAMEMBERT

On 3 August 1914, Germany declared war against France. After forty-three years of peace, the guns were heard once more. No one could foresee the horror of the battles to come. On both sides, soldiers set out for the front buoyed up by the enthusiasm of the crowds. They marched off with jaunty step, the better to forget the anxiety they were surely feeling. A well-orchestrated nationalist orgy was in full swing. In France, nothing escaped the jingoistic fever, and Camembert was called upon to play its part. The conflict on the battlefield even spread onto the cheese's labels, which abandoned their traditional peaceful subjects. The "National" brand went so far as to predict Germany's crushing defeat: its label depicted Kaiser Wilhelm, wearing a pointed helmet and astride an ass, being driven out of France by a battery of French 75-mm machine guns. A rooster perched on a frontier marker crowed in victory. On the French side, the sun shed its golden light on a country village protected by an impressive line of red-trousered, blue-jacketed French *poilus,* or soldiers; on the German, two skeletons lay on the ravaged earth, while in the background a castle went up in flames. This picture, one of many, expressed the illusion shared by the majority of the public, which was convinced that the war would be not only victorious, but of short duration. Along with its other patriotic notes, it attests to Camembert's commitment to the war.

Camembert was not the only product to drape itself in the flag and don military uniform as a commercial strategy. However, unlike other products, the cheese did have some qualifications on which to base its claims. It actually took part in the war, in the trenches, alongside the *poilus*. For Camembert, however, the 1914 war was not a defensive war, it was one of conquest. The cheese was already well known in 1914, but its fame was limited to Paris, Normandy, and a few large cities in the northern part of the country, while virtually unknown elsewhere. Working-class people, with the exception of those in Normandy's rural communities, ate very little of it. The First World War was to crown it as the national cheese by spreading its name throughout the country and making it available to every social class. It was in the trenches that grassroots France became familiar with Camembert.

The nationalistic élan that prevailed in the large cities[36] did not carry over into the villages and countryside, where the declaration of war was received with gravity and concern. Men left their farms to join their units at the height of the harvest season. Only the oldest men, invalids, and children were left behind. Farms were suddenly deprived of their ablest workers at the crucial moment when crops had to be brought in. René Viviani, the leader of the War Cabinet of Ministers, issued a poetic appeal to women to step to the fore: "I ask you to sustain the work in the fields, to bring in this year's crops, to prepare for next year's. . . . Arise, women of France, children, sons and daughters of the homeland! Replace on the labor front those who serve on the battle front."[37]

Fervent patriots though they were, the Norman cheese producers nevertheless viewed with concern the sight of their workers leaving for the front and the depopulated fields they were leaving behind. How were they to replace the men who kept the machines turning? What was to become of farms now inhabited solely by women, children, and old men? Would they be able to continue supplying milk to the cheese factories? Owners, too, were called up, at least the youngest among them. In the small, peaceful world of Norman Camembert, no one was more torn than Willi Nothdurft. At the outbreak of war, Nothdurft, a 19-year-old German, had just completed a one-year training course at the Lepetit cheese factory in Falaise. He had come to be trained as a master cheese maker, a profession he hoped to exercise in his own country. As a souvenir of his stay in France, he carefully kept his work papers on his person. "When I left for the front, I carried in my pocket the work paper with its 2.50 franc stamp—gold francs—given me by Auguste Lepetit, which had opened all doors to me. I carried it like a lucky charm," he recalled.[38] Nothdurft survived the hell of Verdun, one of the few who escaped from Dead Man's Hill. When peace returned, he managed a cheese factory in Silesia in eastern Germany. In 1945, his work certificate enabled him to pass as French and to cross the Soviet lines and reach the western sector of Germany.

With the outbreak of hostilities, Franco-German cooperation was ended for long years to come. Men like Nothdurft were no longer welcome in France. Public opinion was fiercely hostile to anything to do with the enemy. In the feverish atmosphere of the day, able men who had escaped mobilization were forced to flaunt an exaggerated patriotism to avoid being accused of malingering. The cheese makers of Normandy waged their own struggle in their own way. In 1916, they concentrated on the casein factory at Orbec, in the Auge, an Austrian-owned business that had been sequestered at the outbreak of hostilities. Syndicate members demanded that the authorities who had carried out the sequestration rent them the facility and allow them to operate it, thereby "eradicating this Boche factory."[39] The Nestlé company came under fire when the cheese makers, blinded by their militant ardor, began to suspect it of having "a German connection or of being of Boche origin."[40] It was true that Nestlé, which was in fact Swiss-owned and therefore had some connections to the German language, at least, had indeed planned to set up a dairy in the Auge.

The cheese makers' actions were not aimed solely at hunting down foreign companies. They also contributed to the war effort. At the syndicate's general assembly on 22 December 1917, "Monsieur Louis Serey offered to turn over one day's production output to benefit the *poilus* at the front. The majority of those present fell in with his suggestion, and the motion was finally adopted."[41] Nor was Camembert's participation in the national defense confined to that. It was to go much farther. Camembert went to the front lines. Supplying the troops was an immense undertaking. The Army Quartermaster Corps had to see to the daily provisioning of some two million men in the field. A number of purchasing cooperatives served as intermediaries between the food producers and army supply depots in both the front and rear lines. The army market was a highly desirable one.

At the beginning of the war, it had been Gruyère cheese, rather than Camembert, that enjoyed the quartermaster's favor. However, it was available mainly in the rear-line stores, where soldiers were able to buy it on their own. Gruyère had several advantages over Camembert: it is less fragile, it is easier to ship, and it keeps better. When Gruyère was in short supply, the quartermaster fell back on Cantal cheese, which had the same advantages, or replaced cheese with chocolate. In practice, cheese was for the most part consumed as a snack and eaten with bread, and rarely eaten at lunch or dinner. During lulls in the fighting at the front, the *poilus* in the trenches would rapidly wolf down food brought to them on trolleys, breaking into their own reserves as little as possible. The delicate task of rationing food fell to the corporals, known as "cabots," whose duty it was to see that bread, wine, and cheese, when available, were fairly apportioned. Paul Cazin, a veteran of the trenches, recalled: "The corporals, seated on the ground with their legs hanging down into the trench, would cut up cheese for their squads." [42] In January 1916, a fourth of all Gruyère produced was requisitioned by the War Ministry. This move drove up the price of the cheese, but was not enough to ensure sufficient stock. Chocolate was also in short supply. To fill out the ration, a portion of the milk intended for hard-up Parisians was made into fresh cheese, a kind of semi-salted cottage cheese. Four thousand such cheeses were dispatched daily to the Xth Army. [43]

The Camembert makers were eager to supply the army's central storehouses. Despite the handicap presented by Camembert's fragility and short shelf life, they hoped to seize a part of this large market. Army cooperative stores were already being supplied with Camemberts, but the quantities they purchased at Paris's Les Halles were far from sufficient to meet the demands of the troops. In October 1915, the syndicate addressed a letter to the police prefect of the Seine asking him to deal directly with the army quartermaster:

In order to deliver Camembert to the armed forces, the Syndicate is prepared to consolidate the direct orders received through the Quartermaster Corps, which will no doubt be able to obtain a reduced fare for the transport of such merchandise. It thereby hopes to realize its keen desire to supply the French fighting man with the Camembert he enjoys, under the best conditions, at the best price, and at the highest quality.[44]

In this way, the syndicate expected to take over from its competition. However, it needed time to set up direct links with the Quartermaster Corps, which was a cumbersome bureaucratic entity and subject to strict regulations. On 13 September 1916, the syndicate finally received from the quartermaster of the IIIrd Army an order to supply Camemberts at the going market rate. The order was accepted, but for reasons that are unclear, this first transaction fell through. Chairman Vignioboul referred to it in an interview with the newspaper, *Le Matin:*

> The Syndicate has on several occasions made an offer to the military administration to supply Camembert directly to the army at prices below those of the market. Last month, the quartermaster of one of the Armies, via an adjutant, accepted our offer and dealt with us directly. We undertook to deliver Camembert at 10 francs below the going market rate at Les Halles. The cheeses, which were stocked at Lisieux, were to have been sent to Paris, where military motor vehicles would collect them. . . . They did not get far. They had barely left Pantin when an order came down to return them to us and for the quartermasters to avoid any future dealings directly with the producers. We sold our cheeses to the quartermaster at 70 francs per hundred (the market rate at Les Halles on that date being 80 francs).[45]

The army's administrative lethargy—it was said that after an order had been received it was common practice to wait for it to be countermanded—deprived the soldiers of the comfort of Norman Camembert. Men in the field had to bide their time while the heavy machinery was set in motion, all the necessary stamps and seals were affixed, and the many quartermasters and deputy quartermasters had done their jobs. In 1917, contacts with the Quartermaster Corps finally bore fruit. The syndicate was to oversee the supply to the army under the direct control of the Central Military Cooperative. In December 1917, the syndicate's chairman informed the governing board of an order to supply four hundred cases of Camemberts per day at a price slightly below the market price at Les Halles. Despite the agreement of principle with the syndicate's board, the Norman cheese makers were unable to completely fill the orders that began to flood in and that grew more numerous by the month. The syndicate urged its members to do their utmost. The supply of Camemberts to the army varied according to the amount of milk available and, therefore, to price. When milk was plentiful and prices lower, the orders were filled, but when the scarcity of milk caused prices to rise, the patriotism of some cheese makers gave way before the opportunity to make greater profits on the Parisian market. M. Dayné, the agent of the Army Quartermaster Corps, complained. At a meeting of the general assembly, Chairman Vignioboul severely reprimanded his colleagues and threatened to have recalcitrants expelled:

> The secretariat had sent all members a circular urging them to make every effort to meet the army's needs. It had been noted that many producers had already responded to this appeal and were reporting a marked increase in output. The committee wished to thank those colleagues, but it was nonetheless obliged to recognize that the patriotic response did correspond to an increase in the amount of milk available. It regretted that many members had turned a deaf ear when the supply had been scarce. This was unacceptable, and the committee had determined that when such sacrifice was called for, abstaining members should be struck from the Syndicate's rolls, particularly when the sacrifice was on behalf of the military. The committee had decided to call upon each member to set aside two days of production per week, and more if possible, so as to supply Camembert to the army cooperative.[46]

Despite such rebukes, the cheese makers did not come up with the amounts requested. On their behalf, it must be admitted that problems of raw material supply, packaging, and labor availability all led to considerable reductions in their production capacity. The demand for cheese was to increase as time went by and the war continued, and it became more and more difficult for producers to satisfy it. Once again, in September 1918, the syndicate's board exhorted the membership:

> The Chairman added that the Syndicate viewed it as a matter of survival to act as supplier to the army. He planned personally to summon every member to attend a general assembly.[47]

In a letter dated 1 November 1918, the assistant quartermaster reported to "The Quartermaster General, Army Quartermaster Corps, Sector 160," on the shortage of food supplies:

> In order to satisfy overall the orders for snack foods *[casse-croûte]* received by the M.C.A. [Central Military Canteen], we require . . . per day 120 quintals [12,000 kilograms or 13.2 tons] of Gruyère, 10,000 Camemberts. The M.C.A. is far from receiving such amounts; in October we received only 94,380 Camemberts in toto. . . . With regard to the latter commodity, the Supply Ministry has fixed at 250,000 per week, i.e., one million per month, the maximum quantities to be supplied to all of the central canteens.[48]

A million Camemberts per month is a considerable amount! The persistence with which the syndicate's board kept after the membership to satisfy the army's demands was not inspired by patriotism alone. Provisioning the army meant a sure outlet, and one far less uncertain than the open market. Such a secure customer was well worth a lower price. However, the syndicate's principal motive lay elsewhere: in ensuring the soldiers' supplies it hoped to burnish the image of the cheese makers themselves, who had come in for violent criticism by a public angered by privation and rising prices. Camembert makers were accused of commandeering milk that was required for children and of being responsible for the rise in prices and for shortages. The syndicate moved to demonstrate to public opinion that it was in no way guilty for the high cost of living and shortage of milk in the cities. In this connection, it was vital that the syndicate demonstrate patriotism, especially when it came to providing for the military. Chairman Vignioboul was very clear on the subject:

> We must not overlook the attacks aimed at shutting down cheese factories or the regional suppression of true Camembert. In this regard, let us serve the military and accept the offer tendered us to provide Camembert to the central military canteens.[49]

The syndicate also attempted to take advantage of its position as military purveyor to publicize Norman Camembert. Dayné ingenuously suggested that a publicity pamphlet be slipped into each box of Camembert shipped to the front:

> A small pamphlet might be inserted inside each box, the wording and method to be determined, stating that the product being offered the *poilu* is authentic Norman Camembert. Soldiers in the front lines and in the rear as well would thus see the Syndicate seal on a daily basis. That daily reminder would remain etched on his memory. The war over, back in his home, he will still remember it. In addition, such a pamphlet would serve to alert him to any product not produced by members of our Syndicate.[50]

This clever publicity ploy was never put into action, the army having placed a ban on any nonofficial propaganda. A few years earlier, the Poulain chocolate company had been placed under a similar ban for the slips of paper it had included in its tablets of chocolate. Once back home, the *poilus* were indeed to remember Camembert, if not its precise regional origin.

The Norman cheese factories were confronted with what seemed like unsolvable problems. How was it possible to increase production when there was a shortage of almost everything, milk most of all? To begin with, there was the problem of replacing the men, who had been called up en masse. Women now had to do their jobs in addition to their own traditional duties. On the farms they helped with the hard labor in the fields, and in the factories they could be seen performing all sorts of tasks, even those hitherto reserved for males. The cheese makers also hired women, as well as employing war refugees. Chairman Vignioboul reported to the authorities on the difficulties cheese makers were facing:

> In the midst of the countless problems you can well imagine, all of us have bent every effort to continue with our work. The different stages of mobilization have successively taken from us, returned to us, or definitively deprived us of our male personnel. We have, to the best of our ability, replaced the departed men with female personnel. We have employed Belgian and French refugees.[51]

Some women took over the management of cheese factories in the absence of their conscripted husbands or sons. Emma Roustang became manager of the Gervais factories at Ferrières-en-Bray. The experience led her to create her own enterprise, which was later to become one of the largest producers of soft-centered cheese.

Labor was not the only thing in short supply. Coal, salt, rennet, and packaging material were also hard to come by. The syndicate asked the prefect to requisition the supplies of salt and coal needed by the cheese factories and to allow rennet to be purchased in Sweden. It also called for a relaxation of the requisition measures that had been adopted in the hope that that might help the struggling packaging manufacturers:

> We have all experienced packaging shortages on many occasions. Our suppliers, Leroy at Livarot and the Tremblay sawmill, lack wood, and they hope, although it will mean our paying the enormous sums being asked, that they will in the near future cease to experience such shortages. However, in this connection they also foresee being unable to continue to produce nails and wire. Such an eventuality, which would necessarily bring a halt to our production, can be easily avoided if the military authorities agree. With some forethought, the latter have commandeered the output of the wire factories at Le Havre and the Moutou company in Paris. Since the amounts in question are very small, such companies could, without causing any damage to the war effort, release the special nails and wire that our producers need. The Leroy and Tremblay establishments thus seek military authorization to contact the two mentioned companies in order to work out a solution to their problems.[52]

To ensure sufficient coal supplies once the coal regions had been occupied by the Germans, the syndicate took direct action. In June 1917, it purchased a sailing ship, the *Cap Pilar,* to bring in coal from England.

A few small cheese factories did have to shut down. The Cléville factory was converted into a hospital. The majority of them, however, continued to produce as best they could, at from 25 to 50 percent below the prewar level. The factories controlled by the Société Laitière des Fermiers Normands, which had processed 7.3 million liters (1.9 million gallons) of milk per year, dropped to 5 million liters (1.3 million gallons). The Ernest Pottier factory dropped from 6,000 liters (1,600 gallons) of milk per day to 3,200 liters (845 gallons). Production at the Saffrey and Bisson factories was halved.

This drop in production combined with an ever-increasing demand inevitably translated into higher prices. The price of milk products overall rose steeply. The patriotic aura they had acquired by furnishing Camemberts to the armed forces failed to protect cheese makers from violent criticism. Not only did they find themselves obliged to defend themselves from being held responsible for inflation and war profiteering, they were also accused of causing the shortage of milk in urban areas. The syndicate's chairman, in a letter addressed to the prefect of Calvados, attempted to exonerate the cheese makers by shifting principal responsibility for the shortage onto the dairy farmers:

> The cheeses of Normandy are in such demand that the poorest brands are bought up at very high prices. The price increase was needed to cope with a nearly 100 percent rise in the cost of raw material. However, the situation . . . has been exploited by the milk suppliers, further encouraged by the abnormally high cost of butter. Milk is up to 0.45 francs per double liter for many factories, especially those producing Camembert. The rise is not over; it will not stop of itself, and for urban consumers it means a huge increase in the sale prices of cheese and milk. In the considered interests of the industry and in an attempt to control the market, we have done all that we could to set up competitive bidding at Les Halles in Paris, but despite our efforts, prices have not returned to any reasonable level, notwithstanding our desire that the soldiers at the front will not be forced to pay so much for bad cheese. Inflated prices remain the rule, but this cannot continue, and we foresee a time when both the customer and the producer will have had enough. A prudent reduction of the price of milk would, we believe, automatically have the same effect on the price of cheese if the farmer could be supplied with bran, cattle cake, etc., at more reasonable prices, and given some assistance with labor costs.[53]

Obviously, these wholly unrealistic proposals remained a dead letter. However, for the syndicate, the important thing was to counter the accusations by demonstrating that it was contributing to the war effort and that it was not responsible for the rise in the cost of living. As evidence of goodwill, Vignioboul called for the reestablishment of a bidding system at Les Halles. He justified his proposal by explaining that competition would bring down the price of lower-quality Camembert, while the Norman Camembert would benefit from its well-deserved reputation and would sell at above-average prices. Above all, his request was designed, if not to avoid a government price freeze on certain basic foodstuffs, at least to limit its effects on Norman Camembert. In the face of growing discontent, however, he resigned himself to calling for taxation—in other words for an official price-fixing program—so long as it was uniform and took quality into account, and so long as sale by bidding was also reestablished. He therefore wrote to the authorities:

> We are accused of using higher prices to monopolize the milk supply to the deprivation of the urban populations. We are also blamed for contributing to the rise in the cost of living. In order to counter those two serious accusations, we call for taxation. It is our fervent wish that this be enacted, and quickly. Not only are we calling for taxation, we are also calling for the reestablishment of sale by auction bidding, the halting of which has resulted in a leveling of the Camembert market, making every brand equal and confusing prices to arrive at a single price which, of course, has been that of the more expensive and better brands. This is a scandal! Only last week, Monsieur Saffrey, a colleague, was at Les Halles in Paris and was unable to keep from protesting against the sale for 80 centimes of a Camembert containing only 100 grams [3.5 ounces] of the 300 grams [10.6 ounces] of cheese called for. Where is the antifraud commission while all this is going on? [54]

When the urban population began to suffer from the milk shortage, the Camembert industry, which was the largest milk consumer, came under fire. The press made it responsible for the shortage in the eyes of the public.[55] A report submitted to the president of the Republic in 1918 echoed this resentment:

> Since the war, there has been a bitter and violent controversy over the acquisition of milk by cheese makers. They are accused of depriving children, the sick, and the elderly of an indispensable food, of taking the whey needed in the raising of veal calves, and of undermining the production of butter.[56]

Was Camembert, that moral support of the front-line troops, really responsible for the milk shortage that affected the civilian population? True, in a period of relative scarcity, any increase in the amount of milk being turned into cheese would inevitably have an effect on the consumption of fresh milk. The 1918 report duly took note of this:

> The high prices of milk byproducts, especially of various kinds of cheeses
> . . . compelled traditional producers, and then newcomers, to seek out ever
> greater quantities of milk; new factories were set up and the older ones in-
> creased in size and absorbed a greater quantity of the milk available.[57]

In the face of such discontent, the authorities took several steps. A decree of 1 July 1918 obliged all enterprises dealing in milk products to declare the amounts they were using. A decree dated 27 September 1918 set up a quota system. Prefects were given the power to limit the production of the cheese factories, based on the advice of a milk-distribution commission, and to fix the price of milk. Commissions made up of cheese makers and milk producers met on a monthly basis under the chairmanship of the prefects.

As the years went by and the urban milk supply gradually returned to normal, the grievances that had piled up against the Camembert producers would be forgotten. The syndicate's calculated decision to give priority to supplying the front lines to the detriment of the home front ended up benefiting the image of Norman Camembert, which, like that of ordinary red wine, the famous *gros rouge,* would long be associated with the Great War. After the Armistice, the demobilized infantrymen all remembered the cheese, one that most of them had never tasted before. Once back in their home regions, they asked their village grocers to obtain for them the Camembert that reminded them of those few brief and precious moments out of the fray, of the snack times when they could relax and joke together before returning to face the enemy's guns. A historian reported on the effect of the discovery of this new cheese that was brought back from the front at the village level: "A man from the Ardèche, who had been a mere boy at the time, told me that during one of his leaves his father had asked his mother for 'a Camembert,' that strange cheese with its unfamiliar taste."[58] For men who had been at the front, Camembert was a part of the mythology of the Great War, the "war to end all wars." There were many soldiers' tales of shrapnel fragments "blowing up the Camembert."[59]

The 1914–1918 war was a vital moment in the creation of the national mythology. Everything in that period of French history remains marked by the war's carnage and its sacrifices and by the national communion that resulted. Despite the unimaginable horror of the battlefield, the war created a bond among all the French and reconciled families that had been separated by differences of opinion since the Revolution. Both left and right, republicans and clericalists joined to defend the nation under the Republic's flag. Two basic foodstuffs were very much a part of that Republican ritual: Camembert and wine. Before moving out to face the enemy, soldiers, most of them from rural areas, communed in both species. A patriotic equivalent to the Catholic rite of communion, the partaking of cheap red wine and Camembert served to remind the combatants of what they were fighting for: their land and its produce. What the ordinary red was to the consecrated wine of the Mass, Camembert was to the Catholic host, that wafer of unleavened bread. It had the same circular shape, the same white color. The only difference was the sharp tang and soft consistency that evoked for the soldiers both their land, at once rugged and gentle, and the vigor and sensuality of the women who awaited them. Georges Clemenceau himself paid homage to Camembert. The old man the soldiers had nicknamed "The Tiger," speaking in 1919 to the veterans of Hill 504, reminded them of that other friend to man in hard times, Camembert cheese.

If Camembert emerged victorious from the Great War, however, it is not far from certain that the Norman cheese makers enjoyed the same result. They certainly thought so in 1918, despite the criticism that had been directed against them. However, as the years passed, they came to understand that Camembert's success was profiting their competitors just as much as it was them and that their product was on the way to being trivialized.

Increased demand at a time when the production capacity of the Norman cheese factories affiliated with the SFVCN was decreasing meant that the market was opened up to newcomers, both in Normandy and in other areas. The French would continue to want Camembert, but aside from a few city dwellers and gourmets, they paid little attention to its components or where it came from. The SFVCN, which had done so much to promote Camembert, now saw its competitors profiting from its efforts. It realized that it had worked more for its competition than it had in its own interests when it found that, handicapped by postwar conditions, it was temporarily unable to meet the overall demand. Forced to forgo a part of the available milk to supply urban needs, the syndicate had to cut production, while new cheese factories were opening in Brittany, in the central region of the country, and in the east. In 1918, for example, the Bridel dairy, which had hitherto specialized in producing and selling butter, began to produce Camembert in Brittany. The report to the president of the Republic took note of the increase in the number of cheese factories and the resultant widespread drop in quality:

> In Calvados, as elsewhere, a large number of new cheese factories have opened, using milk bought anywhere and at any price, whose mediocre products resemble Camembert only in their shape and outward appearance. The proliferation of new cheese factories and their unfortunate collection practices have played a part in raising the price of milk, on the one hand, and on the other, of putting onto the market under the name "Camembert" cheeses that are far inferior to those produced in Normandy, which owe their delicate taste and special aroma to the classic rules governing their preparation.[60]

Faced with competition at home, the syndicate encountered the same situation when it came to export. The government had banned the exportation of food products because of the shortages the country was experiencing.[61] Foreign competitors, especially the Danes, had quickly begun to offer equivalents to Camembert, particularly on the English market. To foster the illusion that their product was "authentic," they did not hesitate to use French brand names, as one member of the syndicate reported indignantly:

> M. Alba *fils* turned over two specimens of a Camembert-type cheese that he had just bought at a London retailer's. The boxes bore labels that imitated the Normandy ones with the words "Camembert extra-fin" or "fromage Camembert surchoix." These products were made in Denmark and are being sold on the English market in large quantities.[62]

As far as Camembert was concerned, the Great War had had a largely positive result, but for the Norman cheese makers, the concerns and satisfactions balanced out. The war had transformed Camembert's image and had given it a new identity. Having gone off to the front as a regional product, it returned as one that was, first and foremost, French. Henceforth, it would be identified with the nation rather than with its place of origin. The fusion of regional particularities in the crucible of war had the same effect on Camembert as it had on all of the mobilized farmers. The loss of regional identity was compensated for by a national and patriotic insignia. Labels appeared illustrating the Great War. Such a reference enabled the non-Norman producers to shift the emphasis from Camembert's regional origins to its national characteristics. Thus, the "Camembert of memory," whose label piously evoked the struggles of 1914–1918, found itself being produced in the Indre.

This rise to the status of national product and the glory it had acquired on the field of battle therefore profited every producer, but Normandy lost its exclusive rights. For the Normans, it was a bitter pill to swallow. They felt themselves to be the artisans of their cheese's national success without being the principal beneficiaries of that success. What must they do to preserve the advantages of Camembert's "nationalization" without affecting its Norman character? The labels produced in Normandy emphasized the regional aspect, and the syndicate seal reinforced the idea of the product's origin as a criterion for excellence. Nevertheless, the majority of consumers paid little attention to the source of their Camembert. At best, the Camembert of Normandy could hope to be recognized as being the superior cheese, but it was no longer the only cheese. A few years after war's end, the arrival of Joseph Knirim would have the merit of affirming the prior claims and primacy of Norman Camembert. The 1928 ceremony honoring Marie Harel trumpeted Camembert's regional identity and demonstrated that France's prestige abroad could very well be represented by a purely regional product. The myth that sprang from those roots reaffirmed the notion that regional identity was no obstacle to national affiliation. Like the majority of the French, Camembert could serve France without abandoning any of its distinctive regional features.

Chapter 4 | THE REIGN OF THE GREAT FAMILIES

The history of Norman Camembert is a history of families that came from one family. It begins as a tale of the domestic adventures of Marie Harel and her descendants and expands to include tales about some of the other families whose names are now very well known to cheese aficionados. The saga of Marie Harel and her descendants threw light on the early days of the Camembert industry, but the family's decline was not accompanied by any decline in the renown of the cheese that it made famous well beyond the villages of Normandy. By the early twentieth century, other families had taken over.

THE CAMEMBERT DYNASTIES

The Lepetits, Lanquetots, Bissons, and Buquets—the families that came together to form the Syndicat des Fabricants du Véritable Camembert de Normandie (SFVCN)—were to dominate the Camembert industry up until the 1950s. Their stories reflect the story of Camembert over the eighty-some years that stretch from the end of the Second Empire (1871) to the last years of the Fourth Republic. These joined dynasties were to write the second chapter in Camembert's glorious history, the chapter that was to see it spread nationwide, the chapter that concludes with its pasteurization. The consecration of Camembert in the first decades of the twentieth century is the triumph of these families, and their slow decline marks the end of an era and the disappearance of the traditional means of production. Of course, a handful of families did not create the entire history of Camembert by themselves. Dozens of small producers, and even a few larger-scale enterprises without any family connection with the great dynasties, also played a part. However, their influence was limited and transient.

When the last enterprises to be managed by Marie Harel's descendants began to decline or go out of business, other families were setting out to conquer the national market. Apart from a few minor details, the birth and rise of the new dynasties followed a course that paralleled that followed by the first dynasty. Their economic success was not due solely to good management but was, above all, the reflection of a strategy that was centered and based on family.

Marie Harel, Mother and Cheese Maker

Marie Harel did not invent Camembert cheese, but she did found a family that knew how to pursue and expand her fruitful trade. At a ceremony that was held to honor the ancestor of Normandy's cheese industry, the chairman of the SFVCN made mention of two of her qualities—the main one, in his view, having been to create a family of enterprising cheese makers—when he referred to her as "Marie Harel, the farmwife who was the creator of Camembert and a family that occupies such an important place in the national economy."[1] The mother of the Camembert industry, Marie Harel was a model for the success of future generations. It all began with a woman, a cheese maker and mother. An enterprise could enjoy lasting success only if it represented a family. The lesson was heeded, and nearly all of the succeeding family dynasties were founded by a female. They were to follow in a nearly identical way the same path, as though the history of that first family had created a historical matrix for all the cheese-producing families to come.

To begin with, an energetic female founds a small dairy to make cheese. Backed by her husband, she increases the business and hands it on to her children. Enterprising and astute, these creative women are also mothers, which is essential for creating a dynasty. In addition, however, they must pass on to their descendants a respect for the work accomplished and the ambition to build on it. They therefore need good sons or, lacking them,

serious and competent sons-in-law, like Thomas Paynel, the son-in-law of
Marie Harel. In the second generation, the descendants, if they number
more than one, will each inherit a separate enterprise and benefit from the
impetus created by their parents, enlarging their holdings. The first problems begin to arise with the third generation: we find quarrels among
heirs, incompetence, and expensive tastes. The children of the third generation, raised in ease and comfort and eager to enjoy the fortunes accumulated by their parents and grandparents, will begin to squander their
inheritance. If, nevertheless, one of the heirs does manage to keep the
business going and make up for the mistakes of his siblings, the story will
inevitably come to an end with the fourth generation due to either bad
management or the lack of heirs willing to take up the torch. The process
was neatly summed up by one elderly cheese maker who had watched his
own world fall apart little by little: "The mother starts it off, the children
make it prosper, the grandchildren fritter it away."

None of the great Camembert dynasties was to escape this fate, as the
following stories, chosen because they are typical, will show. Of the four
different tales that I shall tell, two concern a pair of the largest and most
important firms, while the other two will deal with more modest, but still
famous, enterprises. I shall also show how rapid growth and success can
be brought to a sudden halt for lack of an heir. All of the stories illustrate
the way in which the economic success of the Camembert producers has
begun with success and good fortune at the family level.

Family Histories

There was a time when the best Camembert cheeses bore on their labels
the names of their makers. When he put his name on a Camembert, the
head of the firm was giving it his personal guarantee, committing to it his
reputation and his honor. A Lepetit or Lanquetot Camembert could be
produced only by someone born with the name or brought into the family by marriage. Of course, keen economic sense prevented a cheese producer from merely discarding cheeses that did not meet the highest standard, cheeses with serious flaws, but his sense of honor and his prudent
good judgment prevented him from putting his name or his label on
them. He could always sell them at a lower price under another label that
did not bear his name.

One of the most prestigious brands, Lanquetot, was already well established in the nineteenth century. Émilie Lanquetot, née Mofras, was a modest employee at the Gervais cheese factory in Paris. Her husband's death obliged her to leave the capital, and to provide for her two sons, Maurice and Charles, she set out to find another job. She worked first at the Le Tremblay dairy and cheese factory in the Eure. An authoritarian, courageous, organized, and clever woman, she rapidly won promotion and soon became the manager of the dairy, responsible for overseeing the fabrication and maturing of Camembert cheeses. In 1890, feeling that she had learned enough about the subject, she left Le Tremblay and set up her own cheese-making business in a former ribbon factory at Saint-Martin-de-Bienfaite-la-Cressonnière, in the heart of the Auge. Thanks to her keen business sense and enormous energy, the firm prospered. Assisted by her sons, it continued to grow: she acquired another cheese factory at Orbiquet and then a dairy in Veys, near Isigny, where she opened yet a third factory. Émilie Lanquetot could now retire with the assurance that her business would be carried on.

Maurice took over the management of the firm after buying the cheese factory at Orbiquet from his brother. From 1930 to 1944, he was the chairman of the SFVCN. His sons, Roger and Pierre, took over from him at his death in 1944 and continued to expand the firm, buying up several others. Unfortunately, there then occurred what so many family businesses fear most: a falling out. The two brothers, who were very different from each other, quarreled. The Lanquetot firm was divided up. Roger, the eldest and heir to the Maurice Lanquetot corporate identity, which was now known as Lanquetot-Deschampes, had little interest in managing his cheese factory. He preferred spending his time on broader technological and scientific questions, with the sole and disinterested aim of advancing knowledge. We must be grateful to him for that and try to forgive him the disappointing quality of his Camemberts. His technological contribution does deserve mention. He prided himself on having perfected a Camembert mold made of plastic, an important technological innovation. He is also said to have conducted extensive experiments on the effects that the antibiotics administered to cattle had on the quality of their milk. Unfortunately for science, his painstaking labors have not been made public. On the other side of the coin, Roger's lack of interest in management rapidly led him to the brink of bankruptcy. He was forced to sell his cheese factories to the Bridel dairy in Brittany.

Roger's brother Pierre invented nothing, but he did manage his share of the Lanquetot inheritance well, expanding it year by year. At his death, the Pierre Lanquetot company was left to his son-in-law, Henri Le Bouc, who set out to prove that he was worthy of having been chosen as the heir by continuing the firm's growth. He was one of the rare cheese makers to resist the switch to pasteurized Camembert. The Pierre Lanquetot companies did begin to produce pasteurized Camembert in the 1960s, but in 1976, realizing that it had been a mistake, they reversed course and returned to the traditional methods. That wise decision enabled them to escape being swallowed up by more powerful entities. In 1988, at a moment when the firm was continuing to grow and was manufacturing seventy thousand raw-milk Camembert cheeses a day, the lack of an heir prepared to carry on the work forced Gilberte Lanquetot, Pierre's widow, to sell. The Bridel group—once again—bought it for more than 100 million francs. Thus, that hundred-year-old dynasty was brought to an end not by bad management but by familial shortcomings.

The history of the Lepetit company, from its lightning growth in the last decades of the nineteenth century to its purchase by the Besnier group, is a perfect illustration of the nature and fate of the Norman cheese-making industry. No other firm had succeeded so well at combining scientific and technological innovation with economic and social conservatism. Prior to embarking on cheese production, the Lepetit family had earned a certain reputation in the butter, egg, and cheese trade. Auguste Lepetit purchased eggs, poultry, and butter from farmers in local village markets and resold them at substantially higher prices in the markets of the large cities. He might well have continued this modest trade for the rest of his life had he not met Léontine Brée. Their marriage marked the birth of the Lepetit firm. The couple set up housekeeping in Saint-Pierre-sur-Dives, a thriving center of local trade.

Léontine's keen business sense was unique. The firm prospered and extended its interests abroad to Great Britain and then to the United States of America. Highly popular Auge cheeses were added to the stock of butter and eggs, and the former *coquetier,* or "egg-cup man"—the familiar term for egg merchants—became a dealer in butter, eggs, and cheeses, a B.O.F. *(beurre, oeufs, fromages)* in popular parlance. But not for long. The slump in the demand for Norman butter, caused by strong competition from imported Danish butter, which was less expensive and of a more consistent quality, led the Lepetit family to switch trades. The difficulty of obtaining quality cheeses caused them to turn to cheese production themselves. In 1884, they bought the Saint-Maclou property in Sainte-Marie-aux-Anglais. In the beginning their output was modest, amounting to some five hundred Camembert cheeses per day. Auguste Lepetit had the benefit of the advice of an experienced cheese maker, his friend and former client Léon Serey. The commercial network created by Léontine Lepetit afforded a broad spectrum of sales outlets for the cheese factory, which was able to increase its production without fear of having to sell at a loss. The output at Saint-Maclou rose from two thousand cheeses a day in 1887 to three thousand in 1891, not counting other products. This sharp increase was the subject of a very favorable report in *L'Annuaire Normand:*

> Every day, 11,000 liters [2,915 gallons] of milk are brought into the factory, transported by seven tankers. On a daily basis, 400 kilograms [881 pounds] of butter, 1,000 Pont l'Évêque cheeses, 500 Livarot cheeses, and 3,000 Camemberts are produced; the firm is also beginning to produce Neufchâtel cheese.[2]

Auguste Lepetit relied heavily on technological progress and was in the innovative vanguard. Beginning in 1891, his Saint-Maclou factory was linked by telephone to his headquarters in Saint-Pierre-sur-Dives, an innovation whose only purpose was to facilitate the transmission of orders, never idle chat. In 1891, the Association Normande honored him with a *coupe d'honneur* award. He was one of the first small local industrialists to install a "dynamogram," which was activated by a 40-horsepower steam engine. This alternator provided light and the electrical current necessary to operate a hoist, a refrigerating plant, several pumps, mixers, a churn, and two skimmers, or cream separators.[3] On the farm, Auguste Lepetit and his sons adopted modern methods of cattle breeding and raising. Their dairies regularly won prizes at agricultural fairs.

By 1914, the Lepetit family was producing seven thousand Camemberts a day. They owned eleven farms totaling 550 hectares (1,360 acres), 200 hectares (500 acres) of which were under cultivation. They owned 150 horses, from four hundred to five hundred cattle, and were fattening two thousand pigs. Part of the firm's prestige came from the success of its dairy herd. Several of its cows won top prizes at agricultural fairs, and one of them was given the highest honor, that of having its portrait, in an oval frame against a red background, on the label of the top-grade Camembert cheese. The herds of cows raised on the family's farms provided a large part of the milk needed. To make up the remainder, the firm also collected milk from some 1,600 farms. The cheese factory included several associated workshops: there was a wheelwright to see to the making and upkeep of the carts used in milk collection; a blacksmith shop for shoeing the horses; a tinker for the fabrication and repair of milk cans, basins, and molds; a woodworking shop for making and repairing the planks, racks, and drying shelves for the cheeses; and a fittings workshop for machinery repairs. Modern technology went hand in hand with highly traditional management. The firm was a virtual autocracy, and the larger part of its investments went to increasing its holdings. The workers were housed at their workplace and fed largely on farm produce.

Business boomed, and the Lepetit firm continued to expand. It took over other cheese factories, including one at Bretteville-sur-Dives in 1898 and the Rocher cheese factory at Falaise in 1900. Following Auguste's demise in 1909, his wife, assisted by her sons Henri and Joseph, took up the reins. Professor Pierre Mazé from the Pasteur Institute was regularly called in to inspect the maturing process. He sometimes took a hand in correcting production mishaps with the help of current scientific knowledge.

The Lepetit firm reached its peak between the two wars. The 1960s and pasteurization proved to be its undoing. In 1978, the Besnier group bought what was left of it, a large milk-collecting network that made milk available to other firms and a name whose fame remains unsullied among cheese aficionados.

The dynastic principle prevailed not only in the large firms but also in those that, notwithstanding their modest size, were to become famous for the quality of their products. The Leboucher and Courtonne firms are typical. Philippe Leboucher, the manager of the Bernières-d'Ailly cheese factory, one of the last independent firms producing raw-milk Camembert, is the offspring of two great cheese-making families. The recognized quality of his cheeses owes a great deal to the accumulated experience of several generations of Auge cheese makers. On both his father's and his mother's sides, all of Leboucher's ancestors have produced cheeses. His father, Bernard Leboucher, himself the son of a cheese maker, was one of the most active members of the Auge interprofessional dairy syndicate. Philippe's mother is the heir to the Bisson family, which founded one of the Auge's largest cheese factories. Désiré Bisson had set up a small cheese factory at Quevru in 1874, which his son, Georges, had transferred to Livarot. Bernard Leboucher's maternal grandmother, the aptly named Marguerite Fromage, had also been the daughter of a well-known cheese maker.

Daniel Courtonne, of Saint-Germain-de-Montgommery, was not a prominent cheese maker other than in the unquestioned quality of his product, but in that realm he was undoubtedly the greatest. His output was never more than one thousand cheeses a day. Now that he is retired, his small cheese factory has been shut down. He told me his family's story. His grandfather had begun making Camembert in 1884: "Seeing that it was going well, he bought some milk and it just grew from there." His own father took over in 1908:

> At the beginning of the last century, my parents were making one thousand Camemberts a day, which was a factory amount at the time, but which is no more than a drop in the bucket today. They bought milk in the surrounding area to a distance of fifteen to twenty kilometers [9 to 12 miles], using horse-drawn carts; the whole thing was horse-operated. They had to collect it twice a day.

The small scale of the Courtonne cheese factory did not prevent it from exporting:

> Desgieux took care of transport from Honfleur. It went by ship. This was during the 1920s, when I was a boy. I remember Brumm—that was the client's name—in Manchester got a regular delivery every week. We would batten down the cases to make the transport easier. We exported maybe three hundred to four hundred Camemberts per week.

Courtonne took part in the constituent general assembly of the SFVCN in 1909 and welcomed Joseph Knirim in 1926 when he arrived at Vimoutiers. Saint-Germain-de-Montgommery is, in fact, very near Vimoutiers.

Daniel Courtonne, with the help of his experienced wife, then took over from his father:

> It was right after the war. We had to readapt to new conditions. I was making only two hundred Camemberts, 400 liters [106 gallons] of milk. I had forty cows. Little by little, I grew. When I retired in 1981, I was making three hundred Camemberts.

In 1981, Camembert-loving gourmets lost their favorite cheese. Royal Montgommery disappeared from the cheese-shop shelf. Courtonne and his wife retired without finding any successor.

Is it really necessary to be born in a curd basin to turn out good Camembert cheeses? It would almost seem so. But there is nothing magical about the superiority of firms that have existed for several generations. Time is an indispensable factor in a firm's success, and the most rapid growth is often the most fragile. How many enterprises have experienced an amazing expansion only to fail within a few short years? The Le Tremblay cheese factory, managed by Léonce Abaye, had been one of the largest cheese businesses at the beginning of the last century, and its history is negative confirmation that familial continuity is essential to the durability of Camembert cheese factories.

The Le Tremblay dairy near Pont-Audemer was founded in 1879 by Abaye, who had bought and restored the ruined Château du Tremblay. At the time, he was sixty years of age. The dairy reached its peak in the years preceding the First World War. The Le Tremblay limited company included two cheese factories and two mechanized sawmills, one of which made cheese boxes. It employed around a hundred people. If we find the Le Tremblay cheese factory unique, it is not only because of its power or geographical location but also because of its unusual status. Whereas the majority of cheese factories were in the hands of a single rural family, the Le Tremblay establishment was doubly unique in being a limited company and in being headquartered in Paris. This had a marked effect on its relations with the milk suppliers as well as on its managerial style and its rapid growth.

At Abaye's death in 1913, his adopted son, Charles, was named as company head. The factory continued to expand for a few more years under the efficient management of Antoine Alba, but the business rapidly be-

gan to decline; it closed down in 1929 and its customers were inherited by
Madeleine d'Orbec's dairy.

The long life span of the Lanquetot, Lepetit, Bisson-Leboucher, and
Courtonne families, four names of importance in the Camembert story,
as well as the rapid breakup of the Le Tremblay cheese factory, all illustrate the importance of power being handed down from generation to
generation. What is the common bond between Lanquetot, who produced seventy thousand Camemberts per day, and Courtonne, whose
output was two hundred times less? Very little, other than the fact that
both firms lasted for three successive generations. Upon close examination, we find that there is no example of lasting success in the Camembert industry that does not also reflect an investment from several generations of the same family. On the other hand, the lack of a family-linked
successor, as was the case at Le Tremblay, has always meant decline. The
importance of dynastic continuity is not unique to Normandy. The
Bridel family in Brittany and the Claudel, Roustang, and Hutin families
in the eastern part of France have also linked their names to the fate of
their cheese factories.

The Difficulty of Patrimonial Succession

Time alone can provide the accumulated experience and knowledge
needed to achieve constant high quality. With time, the cheese maker's
art can be perfected, along with the ability to cope with all of the problems that can arise. Where a neophyte might be brought up short by the
unexpected, the experienced producer will instinctively know what must
be done. Capable of maintaining the quality of his product come what
may, he will attract a faithful clientele. His knowledge and reputation will
increase over time, the confidence he has built up will grow, and his relationships with his milk suppliers will become solid and lasting. A firm's
continuity and stability thus depended on its owner and his family. Anything that threatened family solidity was also a threat to the firm's durability. The weddings of the family's daughters and the paths of future inheritance were critical events for the future of family businesses.

The marriage of a daughter was crucial, since sons-in-law could also be
called upon to manage the firm. The choice of a bridegroom could have
serious future consequences. A happy choice could strengthen the firm's
power, lead to a growth in its holdings, or serve to fill certain gaps, espe-

cially technological or commercial ones. An unhappy marriage, on the other hand, might very well lead to dissension within the family and a dispersal of the inheritance. Every care was taken to avoid making a bad choice, and relationships were carefully nurtured and monitored. Matrimonial unions between the offspring of cheese makers were common. This is not surprising, for in spite of the rivalry among them, cheese makers spent a lot of time in each other's company. The heirs of the large livestock farm owners and of cheese merchants were also prime son-in-law material. Technicians who had graduated from the better agricultural and dairy schools and who could eventually take up responsible posts in the family cheese factory were also highly prized by parents who were eager to add to the family's store of talent. In the early 1900s, the two daughters of Louis Serey, a cheese maker at Boissey, married the two sons of M. Buquet, a cheese merchant and exporter. The two weddings formed the basis of the Buquet-Serey dynasty, which died out in the 1960s after having been among the most famous of them all.[4]

The crucial moment came with the founder's retirement, or demise. If he had no heir, his knowledge and the network of relationships he had built up, which represented the firm's principal capital, would be lost. True, knowledge and experience were not unique to the owner, whether male or female, but were shared by others in the firm and by the most experienced of its cheese makers, but they, too, were part of the firm and shared a bond with its founder or with his descendants. A new owner did not have the legitimacy of the founding family in the eyes of the firm's employees, its clientele, or other producers. Nor, in buying the business, did he acquire any practical experience or build up any mutual trust. Only the succession of a family member—son, daughter, son-in-law—or close associate, a member of the "clan," would, in principle, carry forward the accumulated experience of the preceding generations, enjoy authority over employees, sustain relationships with suppliers and dairy producers, and maintain the firm's reputation with its clients. This was always providing, of course, that the heir could live up to his responsibilities.

Many firms owe their decline to a mismanaged handing down of responsibility from head of family to heirs. An inheritance is more than just some material patrimony that can be negotiated; it is a whole tradition and reputation that must be passed on and preserved. Meaningful authority, respect for tradition, moral probity, and personal involvement in local affairs are more important than managerial skills and technical knowledge. Growing up in a cheese-producing environment and learning manufacturing secrets from one's parents does not necessarily endow an heir with all the abilities necessary to carry on. To begin with, he may lack personal authority. His weakness may lead to a loss of some of his suppliers and to an overall weakening of the firm's reputation. At such times, the assistance of his father's old colleagues can be a valuable support.

The lack of an heir, incompetence, an unwise decision to abandon traditional management methods for modern ones—the moment of succession is fraught with many perils. Not too long ago, the Carel cheese factory near Saint-Pierre-sur-Dives lost its autonomy because the heir, in his haste to modernize, did not prudently manage the family business his father had recently passed on to him. The futures of the last surviving small family firms hang in similar balance. What made their strength— their years of accumulated experience, their network of personal relationships that had been nurtured over time thanks to the family's solidity from generation to generation—is still very fragile capital.

From fabrication to consumption, Camembert is a family product. Produced by the family, it is often eaten in a family setting, each member taking his share as the platter goes round the table. Its creation, its quality, and its enjoyment require family harmony. Just as discord among cheese-producing families can lead to ruin, so too do arguments that arise at the end of a meal destroy all the pleasure Camembert can offer . . . unless, of course, through some gustatory miracle, everyone reunites in a chorus of praise inspired by the perfection of a great cheese. And so Camembert's creaminess can sometimes play a part in resolving family discord for both its makers and for its consumers.

THE BELLE ÉPOQUE OF THE CHEESE BUSINESS

At the end of the nineteenth century, odd-looking buildings began to dot the verdant landscape of the Auge. At the turning of a road winding through hills and valleys, one could sometimes glimpse through a break in the hedgerow a cylindrical brick chimney rising among the apple trees. So did the larger cheese factories announce their presence in the rural landscape. The Lepetit factory at Saint-Maclou was one of these. In 1914, a newspaper article about it read as follows: "From the Paris train line one can see the plume of smoke rising from its metal chimney, soon to be replaced by one of brick."[5]

This was on the eve of the First World War, which would temporarily slow down the growth of the Norman cheese factories—without, however, reducing their profits. After the war, in most of the small communities of Normandy as well as in other dairy farming regions, the number of Camembert producers grew. Chimneys sprang up like mushrooms after rain.[6] Norman Camembert attained the peak of its fame and was everywhere in demand, and prices reached new heights. It is said that money has no odor, but between 1920 and 1930 in Normandy it seemed to have the strong smell of Camembert cheese. Quick to sniff out a good business opportunity, hordes of new cheese makers appeared everywhere: well-to-do farmers, clever wholesalers, enterprising employees, ambitious young men, noble families crushed by a burden of boredom and debts on unexploited properties, adventurers seeking easy money. Mistaking Camembert for a cornucopia of wealth, they all thought that they could already see the crystal chandeliers of their future mansions glittering beyond the brick and metal of their factories. However, for every Lepetit who did manage to make enough money to build his idea of a château, there were countless dashed hopes and dreams unrealized.

Between 1920 and 1930, the Norman cheese factories enjoyed ten years of a prosperity that was far from equally distributed. A few large firms amassed fortunes, many earned what was considered an honest living, and many others were quickly forced to abandon their new trade. After 1930, the depression and competition combined to thin the ranks, starting with the newcomers. The belle époque of the cheese-making business was over.

Camembert had been a rural El Dorado throughout the 1920s, the years in which it really took its place as a national myth. To me, the coincidence of the myth's final realization with the golden age of the small Camembert industry is rich with significance. In many ways, Camembert seems to reflect the characteristics of the period. For a few years, France, having regained its position as a great power following its victory over Germany, could dream of a peaceful world in which the progress made possible by modern technologies would improve living standards without destroying the traditional balance of society. Camembert's success seemed to corroborate that vision. Was it not both rural and industrial, modern and traditional, a product that brought prosperity to the countryside and enjoyed the allegiance of city dwellers and foreigners as well? Was it not bringing a solid economic development that also respected France's peasant roots, as Minister of Agriculture Jules Méline might have wished? The best way to capture the spirit of those years of cheese-making fervor is to go into the places where it was being made. There, one can see how Camemberts came into being, and in what surroundings.

Is it possible, however, to go back inside factories that have long been shut down? What have those few years of euphoria left behind? Labels, carefully mounted and preserved by a few devoted collectors; chimneys on the verge of collapse; a few nostalgic survivors who are stubbornly closemouthed about those bygone days. Secretive people who respect the old saying that a peaceful life is a quiet one lived out of the world's eye, cheese makers as a group have always been men and women of few words. However, there are a few isolated sources of information that help to evoke the belle époque of Norman Camembert. I have been fortunate enough to find three memoirs written by direct witnesses to the activities of two Camembert factories: one of the largest, at Le Tremblay,[7] and a much smaller one at Quesnot. Thanks to those records, we can gain entry to that savory and odorous universe that has disappeared today.

The two cheese factories differed not only in size, but in history as well. The Quesnot cheese factory was old, whereas the Le Tremblay factory was founded as late as 1879, at a time when Camembert had already begun to conquer the Parisian market. Mme Marie-Louise Morice, the goddaughter of Thomas Paynel, set up housekeeping at the Quesnot farm at Lessard-et-le-Chêne, where she began to make the first Calvados Camemberts.[8] Around 1860, her son began his first milk-collecting rounds. After many ups and downs, the cheese factory was bought in 1920 by Jean Neuville, who set out to modernize it. Small in size compared to the factory at Le Tremblay, which took in 15,000 liters (3,975 gallons) of milk per day, it collected only 1,500 to 2,000 liters (400 to 530 gallons).

At the beginning of the last century, an average Calvados cheese factory processed approximately 3,000 liters (795 gallons) of milk per day and produced fifteen hundred Camemberts, more than the Quesnot factory but far less than the one at Le Tremblay. Along with those factories, whose activity continued for some years, there were dozens of small farms that attempted, for the space of a season, to produce Camemberts from a few hundred liters of milk.

To which sphere do these factories whose chimneys were dotted across the fields of the Auge belong? Are they part of some farm, a sideline occupation, or should we view them as representing the industrial world's incursion into the rural environment? In fact, they are both: they are a part of the farm, an extension of its activities, and of the factory, having adopted its rhythm. As noted in a 1903 study of the dairy industry, they were an integral part of the rural world: "The cheese factories are usually managed by the owner or farmer of a rural domain. He processes the milk from his own farm and the milk he buys throughout the region."[9] The Le Tremblay cheese factory, for example, located in the center of a huge agricultural area, was connected to a farm. The property was an imposing one, consisting of 300 hectares (742 acres), one hundred of which were under cultivation; a sty of one hundred pigs; and a herd of one hundred cows, not to mention poultry. The Quesnot property, far more modest in size, was still 70 hectares (172 acres) and pastured a herd of sixty-five cows.

Without exception, all of these cheese factories were extensions of a farm. The two elements complement each other and would have a hard time operating separately; without an attendant farm, there would be no cheese factory. The farm-factory linkage formed a closed circuit: the farm provided the cheese factory with its basic requirements: milk, firewood, draft horses, food for the workers. In return, the whey produced by the cheese factory became food for the pigs. The farm/sty/cheese factory circuit was sometimes enlarged to include other elements, such as a sawmill or container factory, or a cider house. For the property's owner, it was one inseparable whole. When he felt the urge to show the importance of his enterprise to his neighbors, the size of his factory's chimney was not enough, and he would want to build himself a period or modern château or manor house that would add the necessary touch of prestige and increase the owner's authority over his personnel and the respect of his colleagues, suppliers, and clients. During the good years, cheese makers bought up abandoned châteaux, restored dilapidated manors, or erected ostentatious houses that were echoes of their success.

Camembert production peaked throughout the Auge during the 1920s. Paris and other large cities were insatiable consumers, production constantly increased, and the cheese factories did their utmost to meet demand. How was this ever-greater production to be achieved? The cheese factories needed increasingly larger quantities of milk, and that milk had to be brought in from farther and farther away over the Auge's narrow and clogged rural roads.

At Quesnot, three collections per day were enough. But the factory at Le Tremblay collected milk from more than two hundred suppliers within a 12- to 15-kilometer (7.5- to 9-mile) radius. Twenty horses and two tank carts made the rounds twice a day between farms and factory. To transport some 800 to 1,200 kilograms (1,750 to 2,650 pounds) of milk at an average speed of 12 kilometers (7.5 miles) per hour, the strongest Percheron horses were needed, for milk is perishable and cannot be left standing. In the 1920s, a few cheese factories began to use motor vehicles. The Le Tremblay factory had two, a Berliet and a Delaugère et Clayette. However, they did not venture onto the back roads linking the farms to the main highways, but were used to relieve the horse-drawn vehicles, taking on the milk from the five or six carts that collected at some distance from the factory.

A few of the collections were made by factory employees, but the majority were carried out by small local farmers who were paid for their work. The factory furnished the horse and the cart. The milkman, as he was called, bore a heavy responsibility. It was up to him to check on the quality of the milk supplied by the dairy farms, and he could refuse to accept it if it had curdled, which often happened in the summer. At Le Tremblay, the owner paid for his milk by bank check. Other Norman cheese makers and farmers preferred to be paid in cash, in which case the milkmen's honesty was a prime requirement, since they were the ones who were responsible once a month for paying each supplier the amount owed for the milk delivered. The risks inherent in this system—several milkmen were robbed while making their rounds—caused cheese makers to begin paying by check.

Most of the cheese factories were built around a large courtyard that would begin to bustle with activity in the early morning, when the carts would come rattling in with their loads of clanging milk cans. The sound of ringing metal would continue throughout the morning as the cans were unloaded and emptied into the aging vats and then washed out with hot water. As soon as the milk came in, each farm's contribution was sampled by the loading chief, who would determine whether it was of a high enough quality to be turned into Camembert.

Many of the factories were built on two levels, corresponding to the phases of fabrication. The chambers where the rennet was added and the curd was placed into molds, drained, and salted were located on the ground floor; the drying and aging shelves were on the second. The temperature varied from one room to another, and each had a different smell. The warmest room, where the rennet was added and the cheese turned to curd, was adjacent to the molding room. Both rooms were filled with the heavy and pungent odor of curdled cheese. As the process went on, the temperature became cooler. In the drying chambers, where Camemberts underwent their slow aging process, cool temperature was necessary. In order to better control the process, some factories partitioned their drying chambers to create different rooms for different aging phases. The first would be redolent with the acidulous smell of apples, which gradually gave way to stronger, slightly ammoniac odors in the following chambers as the process advanced.

On the third day, the cheeses, after having been salted and sprayed with *Penicillium,* were set on a plank and transferred to the drying chambers, where they were set out on wooden racks. Packaging was usually done on the ground floor. Female employees sorted the cheeses according to appearance, weighed them, and wrapped them in waxed paper before tucking them into their round boxes on which they glued labels to indicate the cheese merchant and the quality of the contents. At Le Tremblay, the cheeses were wrapped in waxed paper; top-quality cheeses were packed in handmade boxes fastened together with studs; the second-quality were packed in machine-made boxes fastened with staples. The top-quality cheese was known as "Le Rêve" and was sold directly to the cheese merchants at 30 francs a dozen. Cheeses with the names "Cyrano le Vaillant," "Renaissance," "Les Près Fleuris," "Le Royal," and "Le Chat" were sold at 28 to 30 francs per dozen, either directly to the merchants or to wholesale purveyors at Les Halles. The "less presentable" cheeses (to employ the understatement used by the manager's son)—in other words, those that had not turned out correctly, were irregular in shape, or had a chalky consistency—were given a flattering label reading "Bon Camembert," and sold only at Les Halles for 18 to 20 francs a dozen. The Le Tremblay cheese factory was so proud of its "Bon Camembert" that it neglected to put its own name on the label. A third of the output was sold to stall-keepers at Les Halles, who took a 4 percent commission; the rest went to other retailers. The factories dispatched their cheeses to Paris's Les Halles on a daily basis, most often by railway. However, upholding the Auge's reputation for quality, the Quesnot factory did not send out its cheeses until they were five weeks old, compared to the three or four weeks of other cheese factories.

The different stages of the process did not all take place at the same times of day but took place in sequence, beginning with the arrival of the milk, then proceeding to curdling, and thence to molding. One or two personnel would also work at night, especially for turning the cheeses. Sudden changes in climate and temperature meant that a constant watch had to be kept over the drying chambers, whose temperature was controlled by adjusting their shutters. Should the wind rise or the temperature suddenly rise or fall, the shutter openings would have to be changed, no matter what time of night or day. It was often necessary to act quickly at night. When he was the technical manager, François Mackiewicz encountered such a temperature crisis:

> You had to keep your eye on the wind and the rain at all times and be ready to adjust the shutters. One oversight or mistake would result in a spoilt batch. . . . It called for constant attention![10]

Producers had always dreamed of reducing the time required to produce enough cheese to meet the demand, but Camembert's aging process could not be speeded up beyond a certain point. Apart from their larger size, the cheese factories of the 1920s were not all that different from those of the preceding century. The laws of nature are not easily modified, and they are the laws that govern the creation of cheeses. The producers were obliged to obey them whether they wanted to or not, even if meant lowering their expectations of profit.

However, some progress had indeed been made since the great early days of farm production. Steam boilers now produced the steam for heating the milk and the water needed for cleaning. At Le Tremblay, a 35-horsepower engine and a 55-volt dynamo were used for lighting and to make ice. The steam engine was used not only to heat the premises and warm the milk in a multitube heater, but also to steam clean the milk cans and to run the mold-washing machinery. Measuring devices—acidometers, cremometers, thermometers—came into use, allowing for more frequent and more accurate controls. Some cheese factories installed refrigerating equipment. At Quesnot, illumination was provided by a dynamo run by a 10-horsepower steam engine, which was also used to wash the molds and containers.

Pressed by the demand and up against competition from the cheese factories in eastern France, which cared little for tradition, the Augeron cheese makers cut back on the time of manufacture. Clotting, which had taken three to five hours a few decades earlier, was now being achieved in an hour or an hour and a half. Similarly, the total aging time had been considerably reduced. Cheeses were being sent out at the end of three or four weeks instead of the six to eight once required. Pasteurization trials had been carried out, at Quesnot especially, but without any conclusive results, and fabrication was therefore still being done with whole, unpasteurized milk.

Did the cheese makers really make much money? They avoided this delicate subject. For that matter, few of them kept any real books. When she arrived from Paris, Geneviève Busnel, who had just wed the heir to the Busnel firm, managed to show her father-in-law that his cheese factory was not earning him anything:

> I wanted to prove to him that cheeses were not earning him a sou. I did the books, which he had never bothered with, only keeping track of his expenses and what he took in over the counter. Unfortunately, I was right. If he had had to factor in my work, that of my husband, the wood he burned, the equipment he wore out, the buildings to be maintained, etc. . . . but none of that was taken into account![11]

Her statement has to be qualified to some degree. It is a fact that, in the 1930s, small enterprises like the Busnel cheese factory were not raking in great profits, but such had not been the case in the 1920s, nor was it up until 1950 for the large firms. According to the manager's accounts at Quesnot, the after-tax profits, added to turnover, seem fairly hefty at around 6.5 percent. At Le Tremblay, they were approximately 8 percent before taxes. Profits were rarely reinvested in factory infrastructure, and only a small portion was used to purchase new machinery. The major portion went to the purchase of more new land, when it was not used to purchase such luxuries as manors, hunting grounds, and luxurious automobiles. In the Auge, the hand of nature was so generous in making the grass grow and the apple trees bear fruit that it was not the habit to invest money in anything other than land.

Managing a cheese factory along with a farm demands constant attention. One must be everywhere at once, calling on the milk suppliers, overseeing the cheese-ripening process, keeping an eye on the Camembert and pig markets, making trips to Les Halles to meet with sales agents, and playing host to local elected officials. It is hardly surprising, then, to find that cheese makers almost never took vacations. In the dead month of August, with production at a low ebb, some would allow themselves to take a week at some spa to deal with their weight or to treat their gout, both results of the many banquets that marked the social life of the country gentry. They had no fondness for idleness or for vacations, but they were nonetheless fond of living well, and they appreciated the pleasures of the table, never letting slip an occasion to sit down to a good meal. Hunting parties were red-letter affairs. Some cheese makers owned hunting properties in the Sologne, a pretext to get away for a few days and escape the domestic routine. A weekend at Deauville was also much prized, for there one could display one's wealth without the fear of encountering disapproving gazes or shocking a supplier.

For some dozen years, Camembert's national—and even worldwide—success made a handful of Normandy's manufacturers very wealthy. Those few fortunate ones lived isolated from social conflicts and change, believing that the world had come to a halt, entranced by the odor of Camembert. The Auge believed that its cheese's success augured an eternal harmonious social order, safe from the crises that were unsettling the world outside. In those days, it was still possible to imagine that France might avoid the general upheaval and enjoy the prosperity it derived from its natural wealth, while at the same time preserving its role as a great power. There was a belief that technological progress and industrial development could be realized and a traditional social order preserved at one and the same time. Factories sprang up in a countryside that continued to resist the pull of the cities. And perhaps it is nostalgia for that short-lived and pleasant, albeit illusory, period that has caused—and still causes—the French to be as attached to Camembert as they are, a Camembert whose taste still evokes that idealized age of prosperity and carefree living.

CHEESE FACTORY WORKERS

When I arrived, in 1930, there were still boys sleeping in hammocks in the stables, with the horses. I said to my husband: I can't possibly run things like that! No, never! The first thing we did was to make small rooms with beds in the grain lofts. There was no running water, but there was a dressing table, a large basin, a ewer, a bucket, and there were sheets. We did the washing ourselves; it created a job for a washerwoman. And it caused quite a stir in the countryside when people heard that at the Busnel farm, the help were sleeping between sheets. The woman is crazy! She comes from Paris and she's completely crazy![12]

Fifty-some years later, Geneviève Busnel still remembered the shock, not to mention indignation, she felt when she discovered how the workers in her father-in-law's cheese factory were living. As a young Parisian working girl, raised to the position of cheese-factory owner through her marriage, she had never imagined that people in 1930s France still lived in such a way.

Every account of the condition of workers in the cheese industry at that period agrees with her main points. Subject to long working hours and required to perform arduous tasks, most employees lacked even the minimum comforts. Were the owners of the cheese factories dreadful exploiters of a labor force that was deprived of any rights and incapable of rebellion? In arriving at a balanced judgment, we must bear in mind the context, the living and working conditions that prevailed in rural areas at the time, and the nature of the relationship that existed between owners and employees in small-scale rural industry.

The status of the worker in Normandy's cheese factories before the war cannot be compared to that of the urban laborer. It was, however, very akin to that of the farm laborer. The treatment of cheese-factory personnel retained the stamp of its origin and was part of its agricultural and rural roots. Having begun as sidelines to the main work of a farm, cheese factories gradually became autonomous but continued to retain strong links with the countryside of which they were a part. Cheese makers who were both farmers and small-scale industrialists thus made little distinction between employees who worked the land and those who worked in their cheese dairies. When the work in the factory slackened, especially during the summer months, some of the workers would be diverted to farm labor. On several occasions, the Syndicat des Fabricants du Véritable Camembert de Normandie (SFVCN) was to maintain that cheese-factory workers were to be regarded as agricultural laborers. Such was the case in 1930, when a social security system came into effect. Cheese makers demanded that their employees be classified as laborers in the agricultural sector. In support of their position, they stressed that the majority of cheese-factory owners were farmers, that their employees were recruited from the agricultural work force, and last, that such employees regularly alternated between farm labor and cheese manufacture.[13]

Cheese-factory workers, although officially classed as salaried employees to be covered by labor legislation, were to a large extent unprotected by the new laws. Their relationship with their employer was a highly dependent one; he guaranteed them and their families a job, a salary, and lodgings. They themselves, when speaking of their work, did not use the term "worker," which for them designated the employee in an industrial factory, but spoke of themselves as servants or domestics or, at the most, used the more neutral word "employee." Everyone working on the owner's property—the farm itself, the "château" or its equivalent, its dependencies, and the cheese factory and its annexes—was regarded as a member of the same family. They owed obedience and respect to their employer, the father of the extended family. And the employer, for his part, took on the obligations of a father: he was expected to deal with them fairly and to ensure their livelihood and that of their family, even when they were no longer able to work due to illness or old age. The cheese makers acted as heads of household whose rightful authority extended over all, family members and employees. Maidservants and manservants, domestic workers, farm workers, and workers in the cheese factory all came under the same authority. As in a family, two qualities were viewed as particularly estimable: devotion to the firm or household and loyalty. In this connection, seniority had its benefits. The syndicate encouraged owners to reward their best employees. At one of its very first meetings, it urged its members to give bonuses and medals to the most deserving: "One article that has not yet been implemented is the one concerning the bonuses to be given the most senior employees of cheese factories. Monsieur Lavril noted that in his company a medal was awarded. The owner himself gave a banquet for his employee."[14] In 1911, the "old retainers" of cheese factories were given a banquet and party at Evreux. In 1933, the syndicate voted a subsidy to award "the oldest and most accomplished dairymaids."

Owner control was made stronger and was seldom questioned because cheese-factory employees were usually fairly few in number. In order to ensure production, an average cheese factory employed three to five milk collectors, one head cheese maker and his two assistants, one molder, and one salter—a total of eight to ten persons. The employer housed and fed everyone who worked for him. Until the Second World War, most firms provided fairly rudimentary lodgings adjacent to the factory itself. In 1914, the Lepetit firm at Saint-Maclou housed ninety employees: "Single men occupied a wing with rooms containing five to six single beds. Families had individual apartments in another wing of the factory."[15] Meals were communal affairs eaten in a canteen. At Saint-Maclou, for example, "meals are taken in common promptly at 7:30 A.M., noon, and 7 P.M. The workers eat at tables for ten, the men engaged in each specialty or members of the same trade eating together at the same table."[16]

Most of the food served came from the home property. At the Quesnot cheese factory, the cider served the workers was made from apples grown on the farm.[17] The cheese makers were often fairly generous in providing alcoholic beverages. While quick to complain about the ravages of alcoholism, some actually kept their employees dependent on them by offering them all the cider, and even Calvados, that they wanted. Mackiewicz, who had worked at several Auge cheese factories, reported with some indignation events he had witnessed when, coming from his native Lorraine, he had discovered the darker side of the employment of farm workers at the widow Pottier's establishment in Boissey:

Five teams of twelve to fifteen dairymaids were supervised by "guardians." They lived in the fields in comfortless dwellings and were housed, heated, lit, and paid, to the extent possible, in produce: milk, butter, cheeses (low grade!), cider, eau-de-vie, they had access to a small garden. Alcoholism was widespread. I had the impression that the foremen encouraged it, generously handing out alcohol as bonuses.[18]

Such practices, however, were rare, and most owners usually exercised an almost parental responsibility with regard to their employees. When the need arose, they saw to family needs. Thus, after the Great War, the syndicate organized a subscription to assist the widows and orphans of employees who had been killed in the war. At the 23 January 1920 meeting, the syndicate's board reported on what it had undertaken:

> The report submitted by Monsieur Saffrey, vice-president of the Syndicate's Committee for Aid to War Widows and Orphans, was read. Monsieur Saffrey proposed the immediate allotment of the 5,800 francs collected through subscription to the nine widows and thirteen orphans reported by firm owners. Each widow is to be given 350 francs and each orphan 200 francs. The payments will be made by the owners directly to the parties concerned. The resultant operation can be broken down as follows: nine widows at 350 francs each, thirteen orphans at 200 francs each, total: 5,550 francs.[19]

When family allocations were established at the initiative of various employers' groups, the cheese makers were quick to sign up. At the syndicate's general assembly in 1925, the chairman's subscription proposals were unanimously approved. In a surge of generosity that reflected both their interest in the common weal and their desire to preserve a tranquil atmosphere within their firms, the cheese makers were heavily in favor of encouraging large families:

> At a time when the birthrate in France is disastrously low, and in face of the acute population problem, it is the duty of all to encourage large families. It is all very well to tell the worker to "have many children," but he must also be given the means to feed and raise them. Nor is it fair that the worker who undertakes to shoulder family responsibilities should be placing himself in a financial position inferior to that of his unmarried or childless colleagues. Offices to aid dependent children and to provide financial support to heads of household have been set up all over France and are yielding excellent results. We, dear colleagues, consider that similar social measures could also be

undertaken in our own factories, since, aside from its humanitarian aspects, the step could work to our advantage by helping us to retain our married personnel and win their allegiance. A worker with several children who has an employer who comes to his assistance will be less likely to be tempted to leave him. He will hesitate quitting work at a factory where he is sure of receiving a salary that enables him to raise his small family and where he is certain that his salary will rise in proportion to the number of children he may produce. To determine a practical method of implementing family allotments in our cheese factories, we have asked the prefect of Calvados to provide us with documentation, and, should family-assistance programs exist elsewhere in the département, we have asked him to furnish us with their regulations.[20]

It is evident that the owners were thereby hoping to win the lasting allegiance of their workers, obviously one of their principal concerns. Nothing worried them more than the regrettable tendency of certain employees to switch factories or even to go off to work in other industries that offered higher salaries. Indeed, some employees went so far as to put their own interests or their desire for freedom above their loyalty to the firm. Even the most highly qualified did not always reject attractive offers held out by competing, and unscrupulous, cheese makers. Indeed, many cheese factories could not have gone into business without the experience and expertise of workers from other famous firms whom they had attracted with the offer of high salaries.

The syndicate, which, as we have seen, was concerned with this problem, attempted to prevent employees from seeking work with another cheese maker. It attempted to prevent the introduction of salary competition, fearing that it would not only cause salaries to rise but that it would also, and more importantly, imperil the very foundation of employer authority, namely, the employee's devotion to his firm.

Fortunately for the cheese factories' prosperity, most employees did not have the impertinence to give heed to outside blandishments. Their devotion to the firm in which they worked was rooted in their family's age-old links with that of their employer, in recognition for services rendered, and in their pride at being part of a prestigious firm. Thus, in the words of a former technical manager at the Lanquetot cheese factory in Saint-Martin-de-Bienfaite-la-Cressonnière: "It wasn't that Marie-Louise, the chief cheese maker, was paid all that much, it was the honor of working for Lanquetot." However, the idea of belonging to a firm was not universally cherished, especially when the business had a bad reputation. In that case, other means of retaining the labor force had to be found, and this became more difficult as its composition began to change. Young people learned that salaries were higher in the cities, that the workweek was shorter there, and that no one worked on Sundays, any of which considerations was a pretext for leaving.

In order to win their employees' loyalty, cheese makers understood that they had to find an answer to the material argument. In 1930, Henri Lepetit came up with the idea of reimbursing his employees the following year for their contributions to the firm's mutual assistance fund, with the proviso that they still be working for the company at that time.[21]

The most difficult challenge was to retain unmarried workers with no family responsibilities. The cheese makers preferred to put their money on the family. They gave priority to persons whose family had a long connection to the cheese factory, either as milk suppliers or as paid workers, and to those who were married with children. Bound by multiple ties, such employees had little incentive or desire to leave.

Whether in the field of recruitment or in that of training, the owners gave priority to personal relations. Cheese-making savoir faire was not something to be learned at school but through direct contacts with experienced workers. The most valuable secrets and know-how were handed down from father to son:

> Each firm has its little secrets, its own know-how. According to Monsieur Lefebvre, manager of the Vallée de Berjou cheese factory, that know-how was essential to the final product, especially when it came to molding. And Monsieur Lefebvre knew what he was talking about: as a great-grandson, grandson, and son of cheese makers, he had also handed down his passion to his own son![22]

As a result, it was preferable to hire the children of employees, especially if they were known to the manager:

> We hired young people. . . . In the main, they were the sons of men who had done good work; when the father was a good worker, well, his son

would have priority when it came to hiring. . . . Since the manager was born here, he knew everyone, he had gone to school with the parents, his children had certainly gone to school with a part of the dairy's workforce.[23]

Although in the larger cheese factories employees could be called upon to perform various tasks, the posts themselves were highly specialized. Molders and salters, for example, always performed the same jobs. Their qualifications were the aptitude that they had acquired. Different jobs had a different status. Collectors, known as milkmen, were more independent than other workers. They were "real nobility," to quote a former technical manager. Their responsibility was great, since they also handed the "milk money" over to the suppliers. Nor was their role limited to mere milk collection; they were also the cheese factory's "daily ambassadors" [24] vis-à-vis the farmers. Whether they made their rounds by horse-drawn cart or by truck, they had to be good drivers. Probably the most difficult part of their jobs was not staying sober, which was impossible, but keeping within the limits of sobriety, since the Auge is rich in occasions to have a drink. Every farm was a potential pitfall. At each of them, the milkman would be invited in to have a bite to eat or a coffee laced with a "little drop of something," usually formidable and homemade Calvados. One "laced" coffee would follow another, for such invitations were hard to withstand. The milkman's day began very early, usually before 5 A.M., and it did not end until 10 A.M. or noon. In the summer, it began an hour later, but the second collection round meant that the men would be back at work at 5 or 6 P.M. and continue on until 8 or 9 at night. In addition to collecting milk, they would also perform little services for the farmers, carrying packages and messages and reporting news of local events from farm to farm.

In general, a female was in charge of the cheese-making operation. However, at the Le Tremblay factory, which had thirty-five employees, most of them women, the master cheese maker was a male. The dock chief recorded the quantity of milk provided by each supplier. He would grade the milk on its arrival in order to prevent the supply as a whole from being contaminated by a few unclean cans. He tasted it[25] to detect whether it had been "wet," in other words watered down, and to screen out any milk that was acidic or that had too pronounced a flavor. Females held the majority of the jobs in most factories, although the Saint-Maclou cheese factory was an exception. Among the various tasks, molding, in which the curd is ladled out of a basin and delicately poured into molds, required the greatest number of personnel.

Salting required a real knack to ensure that the barely 5 or 6 grams (0.1 to 0.2 ounces) of salt needed to make a good Camembert were not exceeded and to see that the entire surface was uniformly salted, starting with the outer edge. Experienced female salters were highly sought after, for the good taste of the Camembert depended on their skill, which often provided them with higher-than-average salaries.

The ambient heat and humidity in the curding and molding rooms made the air oppressive. The molders had to work in this close, heavy atmosphere for several hours at a stretch, repeating the same movements thousands of times:

> It was most unhealthy. All the women, and even the men, had very bad legs. You were constantly in a 35°[C 95°F] temperature, with humid air rising from the damp floor. Everything had to be kept very clean, so you were always wet, it was always damp and hot. Always standing, never sitting down. There was no way to work sitting. Your legs! The varicose veins . . .[26]

As with farm labor, nature imposed its laws, its rhythms, and its schedules. There were no set working hours. The cheeses often had to be turned at night, especially in winter when the draining process was slower:

> In winter, the cheeses couldn't be turned in the evenings before going to bed. They would not have been sufficiently drained, so you had to set your alarm for 3 A.M., get up, and go to the factory to turn them. Obviously, a woman who turned at night was paid more. But being a night turner did not mean that she did not have to be on time the next day if she were also a molder.[27]

This is not to say that the hours and rhythm of the work were necessarily inhumane. However, one had to be available at any hour of the day or night and every day of the week. At certain times of year, especially in the summer, the pace would slacken, and some workers would be laid off, whereas at other periods the workdays were endless. It was an accepted fact that work hours in the country cannot be regulated. "When there is work, it has to be done," as the saying goes. Legislation governing working hours was obviously incomprehensible to the cheese producers, who attempted to be exempted from it or to obtain dispensations.

Whenever a law regulating working hours was up for adoption, the syndicate sprang into action. Whether it involved weekly time off, the eight-hour day, or the forty-hour week, the syndicate would emphasize the special character of cheese making, subject as it is to the rhythms of nature, and the urgency inherent in dealing with such a perishable product as milk.

In 1911, after several syndicate members had been fined for contravening the law establishing weekly time off, the syndicate asked Albert Viger, the minister of agriculture, to grant it permission to "split the weekly time off of its personnel to two half-days." Negotiations went on for several months, and a new attempt was made in May 1912. The mayor of Lisieux contacted the prefect at Calvados, who set up a meeting between the syndicate and the labor inspectors at the Lisieux town hall. The minutes of the 28 February 1914 meeting of the syndicate's board noted the following:

> After examining the situation and following lengthy discussions, the inspectors proposed the following time-off schedule: ten hours of work for females, eleven for males, time off on Sunday afternoon, one full day per month, fifteen days of paid vacation during the slack season, i.e., in May or June.[28]

At that time, the workweek must have varied between sixty-five and seventy hours. Extension of the law mandating an eight-hour day to the dairy industry in 1925 and the ensuing reduction of the workweek to forty-eight hours once again aroused the syndicate's concern, and it asked for dispensations because of milk's perishability:

> Our industry, which is wholly based on perishable materials, cannot be compared to others. We cannot observe set working times for starting work that is dependent on the variability of milk deliveries.[29]

The labor minister, sensitive to the cheese makers' argument, hesitated to impose the law. The syndicate negotiated with the departmental labor inspector, who tacitly granted exceptions and ordered his staff to be understanding. In practice, the law was far from fully implemented. At the Le Tremblay cheese factory, for example, the workday in 1925 always far exceeded eight hours. Employees worked from between nine and a half and ten hours per day, six days a week—more than fifty-five hours per week—at salaries that varied between 180 and 250 francs a month. Indeed, one wonders whether the eight-hour workday law was ever implemented in the Norman cheese factories!

The question came up again after the 1936 Matignon Accords, which established a forty-hour workweek. In May 1937, an exchange between two syndicate members during a meeting reveals that the cheese factories were still setting long working hours:

> M. CLAUDEL: I should like to know whether they are working a forty-eight-hour week in every cheese factory.
>
> M. LANQUETOT
> [CHAIRMAN OF THE SFVCN]: Yes, almost everywhere.
>
> M. CLAUDEL: They are still working fifty-four hours a week at my place.[30]

The situation had hardly changed in 1939, as another exchange makes clear:

> M. LANQUETOT: The workers in my factory put in eight and a half hours a day.
>
> M. LEBOUCHER: The labor inspector knows that my workers are putting in fifty-four hours a week, but he has said nothing.[31]

Long working hours, a reduced weekly day off, arduous and repetitive tasks—all were considered normal in the rural world, and no one protested against them. Workers in cheese factories did not complain. They were better treated than salaried farmhands, and their lives were easier than those of small farmers. Cheese producers had little difficulty in recruiting help and in exercising authority. Toward the end of the 1920s, however, the rural labor force began to be more demanding. Aware of the status achieved by wage earners in the cities and in heavy industry, the rural labor force attempted to improve its lot and to benefit from the new social legislation. Various strategies were employed, for the owners' close supervision, their local prestige, and the weight exerted in the rural sphere by traditions of obedience made the workers eager to avoid confrontation. There were no unions, and strikes were inconceivable. Not until the social upheaval of 1936 did the first hints of strike occur in the cheese factories. Nevertheless, despite the general unrest, few firms were affected. Maurice Lanquetot was the only person to complain of a strike. Instead, employees acted individually to better their lot. The most qualified attempted to obtain higher salaries by playing on the competition between owners, but the syndicate kept a sharp eye on them. At a time of labor shortage, less qualified employees had the option of seeking work in other sectors, and many did so. Rural notables had long been concerned by the exodus of women, who were leaving the extremely harsh working conditions in rural areas, and they were fearful of the bad influence of the cities, as is witnessed by the following diatribe from the turn of the century against rural women moving to the cities in search of higher wages:

> As for young women, they have but one ambition: to doff their clogs and bonnets and set out for the city, there to find employment as cooks or housemaids and dress up like a lady in a fancy hat. This exodus to the cities, this migration of the population, is an open wound today, and when our travelers return disappointed to the fields, having failed to find what they had hoped for in the city, they bring with them ideas of luxury and pleasure that are far above their station.[32]

In the factory dormitories, "pleasure" was strictly supervised. According to Geneviève Busnel,

> The profession of cheese worker, male and female, was one in which a bit of nooky was frequent and common. There was a great deal of toing-and-froing from room to room. In all the large cheese factories, small cell-like rooms opened onto long corridors, and you can imagine the kinds of things that went on. The Lepetits couldn't have cared less. At the Busnels, nobody

paid any attention. My housemaid used to complain that she couldn't sleep because the others were so noisy. So we told them: "We don't want anything going on in the rooms. No guests in the rooms." [33]

Eventually, the strict moral edicts, added to the hard working conditions and low wages, led to a progressive disaffection in the work force. Many cheese factories were forced to shut down for lack of available employees. In 1925, the Le Tremblay factory had a hard time finding workers to replace those who moved on to other jobs and was forced to resort to Polish and Czech laborers.

Even today, although working conditions have improved and the rigorous ethical standards have been relaxed, small traditional cheese factories have difficulty in recruiting personnel. One of the owners of one of the last of the small-scale traditional factories told me of the disaffection with a job that offers few attractions:

Ladle-molding is still a difficult job . . . not onerous, but still demanding. You work all year round, sometimes even on Sundays, so it is somehow out of step with the way things are. Today, we still have good teams, but you have to be careful. I try to recruit young people, I try to enable them to work toward getting professional work papers [C.A.P. = *certificat d'aptitude professionnel*] so that they can get ahead, and to bring young people into a job market that a lot of people don't know about, one that is somehow looked down on and neglected. [34]

Because their status was that of factory-employed servants, even when they were well treated the workers in the Auge cheese factories were to be the casualties and social rejects of Camembert's golden age, although, in fact, they were its real creators. Because of their mistaken confidence that their distant expressions of esteem would be enough to retain this irreplaceable sum of experience, the owners of the Camembert factories lost what would have been their principal advantage when faced with competition from industrial producers. Today, the Auge countryside, which has been gradually depopulated, is losing its last rural laborers. Those who remain have acquired technical training and diplomas that keep them away from the painstaking, difficult, and ill-paid work offered them by the small, traditional cheese factories. And such factories will have ever-greater difficulties in finding the labor they need.

THE RISE AND FALL OF THE DOMESTIC ORDER

The commercial success of Norman Camembert propelled a new elite onto the social scene: a handful of wealthy Augeron cheese makers, all flushed with their success. This new nobility sprang up in the Auge countryside and established itself there in the regions' châteaux, which had been taken over by the government or been abandoned for lack of heirs. Year by year, their holdings increased, and a new landed aristocracy took the place once occupied by the old nobility. Our cheese makers, like the nouveaux riches everywhere, were eminently self-assured. They firmly believed that they had contributed to the common weal by creating an income-producing industry and by upholding a harmonious and just social order. For a dozen years, before being shaken up by the city-bred depression, the new, cheese-based order was to spread well-being throughout the valleys of the Auge. Now that it has almost completely disappeared, how can we bring back that very special world, that golden, soft-centered age of the Auge? None of the cheese producers has left us a diary or memoirs. The pressures of work left them no time for leisurely pursuits, and even had they had the time, their innate reserve would have dissuaded them. They were people who did not open up easily. Thus, that is not the direction we should take in seeking to penetrate the closed universe of the Auge cheese factories.

Given the dearth of written records, we can always try to get the survivors to talk, but that, too, is no easy task. To say that the typical rural Norman is not loquacious would be a vast understatement. I did manage to talk to several cheese producers, some of whom had been active in the 1930s. Their conversation always stopped at the brink of any confidence or possibly compromising tidbit of information and avoided anything that might allow a glimpse into what they might really be thinking. With some skill, and a lot of perseverance, I did manage to glean some information on the way in which the cheese producers did business and on their view of the social order. I shall rely especially on my conversations with one of them, an 80-year-old man with the airs of a patriarch and a fund of false modesty, with whom I played a real game of cat-and-mouse, I trying to get him to talk about his experiences, hoping for some revelations about the more hidden side of the bygone lives of the great prewar cheese makers, he hinting that he knew a great deal about which he would not or could not speak. And yet, he was unable to avoid talking about himself, stopping only when he realized that he was about to say too much. I have filled in the blanks in the accounts of these taciturn survivors by combing the records of the SFVCN and contemporary newspaper articles.

The Norman cheese makers formed a new social category within rural society. Because they were simultaneously farmers, industrialists, and merchants, they had trouble defining themselves and obviously preferred the resultant confusion because it helped to protect the secrets of their business; according to circumstances, they could surface in any category. If it were a question of dealing with the milk suppliers' desire to raise the price of milk, they became industrialists, which enabled them to justify the low purchase price of milk to the farmers by emphasizing their own operating costs and the risks involved in transforming milk into cheese. However, when it became incumbent on them to implement labor laws, they would emphasize the agricultural nature of their business in the hope of being granted exemptions. In 1938, they asked to be classed as an agricultural activity. They also rejected the provision that every milk truck should keep a logbook, on the pretext that the law did not apply to rural pickups and collections. They were also merchants, in that they controlled the commercialization of their products, either in part or totally. Auguste Lepetit, for example, had begun as a merchant and wholesaler. In some listings, Camembert manufacturers are entered as merchants. However, faced with the demands of the wholesalers at Les Halles, who were seeking higher commissions, they immediately brought up their industrial expenses. Farmers, industrialists, or merchants?

The majority were all three at once. The smallest cheese makers were principally farmers, and the largest operated almost totally in the industrial sphere. But they were all rural notables, and their success was measured, in the end, by the extent and size of the property they owned. The cheese factory, even when it was the principal source of revenue, was part and parcel of a broader agricultural domain, and the mark of success, the true source of pride for the large cheese makers, was not the volume of their output or the size of their profits, but the acreage they owned, the size of their herd, and the distinction of their châteaux. They enjoyed showing that they were expert and high-class farm owners, and they were especially fond of medals. They valued all medals—medals to hang around the necks of their cows or horses at agricultural fairs as well as the medals their cheeses could win for them at the big agricultural exhibits in Paris, not to mention the medals awarded them personally in recognition of their accomplishments. Maurice Lanquetot, for example, was awarded the Légion d'Honneur in 1935. Such distinctions buttressed the cheese makers' reputations and their authority with the farmers of the region and helped to maintain links of dependency and strengthen or enlarge their collection area. The new notables saw themselves as replacements for the former landowning aristocrats, whose châteaux or manor houses they often occupied and whose heirs they visited with. Many were mayors of their communities, but their political ambitions stopped there. Conservative, they were wary of any undue political commitment. Their ambition and interests were confined to their region and were based on the promotion of local resources and the maintenance of the traditional social order. Such were the bases of their success, but such too would be the cause of their decline when industrialization invaded the Norman countryside and began to affect agro-alimentary activities.

The Norman cheese producers of the 1920s were fervent promoters of technological progress, and their cheese factories were equipped with steam engines, alternators, and refrigeration devices; some even had motorized tank trucks. They exported a part of their produce overseas and knew how to utilize the techniques of publicity. In 1924, Joseph Saffrey, at his establishment in Saint-Loup-de-Fribois, experimented with salting cheeses in brine. A report on the experiment was submitted to the general assembly of the SFVCN in July 1924, and samples of brine-cured Camemberts were set out to be tasted in an attempt to convince the meeting of the value of a process from a technological point of view. Notwithstanding its advantages, however, and the savings in labor and salt it represented, the technique was abandoned after a few trial months when it was found that the brine bath became contaminated by Camembert flora.

During that period, the cheese factory at Saint-Loup-de-Fribois set up a laboratory that enabled it to perform certain milk and Camembert analyses on the spot. Several cheese factories opened their doors to scientists and sought their advice. The SFVCN promulgated and distributed the results of the latest research into cheese-making techniques. In December 1924, Saffrey moved to send each SFVCN member a copy of Professor Guittoneau's work, *La Technique Rationnelle en Industrie Laitière (Rational Technology in the Dairy Industry)*. In 1923, the syndicate contributed 5,000 francs toward a trip to Washington by Professor Charles Porcher, the editor of *Le Lait (Milk)*, a scientific journal. In 1924, it granted a 1,000-franc subsidy to the same publication. It warmly encouraged the move to Lisieux by the Roger laboratory, which produced bacilli for the cheese factories and analyzed their cheeses, and urged its members to work with it.

Thus, the Auge cheese makers appear to have kept up with technological and scientific advances. However, there were limits to being modern, including modern technology. In certain sensitive areas, they remained attached to traditional methods and disagreed with scientists who maintained that there was no such thing as "vintage" milk. They were wedded to the notion of Normandy as a region with special qualities, a notion that justified their claim that the term "Camembert" should be limited to that province. They also rejected pasteurization in cheese production, in contrast to their competitors in eastern France. Their stubborn adherence to traditional methods gradually led them to mistrust a technological progress that they came to view as a threat.

The 1930s represent a turning point in the manner in which they would come to regard certain advances. Their aversion to the economic and social changes that occurred during the interwar years explains their abandonment of a position poised between tradition and progress and their gradual move toward a fundamental traditionalism. The majority of Normandy's cheese factories were to hew strictly to tradition, forgetting that they had once managed to ally change, technology, and respect for the old ways. The gap between innovative and traditional cheese factories, which had begun to widen even before the war, increased to the benefit of the non-Norman cheese factories and a handful of cooperatives that did not hesitate to jettison traditional ways to sail more freely on the seas of industry. Camembert found itself divided: on the one hand, tradition and decline; on the other, triumphant modernity. Only a few firms managed to maintain or recapture the old tradition without forgoing technological progress.

Progress was accepted so long as it did not threaten the social order on which the firm's prosperity was based. Machines, measuring devices, and technical expertise were all brought into the factories without any problem. On the other hand, social legislation and competitive relationships with suppliers and colleagues were met with resistance because they loosened the bonds that had united people and replaced them with relationships that were unstable or controlled by some external body. The cheese maker wished to remain the master of his domain and to retain control over the economic relationships he had established with his suppliers and his clients. Opposed to social legislation and to any move toward a free-market economy, he attempted to keep his village or town uncontaminated by the social changes that were affecting the cities.

The owner's authority was a capital factor for Normandy's cheese producers, not as a thing in itself or because of some authoritarian urge, but because it was at the basis of the traditional social order upon which their prosperity was built. It was an order based on the family. The firm was viewed as a kind of special extended family. The owner was like the head of the family to his clients, to the farmers who provided him with milk, and to the employees he fed and housed. Given that kind of structure, relationships, including economic ones, were only possible among people who were personally acquainted. This proviso necessarily limited the firm's size, since its owner's circle of acquaintances was necessarily restricted and his physical presence was required if he were to exercise real authority. The quality of his product depended on experience acquired over generations and on familiarity with the environment, the land, and the people living on it. It therefore assumed both stability and a deep-rooted attachment to the region. All of the traditional cheese makers I met told me the same thing, each in his own way.

M. Lebaron, my reticent eighty-year-old informant, told me of a world that has largely disappeared, speaking with a feigned detachment that did not completely hide his bitterness and dissatisfaction. His remarks were tinged with a hardly concealed resentment of all the "big-money interests" that had swallowed up the small Auge cheese factories. Once the owner of a famous cheese factory, he had been a prestigious figure in the profession. When recalling his former high reputation, he made a great effort to avoid allowing his pride in his past success to show. He presented himself as a wise old man with a vast experience who was eager to impart to me the precepts for how to achieve success in the Auge.

The first item on his list was, "Stay where one belongs," in every meaning of those words. To remain in one's home region as well as in one's sphere of activity, to know how to maintain one's position despite one's success—those were the guarantees against all error. His statement was a golden rule to be respected absolutely. An expansion of one's cheese factory must not lead to risky investments in other regions. In his eyes, the failures of the investments made by Lepetit in Brittany or Lanquetot in the United States of America were the logical results of their having ventured beyond their home region. For a man who had made money, the best possible investment was land, his native land, which he should never leave. Of that, Lebaron was utterly convinced, and he pointed to the example of his father-in-law to support his thesis: "Every year, my father-in-law bought preferred stock, but always in our own sphere." Like Antaeus, who renewed his strength from contact with the earth, the Auge cheese maker owed all his strength to his permanent contact with his native soil.

The length and purity of his ancestral line lent him strength and greatness. The most productive firm was not necessarily the most prestigious. Greatness was not measured in profit or turnover, but in span of years. Lebaron believed that his firm, which had never managed to reach the same level as that of Lanquetot, was nonetheless more prestigious because it was a generation older:

> We were all from the Auge. My wife comes from one of the oldest cheese-making families. I believe that my son, who manages a small dairy, is the only one who can boast of being directly descended from three or four cheese-manufacturing families, even more than some with more familiar names. Lanquetot, that is a generation later. For that matter, today there is not one Lanquetot in Camembert.

Belonging locally, a condition for a firm's stability and success, implies strict rules that are often hard for the large firms to respect, tempted as they are to neglect relations with small farmers. Both envied and respected, the local cheese makers also gave rise to jealousy, as one of them admitted: "They called us the Auge barons, and there was jealousy." Their success put them in a delicate position. So long as it was reflected in the size of their property holdings, it did not offend farmers, who respected a big landowner. On the other hand, ostentatious displays of wealth, nouveau-riche behavior, fancy clothes, and "Parisian" manners were very poorly regarded. Wealth should remain discreet and rural. An elderly cheese maker told me about a small scandal involving one of his colleagues, an industrial cheese maker from eastern France, who had turned up at a meeting wearing riding breeches. Cheese makers should never forget their duty to be a part of the rural world and always avoid giving offense or causing shock. The owner of one of the largest cheese factories made the rounds of his milk suppliers in a modest Deux-Chevaux, keeping his Jaguar for Paris and visits to the Normandy coast. Hunting parties, races, manor houses, and banquets were all acceptable evidences of good living, so long as they remained regional. One of the best ways to create or strengthen good relations with the region's landowners and businessmen was the hunt. Dairy farmers regarded it as a great honor to be invited to be part of a hunting party given by the cheese maker to whom they supplied milk. When Nestlé opened a plant in a former chocolate factory at Lisieux to produce concentrated milk, the manager allayed the apprehensions of the region's cheese manufacturers by inviting the more affluent to take part in a hunt.

Similar trusted relationships also extended to include faithful consumers, who were much more than mere customers. The solidity of such links withstood the inevitable production mishaps. According to a former cheese maker, "Before, we had friends; I provided Camemberts to people with whom I was friends. Even if work didn't go well for a few days, they still trusted me."

As legitimists, the Norman cheese makers recognized governmental authority. They often took the opportunity to address deferential letters to a minister or a prefect to express a desire or voice an opinion. They might contest a particular legislative or governmental measure, but they never questioned the authority of those in power. On the other hand, they protested anything that weakened their power and fought against any kind of outside interference in their affairs. They expected the state to adopt measures to buttress the social order of which they were a part and could not understand why the government could not guarantee for the country the same kind of order that they achieved in their factories and on their lands. Their demands were all focused on strengthening and cementing their own position. They pressed the government to restrict the use of the name "Camembert" and spare them a competition that threatened their firms. Their rejection of the laws fixing a shorter workweek was inspired as much by the limits it imposed on their power as by the inconvenience it caused them. From their viewpoint, nothing should be allowed to hamper the owner's power and control. They considered themselves the sole judges of their employees' well-being and recriminated against forced benefits and tax laws that allowed the government to pry into their business. Any control imposed from the outside was rejected. On several occasions, and in quite different contexts, the syndicate spoke out against what it termed a "State-controlled economy." During the First World War and the penurious days that followed it and during the occupation in the Second World War and the ensuing reconstruction, the agro-alimentary industries were subjected to severe controls. Cheese makers had restrictions placed on their production, limits for fat content were set, and price controls were put into effect. In all situations that impinged upon the owners' authority, the syndicate's protesting voice was sure to be heard. There were many causes for the decline of the Auge cheese factories in the 1950s. All of them, however, boiled down to a refusal to depart in any way whatsoever from the family-oriented framework. Given that, it was impossible to grow beyond a certain point or to enter into large investments. Lebaron, in looking back over many decades in the cheese industry, was aware that any unduly large family firm was fated to pass to other hands:

> Given the fact that we were still a family business without outside capital, we were almost inevitably fated to reach a size that could not get any bigger because it could no longer be passed on intact. So it was easy for me to hand my business over to my son, it was human in scale, whereas someone like Besnier—suppose he were to be killed in an automobile accident tomorrow. His firm cannot be handed over, so it gets taken over by someone bigger than he is.

For the Auge producers, family control ensured the firm's independence and preserved its managerial secrecy. On the other hand, family problems had a direct influence on the way the business went. As we have seen, many firms lost their autonomy because of family discord.

However, there are other reasons for the disappearance of the majority of the nineteenth-century cheese factories. Lebaron mentioned one of them:

> Those people did not have enough of the industrial mentality. Their minds were attuned to living the good life, living pleasantly and well.

Some of them, probably, but such refined pleasures were not shared by every cheese maker. Why were they so unable to enter the industrial age? The heart of the problem lay in their attachment to the land, in the most basic sense, and that attachment is what made them hang back when it came to industrial organization. Lebaron explained:

> None of them were really industrialists. They were like my wife's parents, farm people, who began by turning out one thousand cheeses, then two thousand, then three thousand, and it kept going up. And we retained something of that, a bit of land under our feet. The majority of those who changed things were the sons of producers. They still had something of the land about them.

A still-active cheese maker—he could be Lebaron's son—said the same thing to me. The Auge cheese makers could not bring themselves to remove their boots or their clogs and enter the industrialized world. When they were forced to choose between their land and industry, their gaze went back to their herd of cattle.

> The Augerons were farmers. They joined the flow and became cheese makers, but they were not industrialists. Take Monsieur Bongrain, for example, if you want to see someone with an industrial sense; he had none of the advantages of the Augerons. Or take Monsieur Besnier, who started from nothing, without the advantage of being born into an Auge family—he had the industrial sense. We were country people first and foremost, farmers who

became cheese makers, and we have always had mud on our boots. We had no industrial sense. We had a feeling for work, not for economics.

There was one exception to this congenital lack of industrial spirit, and that was Pierre Lanquetot. Unfortunately, according to my interlocutor, fortune had not dealt kindly with him, since the poor fellow had produced nothing but daughters:

> Pierre Lanquetot had a bit of industrial sense, but all he had were daughters and one son-in-law who worked with him. But a son-in-law—it takes a lot of money to compensate for that. You have to be able to think financially, and that's even more complicated than thinking industrially.

The characteristics of past Augeron cheese production compared to the anonymous situation that prevails today were even more clearly brought out by Lebaron: "They are anonymous businesses. Like the managers who are running Besnier's firm today, they could be dealing with lumber or anything, they would be using the same methods. It doesn't matter where it comes from, all that matters to them is earning a million a year, whereas with us, it wasn't like that."

Lebaron was unable to understand the anonymity of industrial companies and their managers' supposedly detached view of their product, finding it completely foreign to his notion of an owner's role. The Augeron firms had proudly borne their founders' family names. He also found it hard to understand the equally anonymous relationship with the consumer, and launched into a colorful diatribe against marketing studies:

> Today, everyone is doing marketing studies. I've never really understood how that works. Because they do marketing studies for a product that hasn't been produced yet. Now, for me, a guy comes along to sell you wine, and he says, "Here, let me open a bottle for you," and if it's good, you tell him, "Fine, I'll take twenty bottles."

His words clearly demonstrate the irreconcilable gap between the traditional cheese factories and present-day industry. He could not conceive quantity's winning out over quality:

Besnier, he said, "I respect those who have come before me," but that's not my problem, that's not the future problem. The future problem is not to make cheeses that everyone will want to have again, that will make them say, "God, that's good. It's as good as that cheese we had a couple of weeks ago!" That's what we were after, that was our goal. While he says, "All I care about is that someone buys a pallet of cheese from me. I really don't care whether anyone likes them, I just want them to eat them." We didn't work out of altruism. For us it was a question of pride, taking satisfaction in what we were doing because we had made them, and knowing that people would say, "God, they're good!"

However, this clear-cut antagonism between the two systems does not give us all of the reasons for the decline of the small cheese factories, and we must seek explanations for their disappearance beyond the rejection of mass production and anonymity. Later, I shall show that their loss was due not so much to those principles per se as it was to their rigid implementation and to the firms' failure to absorb social and technological changes.

The particular order illustrated by Normandy's cheese factories, with its alliance of technological progress and social conservatism, the search for broader markets and the deep-rooted attachment to the soil, was not their invention. It had been one of the dominant characteristics of the Association Normande, founded by Arcisse de Caumont in 1833. That association, which had brought together many aristocrats, had worked to preserve the traditional social order from the effects of industrialization. For its members, economic prosperity was to be grounded in the spread of modern agricultural techniques and in small local factories, all within the framework of the existing social structures. That is undoubtedly the reason why the association encouraged the early Camembert industry, which it viewed as an alternative to the large-scale industry that posed such a threat.

In 1856, Jules Morière, who was one of the first to realize the importance of the cheese industry to Normandy, wrote a vindicatory article about the lace-making industry, emphasizing all of its social virtues. His words could apply equally as well to the Camembert industry:

Of all the industries being carried out in the Calvados region, none is more deserving of attention than the lace-making industry, not only because it engages from fifty to sixty thousand female workers, but because it is in essence a moral one. Indeed, instead of working in the large workshops that are all too often nothing but hotbeds of corruption, our female lace makers work at home, sheltered from all pernicious contact; theirs is a family life, to which they grow accustomed and which they come to enjoy.[35]

A short time after that edifying picture was set before the readers of *L'Annuaire Normand* for their reflection, the lace-making industry and most of the other small textile industries operating in rural villages went into a swift decline. In a very few years, they had all disappeared, throwing out of work a large female—and to a lesser extent, male—workforce. The cheese-making industry emerged at an opportune moment to take up the slack and ensure local employment to those who could not find full-time jobs in the agricultural sector.

Industry without industrialization, factories in rural areas, technological progress without social upheaval and without bringing into question the traditions and values of the past—this dream, cherished by the dynamic leaders and influential thinkers of the Association Normande, was shared by a majority of the French people and their leaders right up to the eve of the Second World War. The Camembert industry, which embodied this conservative utopia while still managing to conquer the national market and export to the United States of America, was a reassuring symbol of the "true" France, at the cutting edge of progress without abandoning its rural roots or changing the traditional social order.

Today, we know how unrealistic and dangerous that rejection of industrialization and social change really was. However, following the spread of industry into the countryside, many French were still nostalgic for the old ways, forgetting their concomitant constraints, which most of them had not experienced. Rural industry, technological progress that served the gastronomical tradition, small businesses harmoniously blending into their surroundings, the family spirit in trade—all of those aspects of Normandy's prewar cheese industry, setting aside its labor constraints, still exercised a strong attraction. Camembert, with its soft and creamy center, seemed to be the ideal, savory synthesis of all those contradictory traits that made France what it was. And it is obviously one of the reasons that the cheese retained its popularity even after nearly all of the small traditional cheese dairies that had produced it had disappeared.

Chapter 5 | THE WAR OF
THE TWO CAMEMBERTS

Toward the end of the 1950s, a storm broke over the Norman cheese factories. Sweeping away everything in its path, only a few of the region's dozens of establishments were left standing after its passage.[1] The storm's name was pasteurization. The process was to wipe out the small cheese factories as though they, too, were so many bacteria. The pioneers in the introduction of the new technology to the cheese industry were the newer companies in the eastern part of France, which lacked the advantages of top-quality milk and tradition. For them, industrial expansion was the only way to outdo their Norman competitors in the marketplace. The Norman cheese makers, solidly entrenched in their traditions and convinced of the superiority of their product, were to persist for some time in their hostility to what they regarded as a newfangled process, one that they viewed—quite rightly—as a threat. The Syndicat des Fabricants du Véritable Camembert de Normandie (SFVCN) had spoken out against it in 1943 before the Fédération de l'Industrie Laitière (Dairy Industry Federation):

> We protested cheese pasteurization by pointing out that the widespread pasteurization of the milk we used would have a negative effect on the quality of our products, based as they are on whole raw milk. We spoke out against

that standardization, embodying as it does the east's battle against Normandy, its only goal being to target our products and seriously undermine their superiority.[2]

Thus did the tradition-bound Norman cheese makers define the major drawback inherent in the process: standardization. And indeed, pasteurization does result in a standardized milk, eliminating the differences that exist among different milks from different sources and wiping out the Normans' claims that their cheeses were special because of the region from which they came. If the triumph of pasteurized Camembert over traditional raw-milk Camembert did not mean the end of regional significance, it certainly made it less important.

France had been an industrial power prior to the Second World War, but it was still an agricultural country in which the rural population was in the majority. Aside from a few industrial zones, its countryside was a stranger to the rhythms of production and the norms of urban consumption. A large part of its food production was nonindustrial.

All of that was to change in the 1950s. With industrial growth, pasteurized Camembert became inevitable. France's symbolic food could not escape the wave of industrial modernization, caught up as it was in the overall changes taking place in the country as a whole.

THE PASTEURIZATION CRISIS

In 1950, pasteurization was hardly something new; it had been employed for years in many sectors of the dairy industry, especially with regard to the milk intended for domestic consumption. Heating milk for a few minutes at a temperature of approximately 70°C (160°F) kills the Koch bacillus, which causes tuberculosis. It was for that reason that health authorities had imposed the process. In the cheese industry, however, pasteurization was not necessary, since the Koch bacillus was automatically destroyed during the aging process. Nevertheless, scientists urged the pasteurization of the milk to be used for cheese making, not for reasons of health but to gain better control over the entire process, for milk is a highly complex and recalcitrant substance. Milk, the source of life, has always fascinated and irritated scientists. The mutations it undergoes from its natural state are so uncontrollable and difficult to understand that it is impossible to handle it with confidence. Scientists know that this unpredictable behavior is caused by myriad different bacteria and microorganisms, most of which escape their observations. Raw milk is fragile, unstable, and difficult to work with industrially. By pasteurizing it, scientists believe, milk can be brought under control. Once rid of all of its microscopic hosts, it becomes controllable, obeying the instructions of scientific authorities rather than acting with a kind of unpredictable anarchy. Pasteurizing the milk intended for cheese therefore meant making it obedient to discipline.

On paper, pasteurization has nothing but virtues, at least from the scientific and industrial viewpoint. Furthermore, nothing could apparently be simpler. Beginning in the early years of the twentieth century, scientists conducted experiments into ways to use pasteurization in cheese making with the aim of eradicating chance and standardizing the production process. They were hoping to find a way to free the cheese industry from its willful empiricism, which they viewed as based on ignorance or, worse, superstition.

Professor Pierre Mazé of the Pasteur Institute was one of the most active propagandists for the use of pasteurization in conjunction with the practice of reculturing the pasteurized milk with select, laboratory-grown bacilli. His experiments were not confined to the laboratory, and a few cheese factories agreed to serve as guinea pigs. Marcel Monteran, an agricultural engineer, had attempted to introduce pasteurization into the cheese-making industry in 1908.[3] However, his impertinent experiments had not been successful. The syndicate reported on them with some derision: "Some scientists in the dairy industry who have set out to produce pasteurized Camemberts have been sadly disappointed by the results obtained and have been forced to shut their factory."[4]

Professor Jean Keilling, who had been a technical manager in the early days when there had still been some uncertainty about the pasteurization method itself and questions about the need for it, told me of his own trials and tribulations:

The first time that I pasteurized milk was before the war in Beuzeville, near Honfleur, at a young cheese maker's establishment in the Auge. He told me, "I have milk, make it into pasteurized Camembert." So I took a container, built a fire, heated the milk. . . . Instead of shrinking in size, the cheese swelled up overnight because of the fermentation, a bacteriological accident. That spoiled 500 liters [132 gallons] of milk, so it made me more careful.

It would take no less than eighty-five more years for the method to become widespread. Norman Camembert resisted pasteurization and refused to allow its behavior to be dictated to it by some laboratory. At the time, large-scale pasteurization of the milk to be used in cheese proved to be nearly impossible in practice. Everything seemed to work against that apparently simple operation. It was, in the end, a question of forcing empirical methods of fabrication to bend to industrial standards, but nothing was more difficult to standardize than the production methods for Camembert cheese, a little country cheese that had been created by two clever Auge farmwives, Marie Harel and her daughter. Dairy products were considered more difficult to industrialize than any others, subject as they are to climate change and the unpredictable moods of cows. For scientists, nothing was more baffling and unscientific than the skill of the cheese makers, who managed to produce savory Camemberts without knowing anything at all about microbiology. The industrial offensive against this apparently impregnable bastion of empiricism was to be a lengthy one. As we have seen, it had begun over a century before, with Louis Pasteur.

Technical considerations were not the only reasons that the process of bringing Camembert under control was so drawn-out an affair. Prior to 1950, no one in France, apart from some scientists, was interested in the pasteurization of Camembert. In rural areas, pasteurization was unheard of prior to the Second World War. For it to become common practice, everything had to change: the way in which the dairy farms were worked and the methods used in milking, collection, and fabrication. Pasteurization first requires milk collected under good conditions, milk that has not been tampered with or adulterated. When acidic milk is heated, it "turns," as everyone who has attempted to boil slightly stale milk knows. Milking and milk collection therefore must be carried out in a way that can ensure the milk will be rich in bacteria and have a low acid content. Pasteurizing milk upon its arrival at the cheese factory halts the maturation process that is essential for cheese production. In order to achieve maturation, therefore, the milk must be recultured with lactic bacilli.

Cheese pasteurization therefore entails both measuring and controlling milk acidity and relying on laboratories that specialize in creating lactic bacilli. It also means allowing into the cheese factory the technologies, equipment, and products that are used in laboratories. In a way, it implies a devaluing of the empirical knowledge of the cheese makers, forcing Marie Harel to obey the dictates of Louis Pasteur.

There was yet another large problem. The curd of pasteurized milk does not drain well. One effect of pasteurization is to coagulate the soluble milk proteins in the curd that alter its consistency. Given a denser curd, the liquid portion does not drain properly. The problem does not arise with cheeses made of cut curd, like Livarot or Pont l'Évêque, but with Camembert the curd should remain whole, and draining should be spontaneous. The only solution is to break that rule and to cut the curd to enable the liquid to drain away. If one risks flouting long-standing rules, one must do so in the belief that some real benefit will result. The scientists were happy just to manage to control the process, but this did not convince the cheese makers. Nor did pasteurization in and of itself especially attract the industrialists. However, its necessary corollary, a cut and separated curd, did have an appreciable effect on productivity. It enabled industrial cheese makers to forget the ladle, which would henceforth be a museum piece, and to use a separator. Instead of lifting off the curd from a basin, ladle by ladle, the cut curd could be put into a separator, which would then pour it into a series of molds. One worker could thus replace ten or twenty molders.

If we go by the definition of Camembert as "a cheese with a homogenous curd,"[5] then the result obtained clearly did not have the right to be called "Camembert." Despite some protests, however, the rules were allowed to be bent. Pasteurized Camembert was only required to preserve the outer appearance of true Camembert and have the same fat and protein content as before. It was decided that when it came to defining this cheese, the production method employed was of secondary importance. The historical context may help to explain why a deaf ear was turned to the protests of the traditional cheese makers. In the 1950s, France still had a vivid memory of the shortages that had prevailed during the war and in the immediate postwar period, when the produce available in city markets had been both meager in quantity and poor in quality. Camembert had not escaped the rigors of the Occupation. Because of the fat shortage, the Germans had forbidden the production of Camembert with a fat content of more than 30 percent, a big reduction from the customary 45 percent. The restrictions imposed on Camembert by the occupying forces had meant that the French had been deprived of most of the better brands. Such privation must have got to Antoine Blondin, who was an aficionado of the cheese. The memory was still vivid in 1951, when he wrote the following:

> Although [Paul] Claudel still showed up on our stages during the Occupation, the other Claudel [a famous brand of Camembert with a 45-percent fat content] totally disappeared from our tables. Of the two, the latter was the real resistance fighter. Let us pay a disinterested tribute to the Claudel that preferred absence to collaboration.[6]

As that period drew to a close, considerations of quality did not return immediately to center stage. For the majority of consumers, it was enough that the shelves were once again filled. Productivity experts returning from visits to the United States were also urging the adoption of American methods of mass production. The primary concern was to produce in quantity and at the lowest cost in order to meet the growing and widespread demand. The argument based on price and production costs won out over devotion to tradition.

For industry, pasteurization offered nothing but advantages. Retaining the soluble proteins that had formerly been lost with the whey meant that the cheese-producing capacity of the milk was increased by some 10 percent. After the curd was cut up in the vats, filling the molds became an easy process. The curd, cut into centimeter-sized cubes and floating in the whey, could be worked as liquid and poured. The women who had been employed as molders were sent home to exercise their ladle-wielding talents in their own kitchens.

Theoretically, the curd could be cut up and molded in a separator without having been pasteurized. In fact, some firms did do this, and also charged more for their raw-milk cheeses. In 1950, however, pasteurization was a necessary prelude to the general change in production methods. It was an obligatory security measure when dealing with large quantities of milk, some of which might not meet the very highest sanitary standards. Furthermore, the curd produced by raw milk is more fragile, and its handling was too delicate a matter for the crude machinery of the period.

Throughout the 1950s, the Auge cheese factories had still been hoping to avoid pasteurization. They were finally forced to face the fact that even the high reputation of their product could not protect them against the competition being brought to bear by industrial Camemberts. In the 1960s, therefore, most of them embarked on the adventure of pasteurization and mechanized their production. The increased productivity that resulted from large-scale production also meant a reduction in cost and lower sales prices. Unable to keep up with the increased pace, the small cheese factories disappeared. Only a few mid-sized firms managed to retain a position in pasteurized Camembert. Of the cheese factories that remained faithful to traditional methods, the sole survivors were firms whose reputation for high quality had earned them a clientele that cared little what they paid for their cheese.

Between 1950 and 1960, Camembert became an industrial product, and the world of traditional cheese making virtually disappeared. Its collapse took some twenty-five years, from 1955 to 1980—a quarter-century that witnessed the annihilation of a century-old network of interwoven local activities. The change went hand in hand with similar innovations in farming, especially in cattle raising. The Norman countryside, with the exception of the plains region, had remained practically unchanged for more than a hundred years. After the Second World War, changes took place with lightning speed and affected everything. Norman cattle were replaced by black-and-whites and artificial insemination became the rule; silage and fodder crops replaced hay as the principal livestock feed. Dairy productivity increased fivefold, as did the average size of such establishments. After penury, the region began to experience surplus.

Industrial Camembert

Thirty years after the spread of pasteurization in the Auge region, a white sea of industrial Camembert stretched as far as the eye could see. Today, nearly 90 percent of all Camembert cheeses are produced industrially. Almost all of them are made by the same identical processes and machines. We have entered the age of mass-produced Camembert. Television advertising attempts to give these many cheeses, which differ from each other by little save price and label, the touch of uniqueness that they lack. I shall leave it to others to bemoan the situation. If industrial Camembert has taken over the market, it is because of its own qualities. As one who loves distinctive and individual cheeses, I rarely eat supermarket Camembert. Indeed, I have done so for only two reasons: first, when served some as a guest, I have eaten it out of politeness; second, when working on this book, I have done so for experimental purposes. I can therefore speak from taste experience. However, I shall attempt to adopt a neutral stance with regard to this product of triumphant industrialization.

To capture the real nature of this industrial Camembert, we must follow it through the whole chain of its production and enter the world of vats and pipes in which it is created. It is much more than just Camembert made from pasteurized rather than raw milk. It is an industrial product up to and including its very crust. Strategically placed stacks of it have taken over the refrigerated shelves of the large supermarkets, sometimes to overflowing. However, like all products of mass consumption, its familiarity goes hand in hand with the average consumer's total ignorance about where it comes from and how it is made.

Camembert making, once an art, has become an industry. The industrialization of Camembert is not confined to its production; it affects every operation connected with it, including the relationships and the people involved in its creation. From start to finish, from the production of milk on the dairy farm to the final sale of cheese to the customer, from cows to bacteria, from farmers to consumers, nearly everything has been subjected to industrial discipline. Standardization, stabilization, and productivity, the pillars of the industrial order, have had to deal with the nature of the substances involved, the complex changes those substances undergo, and the interrelationships of all the people who play a part in the chain of production. There have been many clashes between industrial logic and the complex nature of materials and people. Industry requires a milk whose supply will be constant, stable, homogenous, and subject to precise standards. Industry demands a supply that will be regular, or at least flexible, whereas milk production depends on the cow and its cycles—in other words, on the caprice and mysteries of nature. At one with the growth of the grass and the calving cycle, milk production is at a maximum in the spring and at its lowest in late autumn. Milk's composition, taste, and properties all vary throughout the year and from one cow to another. The industrialist is forced to buy all of the milk his producers offer him, notwithstanding his needs and his production capacity. When the supply is superior to his demands, he turns to producing powdered milk and butter.

Industry affects the dairy farm, starting with the selection of cattle. Cows are no longer familiar domestic animals like cats and dogs, with known antecedents. Farewell to the good Norman cattle with pet names; hail the F.F.P.N., or Française Frisonne Pie Noir,[7] a new breed of dairy cow. Tagged, numbered, and—in the most modern establishments—managed by computer, this new milk-producing phenomenon is the result of a process of programmed breeding and subjected to regular checkups and inspection. There is no question of leaving the reproductive cycle of the modern cow to mere chance. The farmer determines when they are to be fecund. Here, too, the demands of productivity reign supreme. Dairy cows are artificially inseminated with specially selected semen from licensed sires who are recorded in the herd book, the official birth record of elite cattle, and comfortably ensconced in registered centers. Functions are even beginning to be specialized with regard to calf-bearing cows and dairy cows. The calf-bearing cows receive embryos that have been removed from donor cows with high milk-yielding capabilities. Twins can easily be produced by embryonic manipulation. Are they cows, or are they milk-producing units? The question may well be asked. The spacing of calving periods and the food supplements added to the diet in winter serve to control the level and quality of milk production. All that notwithstanding, the cows are not yet as completely free from natural cycles as the industry would like or as scientists may hope. The cheese-making industry is engaged in a struggle to correct nature's last foibles and fantasies. The matter is a serious one, and a great deal of money is involved. No one can allow such huge investments to be endangered by a recalcitrant cow or by some farmer reluctant to adopt modern methods. The cooling and storing of milk in refrigerated tanks at the dairy farm protect it from bacteria until it is moved to the factory. Huge 125,000-liter (34,000-gallon) tank trucks go from farm to farm to collect the milk on a daily basis rather than the twice-daily pickups made when 20-liter (approximately 5-gallon) milk cans were the norm. The industrialists welcome this milk, which they refer to as "broad mix" milk. According to one dairy manager, "With such large quantities, a highly homogenous basic material is achieved, and this type of collecting yields a very clean and very stable milk with the least possible amount of bacteria."[8]

The product that arrives at the factory is already standardized. However, many problems that can affect industrial production still remain to be solved. One of the most dreaded threats is the presence of bacteriophages. These microorganisms attack without warning, and in a few hours they can decimate a population of wholesome lactic bacteria and prevent the milk from aging. Aging and clotting times can vary greatly and complicate the workers' task. In order to avoid the unexpected, technicians have increased the standardization of the various elements involved and carry out constant monitoring. Industrial fabrication, therefore, begins by eradicating the original characteristics of the principal raw material, especially its inner life, its local and temporal qualities—in other words, anything that might recall the odor of the cow. The bacteria added to the milk to replace those killed by pasteurization are also closely monitored industrial products. None are allowed into the factory unless their identities have been fixed and normalized. The industry creates a break in milk's spontaneous cycle of change in order to inject its own norms. In this respect, the creation of Camembert is no different from that of any other industrial product. We need only note the words of a floor manager in one industrial cheese factory that turns out 250,000 Camembert cheeses per day:

> The product has material, psychochemical, and bacteriological characteristics; it must meet the specifications that have been set. To produce it requires a certain amount of milk, a certain amount of additives, a specific wrapping. It is required to leave the factory weighing 250 grams [8.8 ounces] before packaging, and in order to arrive at that 250 grams we need 1,850 liters [490 gallons] of products, of—

The floor manager hesitated over the correct term to use, as he clearly no longer knew how to describe the basic material out of which he was making Camemberts. I tried to help him out by murmuring the word "milk," and my suggestion started him off again: ". . . of milk, yes, but milk with a fixed content, because if there is any variation . . . the composition of the milk is not . . ." And again he hesitated, because milk is not stable, it is different every day, and technicians are forced to make daily adjustments:

> We adapt the liter intake according to the amount of solids the milk contains, which changes daily. To make Camembert, you need 68 grams [2.4 ounces] of protein and 58 grams [2 ounces] of fat. So you analyze the milk, and if something is lacking you raise the liter amount. It is adjusted according to the result of the milk analysis.[9]

Milk's living, complex, and fragile nature is just another obstacle to its complete normalization and to total control over its transformation. Research is under way to achieve this control. For example, one of the concerns of industrial cheese manufacture is controlling the milk's acid content at the time the rennet is added. The development of a lactic-acid activator would solve that problem.[10] Such an activator, which would make it possible to alter the acid content, would serve to increase the technicians' control over cheese manufacture. It would also mean a speedier aging and maturing process. The advertising of one producer of such a product states: "Your choice will be reflected in the quality of your product," a slogan that perfectly sums up the industrialists' obsession for exercising total quality control and achieving uniform mass production.

With continuous clotting, the total automation of production is in sight. The continuous clotting machine, with which the largest cheese factories are now equipped, consists of a flexible belt moving along a semi-cylindrical steel base some 50 meters (164 feet) in length, which carries the clotting milk.[11] At the end of this concave belt the curd is cut up and poured into molds that have been pierced with small holes. After they have drained, the cheeses are salted by being plunged into a brine bath. They are then sprinkled with a solution of *Penicillium candidum,* after which they are aged in a drying chamber for two weeks. The Camembert cheeses, in their white coats, are wrapped, put in boxes, and shipped off to be sold. Today, the largest factories are turning out four hundred thousand Camembert cheeses per day—the equivalent of ten years of Cyrille Paynel's output—with a workforce of under one hundred.

The industrial cheese manufacturer takes care to produce cheeses that weigh the correct amount: 250 grams (8.8 ounces) total, not one gram more or less. More means loss, and less means that the cheese may be

downgraded and sold at a lower price. Weight variations are closely monitored. One dairy manager has said, "One tries to make them as equal as
possible. Since I came on the job they have worked to improve the equipment in order to produce the maximum number of cheeses possible."[12]

As the manager of the Besnier firm in Domfront in Normandy, where
more than three hundred thousand Camemberts are produced daily,
so candidly remarked, "No cheese here has been touched by human
hands."[13] A workforce trained as electromechanical engineers and versed
in electronics is required to produce such cheeses. According to another
manager, "Electromechanical engineers are at the heart of modern cheese
production." Knowledge and experience in dairy work and cheese making are deemed necessary only for a few senior technicians and laboratory
personnel.

The modern cheese factory conceals its true function. The visitor will
search in vain for any sign of milk. Everything travels by pipes and tub-
ing, and the prevailing odors are those of cleaning products. The white
tile floors are damp, but not from milk; the moisture comes from cleans-
ers and water. The overall effect is of a chemical laboratory. One must go
into the drying chambers and see the hundreds of thousands of flat cylin-
ders set out on their stainless-steel wire stands to realize that one is actually in a cheese factory.

Seventy percent of cheese sales are made through large chain supermarkets or local supermarkets and their central purchasing departments.
Upon leaving the factory, therefore, the cheeses also leave the control of
their maker. They are handed over to the transport facilities hired by
the purchasing departments. However, the producers are in charge of
promoting their product commercially, including advertising at the point
of sale. In order to stand up under the handling inherent in mass distribution, Camembert has to be fairly sturdy, with a firm consistency. Dis-
played in refrigerator sections, the cheese can be examined by the consumer, who selects his Camembert without the help of a sales clerk.
Choice is totally dependent on the consumer; therefore, a consumer must
also have been trained and conditioned to evaluate the product he is buying. He wants it to look like it always has, to have the same taste and texture, and he must like its slightly elastic consistency. He will appreciate its
appetizing whiteness, its resilience, its nutritional qualities, and its modest price. For exportation, the Besnier firm makes a Camembert whose

taste and texture, less sharp than the cheese produced for French taste buds, are thought to meet the demands of foreign consumers. Norman Camembert had conquered the world by flaunting its origins and identity, but industrial Camembert has carved out its place in the market by disguising them. Only its package indicates its source.

There are hardly any die-hards to stand up against the industrial output of the five large factories, which produce some 1.5 million Camembert cheeses per day . . . just enough, perhaps, to keep the technicians and scientists on their toes and the managers running. Of course, minor catastrophes do occur: an unfortunate outbreak of *Listeria* contamination, a lightning attack by some bacteriophage, a strike, a dairy farmers' revolt, a machine breakdown, roads closed by bad weather . . . or protests by consumer groups.

Michel Besnier, the Emperor of Industrial Camembert

Today, one firm dominates the Camembert industry: Besnier. Since taking over the Bridel company, the Besnier group has been producing more than 40 percent of all French Camembert cheeses. The three top-selling brands, "Président," "Le Châtelain," and "Bridel," all come from his factories. The firm took off after the Second World War, when the Norman cheese makers were still wallowing in tradition. In 1955, Michel Besnier replaced his father, André, as head of the family's small dairy in Laval. There, as in many other dairies at that time, a whole range of dairy products was produced: butter, casein, and cheeses. Camembert production was fairly constant at four thousand cheeses per day. A small dairy, one out of hundreds of others, the Besnier firm attracted attention for only one reason: the label on its Camemberts. The label depicted a ruddy farmer seated on a train, dressed in a three-piece suit, looking very pleased with life and eating a Camembert depicted as emitting a delicious aroma, while in the background two cows stood looking on in astonishment. It was totally unlike the usual Normandy cheese labels, with their heraldic or worldly references, all of which seemed to look down on the peasant.

Besnier, caring little for tradition, was from Mayenne and therefore lacked the right to label his product a true Norman Camembert. He was also one of the first of the western producers to make pasteurized Camembert. He saw that the lower production costs meant little if they were not linked to an increased demand. At the time, the situation was one of great confusion. Hundreds of brands fought for recognition by the disoriented customer. Most of the cheese producers were selling their products under several different names, often changing their labels. Besnier was the first to pick a national brand name for his cheeses, calling them "Président," a name he had bought from a wholesaler. From the outset, his brand was clearly identifiable; consumers could find it everywhere bearing the same unchanging label. Traditional Camemberts and smaller brands had a hard time keeping up with wide-scale distribution and its refrigerator sections. According to Michel Béchet, the former head of the SFVCN, "nine times out of ten, Camemberts were badly stored and held too long."[14] On the other hand, "Président" fit in perfectly because of its stability and quick turnover. According to Besnier, his Camemberts are "products that are uniform and better adapted to wide distribution. In supermarkets, our pasteurized-milk Camemberts stand up better in refrigerator sections. They change less after they have been packaged."[15] In recent decades, before the resurgence in the popularity of local produce, the bland taste of "Président" Camembert, so disparaged by purists, was an advantage with urban consumers, who dislike strong smells and sharp flavors as too reminiscent of the farmyard with its odors of dubious origin and its questionable hygiene. "Président" had the great advantage vis-à-vis its rivals of being stable and always the same. In selecting it, the consumer avoided unpleasant surprises and could be sure of what he was getting; he had no need to seek the opinion of the shopkeeper. The new, self-service shopping practices, the change in consumer habits, and the increase in consumer awareness all tended to favor "Président's" success.

Besnier required ever-greater quantities of milk in order to meet demand. Despite the increase in milk production, collection from dairy farmers was still not enough. This problem had been a stumbling block for producers in the past. Since the nature of the relationships between dairy farmers and cheese makers had prevented the latter from going to their competitors' suppliers, the only solution had been to acquire new dairies and their milk potential. The impossibility of transporting milk over long distances had, in the past, limited the benefits to be derived from such takeovers, but the advances in rural transportation and communications and the growth in automotive transport now made it possible to bring together in one establishment milk that had been collected over a very wide area. Besnier therefore bought up a number of small cheese factories, some fifty over the course of thirty years. What interested him was not their production facilities, which were often old-fashioned and dilapidated, nor was it the brand or label. What he was after was their milk supply. The scenario was always the same: after purchase, Besnier would keep up production on site for a few months and then shut it down, concentrating activity in a few modernized factories. He generally offered a tempting price, even when the firm purchased was unable to meet its commitments. He made the arrangements with the milk suppliers his priority, thereby winning their gratitude and future fidelity. Many cheese factories became takeover candidates.

And many of these were victims of pasteurization. They had committed the fatal error of attempting to compete with the big brands on their own turf by producing their own industrial Camemberts. However, the product they turned out was not to the taste of their traditional clientele. Too small and too inexperienced to negotiate with the large distributors, they were unable to break into the system. When the question of succession arose, heirs often preferred to sell their parents' property rather than to cope with the difficulties of managing a family cheese business. In every instance, Besnier was in the foreground and managed to prevail without any problem. Bourdon, Bisson, Buquet, Lavalou, and Fermiers Normands—all of the big names of the prewar cheese industry—fell into his hands. In 1978, he bought the famous Lepetit firm, keeping the name and also a foothold in the production of raw-milk Camembert. He also acquired the Claudel-Roustang business from Nestlé, and in 1990, following a family dispute, he bought one of his main rivals, the Bridel company, and its subsidiary, Lanquetot. More recently he acquired several famous traditional cheese factories: Moulin de Carel, Vallée, and Jort. The only competition he faced now came from the Compagnie Laitière Européenne, the Lutin cheese factory, and a few scattered small private firms that still risk being absorbed in the future. Camembert is the star product of the Besnier firm, but Besnier's output includes most other cheeses and dairy products. In his desire to become the Camembert king, Besnier created France's foremost dairy conglomerate. And he extended his kingdom abroad, particularly in the United States of America, where he acquired Simplot Dairy and Concord Marketing. When Besnier died in June 2000, his son replaced him.

Cooperative Resistance

Up against the Besnier group, the Union Laitière Normande (ULN) had striven to keep for itself a significant share of the milk supply and the industrial Camembert market. In the beginning, the dairy cooperatives in the west did not produce cheeses. They were often denounced by small dairy owners for the tax advantages from which they benefited. Small private dairies were especially fearful that the cooperative example might cause their own suppliers to ask for an increase in the price of milk. The conflict between cooperatives and private dairies became very like a religious war in the west, with two deeply entrenched sides: on one side, the cooperatives; on the other, those who, faithful to tradition, remained attached to a small dairy whose owner they knew personally. The first cooperatives were created outside the Auge. They brought together milk suppliers who wanted to get out from under the butter wholesalers and retain control over the treatment and commercialization of their product. They collected butter and cream, or milk which they transformed into butter and casein. Before the war, few of them were engaged in cheese production. The principal aim of cooperative members was not so much to transform their milk into sophisticated products like cheese as it was to escape being taken over by private firms, and they therefore avoided activities that required a large workforce.

The ULN was formed after the Second World War at the initiative of M. Gustave Grandin. It brought together the small cooperatives in the Manche and Calvados districts and enabled them to work on an industrial scale. The cooperative, which specialized in butter, was slow in turning to Camembert production. It created two profitable industrial installations at Ducey and at Vire, each of which produces more than three hundred thousand Camembert cheeses per day, and it boasts a nationally known label, "Coeur de Lion" (Lion Heart), which is the top seller in the country.[16] Nevertheless, it remains far behind its competition.

Like France itself, Camembert has changed enormously over the course of the past five decades. Having begun as a local and regional product, it has moved into the industrial era and become a product of mass consumption produced by a few semi-automated factories. As it exists today, Camembert has little relationship to what it once was. It has shed its most essential characteristics, namely, its taste and its smell. All it has retained is its name. It is a significant change, similar to the one undergone by the French themselves. The nation cherishes a nostalgia for its rural past and its countryside unspoiled by industrialization, but it has irrevocably turned a page in its history. The countryside it loves so much is now asepticized, cleaned up, deodorized, and prettified, just like pasteurized Camembert, whose name alone recalls its peasant origin.

ORIGIN OF AN APPELLATION

Pasteurized or unpasteurized, temperature-controlled, ladle-molded or poured, the diverse guises Camembert can assume make things difficult for the consumer who is looking for the real article. But what *is* authentic Camembert? This serious question raises a good topic at the dinner table when the cheese platter appears. Do not expect me to provide an answer to it. A mythic object, Camembert cannot be summed up in a recipe or definition; it cannot be fitted into one special box. It is the accumulation of its past, present, and future avatars, without restrictions of any kind. Belief obviously plays a part. If you are convinced that a cheese is Camembert only if it has been ladle-molded, you will feel nothing but contempt for all of the ersatz pasteurized versions. But you should at least be aware that the majority of consumers do not pay much heed to such distinctions. Nor is it up to me to lay out what is or is not in keeping with the authentic norms, which were never precisely defined. On the other hand, insofar as the question has long concerned the cheese world, I shall recount the unfinished quest to find an impossible definition for genuine Camembert.

An undisputed mark of French identity, one recognized worldwide, it has been years since Camembert was exclusive to France, not to mention to Normandy. It is now produced in Argentina, in Germany, in Japan, in the United States of America, and in many other countries. France's Camembert is the powerless victim of blatant counterfeiting and protected by no international law whatsoever, since the crime is recognized neither by the United Nations nor even by the World Trade Organization. How is it possible that the jewel of France's cheese production is not protected from its imitators—as is, for instance, Champagne? Only products that can be defined with precision or that are protected by an uncontested trademark or label can be safe from counterfeiting. The word "Camembert" is neither a commercial brand name nor a geographical description, nor has it ever been properly defined. The official (and hardly restrictive) French definition of Camembert is not even fully respected by most of its French producers. How then can it be expected to be honored in other countries? Several attempts have been made to define and circumscribe Camembert in a way that could guarantee a monopoly for the Norman cheese makers. However, despite all of their efforts, they have never managed to recapture possession of the cheese, which was wrested from them before they were even aware of it. In the meantime, Camembert has become the national cheese, the collective property of the entire nation. Norman by birth, like Pierre Corneille and Gustave Flaubert, its fame has made its nationality more important than its provincial identity and origins.

Normandy's cheese makers created the SFVCN in 1909 in an attempt to retain for themselves the benefits of Camembert's renown. At the beginning of the century, the Parisian market was overrun with cheaper products that devalued the name, lowered prices, and placed the better products at a disadvantage. The Norman cheese makers were perturbed by this competition from other regions, which cut into their profits. Unfortunately, the reaction from Normandy was slow. Indeed, Camembert-type cheeses had already been made outside Normandy for several decades. If we view things from the point of view of conditions as they were then, we realize the problems that the SFVCN was facing. It had to come up with a formal definition of Camembert, demarcate an exclusive zone for its production, obtain a legal protection that did not yet exist, and ensure the quality of its members' products. It was an enormous task. Labels of quality were not yet legally recognized. The law of 1 August 1905 defined and set sanctions for frauds involving foodstuffs and protected brand name labeling, but it contained no explicit recognition of geographical provenance as a factor in a product's definition.

Like most other foodstuffs at that time, Camembert had no accepted definition, no fixed content, no established method of production. In those circumstances, it was difficult to bring producers in other regions to court for counterfeiting. The syndicate therefore set out to draw up a formal definition that would permit fakes to be detected and labeled as such. Defining what is and what is not a Camembert, however, was especially tricky, since methods of fabrication differed from one cheese factory to another even in the Auge, and no one followed any strict guidelines. At the beginning of the last century, the notion of defining an agricultural product was a novel one. The question arose in answer to two concerns: first, the desire to delimit the producing region in order to prevent outside competition—which was the syndicate's motive—and second, the desire to protect the consumer against fraud, which was the concern of the public authorities. For cheeses, the problem had not arisen prior to the late nineteenth century. Only the makers of Roquefort had succeeded in obtaining a ruling forbidding the use of the name "Roquefort" for any cheese that had not spent time in their famous *fleurines,* the limestone caves in which the cheese's natural aging process was carried out. The earliest definitions of dairy products dealt with butter, in 1897, and milk, in 1905. In both cases, it was a question of cracking down on dangerous practices that posed a threat to public health. Milk sold in the cities was often watered down, and animal fats and chemical preservatives were being added to butter.

Camembert, whose recipe had been handed down by word of mouth, had never been precisely defined. In the beginning, the recipe for making it had been a secret, and there was no written record of it. So long as it had been distributed over a fairly limited area, this had not presented any particular problem. Potential profits had not been enough to inspire the creation of new firms. The increase in demand and the obvious wealth being acquired by the cheese makers caused that situation to change. No production secret can withstand the irrepressible laws of the market. Since there was a demand for Camembert, all one needed to do was to produce a cheese that resembled it closely enough to satisfy the customer, if need be by poaching away the best workers in older and more reputable establishments. The descriptions set down by some writers, such as Jules Morière in 1859, provided a certain amount of information to those seeking to produce imitation Camemberts. The only things that remained confidential were specific items of know-how, the fruits of experience. Beyond a few basic rules—aging the milk, ladle-molding—the actual methods of fabrication varied. The syndicate prudently evaded the question by adopting a vague definition at its constitutive assembly in 1909. The only things established were shape, weight, size, and the provenance of the milk. A new definition was proposed in 1909 at the request of the Ministry of Agriculture. The text is somewhat more precise in that it prescribes weight, size, and fat content:

> Camembert cheese is a soft-centered cheese created by draining, uncooked, unpressed, and unworked, slightly salted, with a mold crust, round in shape, weighing a maximum of 350 grams [12.3 ounces], with a maximum diameter of between 10 and 11 centimeters [4 to 4.5 inches] and a thickness of from 3 to 4 centimeters, [1.1 to 1.5 inches], whose dry content is a minimum 36-percent fat and is made from pure Normandy milk.[17]

This is still fairly vague, the only precise element being the region of production (i.e., Normandy). For the syndicate, geographical origin was an integral part of the definition. However, that did not correspond with contemporary legislation and could not be recognized by the courts. On the other hand, as we have seen, the provisions regarding fat content did allow for sanctions against producers who did not respect them. Had the syndicate drawn up a definition that omitted a reference to origin, it would have risked connecting the term "Camembert" solely to a method of fabrication, regardless of where it was made. This is why it emphasized the origin of the milk, which brings us to the question of *appellation d'origine* or label of source and quality.

For a product to be eligible for the *appellation d'origine contrôlée* (a government certification of quality and origin) the definition of its area of production must at least follow objective criteria or be in line with a practice that has been recognized over a sufficient period of time. This was far from being the case with Camembert. There was no compelling reason for making Normandy the region for Camembert. The cheese that bore the name of a village in the Auge was primarily Augeron in origin. The Auge region is a natural area or zone that has the distinctive features of a region. It is the only delimitation with objective historic and pedological bases that compare with other *appellations d'origine.* It is the delimitation that was later to be employed for Livarot and Pont l'Évêque cheeses. In addition, since it was the principal area in which Camembert factories were located at the beginning of the last century, the delimitation was also a de facto legitimate one. Why, then, did the Augeron cheese makers not demand that Camembert's appellation be restricted to the Auge?

The broadening of the delimited zone to include all of Normandy was designed to add more political weight and impact to the demand. To be sure, the Auge was not as famous as Normandy, a province with which everyone was familiar. In addition, it allowed many more cheese factories to be brought into the syndicate, which meant that a larger number of elected representatives could be brought into the fold. Normandy, however, which was an overdiversified area made up of clearly different regions, could not be made a geographical basis for defining the characteristics of a single product. On this point, the syndicate's position was a fragile one, for it lacked an argument in support of anything specifically Norman. Its only references were historic ones, based on the division of the country into provinces under the Ancien Régime. The Duchy of Normandy had then included a part of the Oise. The partial annexation of that département enabled the syndicate to win the support of an additional deputy, but it could only have alienated the Republican government, which was not likely to recognize that kind of delimitation. The Camembert producers overlooked the fact that the Republic no longer recognized provinces, even less dukedoms. They also overlooked the fact that their well-known Camembert legend set its creation during the Revolution, at practically the same time as that of the Republic. Retaining only the legacy of the Ancien Régime and ignoring Camembert's republican character was a fatal political flaw in their demand. Nevertheless, the syndicate based its campaign on this extremely regionalist foundation. In December 1910, the syndicate addressed the "deputies and senators of Normandy, including the relevant area of the Oise," and requested that they support its cause:

> Considering that the struggle against the regional product it is defending is daily becoming more aggressive and more threatening to the future of the region's industry and agriculture; that fraudulent practices are attempting not only to employ the name "Camembert" for a product that merely looks like it and that, in addition, has been made from milk derived from any French pasture, without distinction, but also to call "Camembert" a cheese made from totally skim milk, the Syndicat des Fabricants du Véritable Camembert de Normandie calls upon all the deputies and senators of Normandy and the relevant area of the Oise to support it in the economic struggle it has undertaken, upon whose success depends the existence of the age-old Camembert industry.[18]

So we have a precision of delimitation of the zone of production going hand in hand with a very imprecise definition of the product itself.

The petition of the Norman cheese makers was not an isolated event. All over France, regional producers were asking to be protected from the competition of cheap imitation goods. With the growth in the food industry, the need to protect certain names from competition, especially from abroad, became more pressing. The producers and owners of the great vineyards were in the vanguard in obtaining legal protection. This did not occur until the act of 6 May 1919, which defined the *appellation d'origine* to cover the place of origin and "local, faithful and long-standing practices." [19] That act, however, adopted at the behest of the wine producers, removed the burden of delimitation from the executive branch and placed it on the courts. Government authorities did not see that they had anything to gain by dealing with this thorny problem with all its inherent conflicts of interest. Roquefort, with its centuries of tradition, was recognized and granted protection by the court at Sainte-Affrique on 22 December 1921. Camembert, however, was considered too young to hope for the same recognition. Could it really boast of any historical legitimacy? It did not enjoy the senior status of Roquefort or Brie and was not even as old as its Norman competitors, Livarot and Pont l'Évêque. As for other traditional cheeses, they had rarely been produced outside their places of origin. In the beginning, Marie Harel's descendants had sought the exclusive right to make Camembert. To their mind, the only true Camembert was the cheese produced by families directly connected to the woman who, they claimed, had invented it. On the other hand, the producers who formed the SFVCN lacked that legitimacy of birth. They were all newcomers, and the oldest families among them could boast of no more than twenty or thirty years' seniority.

No government was willing to make the decision to ban the use of the "Camembert" name in regions outside Normandy. To delimit the area in which Camembert could be produced would open politicians to the fury of the non-Norman producers as well as contribute to a rise in prices. The prudent course was to do nothing. Successive ministers of agriculture were skilled in making vague promises and in sending hopeful messages to the Norman cheese makers, but they were very careful not to take any concrete action, not even those ministers who had actively supported the cause prior to assuming office. Camembert had already become part of the common national patrimony and could not now be made the exclusive property of a single province, even if it had been born there! It was now French before it was Norman. The syndicate, therefore, having vainly besieged the minister of agriculture and brought pressure to bear through all of the elected representatives from Normandy—foremost among whom was Henry Chéron, the honorary president of the SFVCN—was forced to take its cause to court.

Between 1909 and 1926, a great many people became involved in the Camembert matter. The majority of those in the dairy industry were against delimiting Camembert. Scientists also contested the Norman claims. Professors Pierre Mazé and Charles Porcher, among others, denied that region of origin had anything to do with milk quality. They recognized only the scientific definition of Camembert and rejected the descriptive definition proposed by the SFVCN. On behalf of freedom of trade, the wholesalers supported the broadest of definitions, one that clearly reflected the position of the non-Norman industrialists:

Camembert cheese should be described as a cheese with the shape, dimensions, and appearance of the cheese that has been known as Camembert for many years now, regardless of its quality or place of origin.[20]

In 1914, a short volume devoted to the question was published.[21] Its author, Francis Marre, was plainly on the side of the scientists and industrialists. He rejected the claims of the Norman cheese makers and denounced their empiricism and archaic notions. Instead of supporting the transmission of inherited expertise handed down within the family, he favored scientific method as the only way in which fully controlled production could be achieved:

The day is long past when, in old rural families, the eldest would inherit as dowry, along with the paternal patrimony, the jealously guarded recipes and tricks of the trade that lent originality to whatever the farm might produce. The investigative curiosity of chemists and bacteriologists has gradually brought to light all of the empirical formulae. Their labors have reached the factory, where methodical and scientific work has led to the perfectly consistent creation of products that are, if not superior to their empirical forerunners, at least more economical than they and of a reliably uniform quality.[22]

Nice scientific optimism! Marre was only forty years too early. Pasteurization would have to become widespread before his hopes would be realized.

The battle over delimitation was thus among the regional traditionalists; the industrialists, who were only interested in standardized production methods; and the merchants, who were against anything that might stand in the way of free trade. Clear positions were taken shortly after the end of the First World War, when a debate was opened that continues today with the European common market.

After a first victory before the Vendôme court, which found against a producer in the Loir-et-Cher département on the grounds that "Camembert" was a name denoting origin, the Norman cheese makers met with a series of setbacks. The courts determined that the term "Camembert" was generic. The only argument that the syndicate could present in its favor was based on the amount of fat content. The SFVCN's last hopes were destroyed by a ruling handed down in 1926 by the court of appeals in Orléans, which rejected a plea to make "Camembert" an *appellation d'origine.* Indeed, the court recognized only one fact, namely, that "Camembert," which was being produced in various regions throughout France, was a national cheese. The Norman cheese makers then turned all their efforts to obtaining stricter rules and to making consumers aware of the superiority of their cheese.

Upon examination, the failure of the SFVCN's request is not surprising. It was due both to the imperfect definition the syndicate had put forward and to the flimsiness of the argument favoring Normandy as the cheese's place of origin. In addition, the syndicate should have devoted greater effort to controlling production and to persuading its members to adopt rigid quality standards like those in force in the wine industry. We have already noted the reluctance on the part of producers to go along with the standards set for the use of the syndicate seal. Although Camembert cheeses sold with the seal were of better quality, the syndicate members also sold as "Camembert" their own second-rate cheeses and even their rejects. Unsatisfactory products were able to use the name alongside those of the highest quality. Merchants sold second- and third-rate Camemberts at reduced prices, just as they were able to sell cheeses that were so overripe that they oozed out of their boxes, "wounded" cheeses (so called because they had been dropped or nibbled at by hungry mice and more or less repaired), and even cheeses that had fallen prey to a variety of microscopic insects that fed on their soft centers (these were described as "moth-eaten"). All of these cheeses were sold with the label "Camembert," without the syndicate saying anything about it. Even if the Auge producers had made the rigorous efforts exerted by those in the wine business, it is unlikely that they would have been successful. Camembert's success had been so swift that it had become a popular and familiar item even before its original makers had awakened to the need to protect its identity.

As long as Norman Camemberts maintained their superior quality, they could expect to be sold at higher prices. However, pasteurization wiped out the differences between cheeses produced in Normandy and those from other regions, substituting another difference between them: Camemberts made of raw milk and those made of pasteurized milk. The producers of raw-milk Camembert did not take steps to distinguish their products from pasteurized Norman Camembert, which, because it was made in Normandy, had the right to use the syndicate seal. That distinction reflected no more than a geographical origin, without making any basic distinction between raw-milk products and others. In 1968, the syndicate managed to win recognition from the Ministry of Agriculture for a red label reading "Véritable Camembert de Normandie" (True Norman Camembert). However, this label was utilized both for cheeses made from raw milk and those made from pasteurized milk. Competitors, as well as the Ministry for Consumer Goods, questioned the legitimacy of the term "Véritable." As a result, the syndicate agreed to stop using it against the promise that there would be approval of an *appellation d'origine controllée* for raw-milk and ladle-molded Camembert. The small producers behind that request were joined by Besnier, who, although the largest industrial producer, was still sentimentally attached to the Camembert of his childhood. Having acquired the Lepetit firm, he was also now a member of the syndicate and directly concerned.

The battle had already been decided when the decree creating an *appellation d'origine* was finally handed down, and the majority of producers had gone down before the offensive waged by the industrial cheese factories. In 1983, seventy-four years after its first meeting, the SFVCN, still alive but barely eking out an existence, was finally granted a decree setting forth the provisions of an *appellation d'origine controllée* reading

"Camembert de Normandie" (Norman Camembert). The *appellation d'origine* fixed production regulations but contained no provisions concerning the origin or quality of the milk used. The only proviso was that the milk be obtained in Normandy.

A control commission made up of professionals; antifraud inspectors; the supervisor of the regional veterinary service; and the chief inspector of agricultural engineering, water, and forests for the Basse-Normandie region was set up to ensure respect for the standards and oversee the quality of the Camembert bearing the label.[23] It did so through the intermediary of a body of experts who formed a so-called "tasting and consent" panel that tasted and graded samples submitted by each establishment. The quality criteria used principally covered "shape, appearance, crust, center consistency, aroma, and taste."[24] A label of *appellation d'origine controllée* (AOC) and the designations "Camembert de Normandie" and "raw-milk, ladle-molded" alerted the consumer to those products that met the regulation standards.

The decree granting raw-milk Camembert an *appellation d'origine controllée* did not put an end to every problem. The AOC only indicated the factories that followed certain traditional norms and protected the last firms that still implemented them. However, the rules laid down in the decree were not rigorous enough. The authorized milk-supply area was too large, and neither the collection methods nor the breed of dairy cattle was specified. The authorization to use the automatic molding machine opened the way for industrial production. And what did an *appellation d'origine controllée* mean if it did not set any restriction on the use of the basic name itself? The only thing protected was the term "Camembert de Normandie," not the term "Camembert."

Sales of raw-milk, ladle-molded Camembert cheeses with the AOC "Camembert de Normandie" label have increased sharply in the 1980s and 1990s. It is not certain, however, that this is due to the labeling. Indeed, there is some doubt as to the commercial effectiveness of the AOC. Raw-milk, ladle-molded Camemberts probably do not need the label to sell well. One wonders whether the label is protecting the true tradition and the small producers. If we examine the situation, the whole thing is still unclear. Some factories that pride themselves on tradition do not even utilize the label. On the other hand, purists consider that some of the brands that do use the label are far from traditional. Further, the commercial exploitation of tradition by several brands that are not produced according to so-called traditional methods only serves to add to the confusion. To see the situation clearly, a distinction must be made between cheeses made of raw milk and ladle-molded by hand, raw-milk cheeses that are ladle-molded by machine, those made of raw milk and molded mechanically after the curd has been cut, those that have been thermalized, and those that are pasteurized.[25]

In 1992, eleven firms were entitled to use the AOC label for their Camemberts. They could not be more different. Four of them—Moulin de Carel, Laiterie de Berniére, Lepetit, and Lanquetot—are now part of the Besnier group and represent more than 80 percent of the AOC-labeled cheeses sold. With their automated molding systems, they are all moving to assembly-line mass production. The other firms—with the exception of the Isigny-Sainte-Mère dairy cooperative, the only cooperative to enjoy access to the AOC label for Camembert—are far smaller.

In principle, the "Camembert" appellation is governed by two decrees, one covering "Camembert" without affording any details,[26] and the second covering Norman Camembert. However, those belated regulations have not prevented the Auge's soft-centered cheese from being copied throughout France and in many other countries, nor have they stopped it from being produced by methods that have nothing to do with the original recipe. Kept as a secret in the beginning, both in the myth in which a priest played a part and in reality, where the recipe was the jealously guarded monopoly of a few Augeron farmers' wives, Camembert cheese has always resisted all attempts to give it a formal definition. Having risen from local specialty to the status of national asset before any classification could be made, it has eluded every attempt to describe it with precision. And is such a description truly necessary? Without any effective regulatory protection at all, Camembert has maintained throughout the world its identification with the French nation. I even feel that its many copies, all tributes to the true Camembert, have served to support the myth. Just as a reproduction does not pretend to be replace the original, the foreign imitations of Camembert are not out to deceive. They are only trying to serve as modest substitutes for a cheese that cannot, in its authentic original version, hope to be everywhere.

TABLE 1 Evolution in Production and Sales of AOC Camembert

Unit = 250-gram Camembert

	1984	1985	1986	1987	2000
Total production	38,932,000	42,838,000	60,548,000	57,344,000	59,088,000
Sales under AOC label	26,894,000 (69%)	30,177,000 (70.4%)	53,120,000 (87.7%)	50,784,000 (88.6%)	52,792,000 (89.3%)

SOURCE: Comité Nationale des Appellations d'Origine des Fromages.

The above table charts the development of the production and sales of AOC Camembert.

THE INVENTION OF A TRADITION

Camembert, as a cheese with many identities or as one with no precise identity at all, which is largely the same thing, has eluded a set definition. We might, however, think that tradition has been satisfied with the *appellation d'origine controllée* that reads "Camembert de Normandie." Alas, no sooner do we feel that we have reached solid ground than we are forced to recognize that Norman Camembert is not an impregnable bastion of tradition but an edifice built on sand and already under siege by those foreign invaders of industry, the robot molders.

The Industrialization of Tradition

Since the granting of the AOC in 1983, an event has occurred that has completely redealt the hand, namely, the automation of ladle-molding. For the small producers, ladle-molding ensured the preservation of the old-fashioned methods of production and kept the playing field somehow level. They could not foresee an innovation that would put everything into question. Today, they are beginning to realize that the AOC regulations are not the ultimate weapon. Industry has taken control of the ladle and endowed that banal kitchen tool with the ability to work like a fiend.

The innovation was introduced by the united dairy cooperative at Isigny-Sainte-Mère. Located in the heart of the one of France's most important dairy regions, it is the only cooperative turning out a traditional Camembert. The cooperative was created by the joining of two famous earlier cooperatives: that of Sainte-Mère-Église, which was set up in 1905 by a group of farmers to preserve and champion the fame of Isigny's quality butter in the face of the abuse of the appellation by various merchants, and the cooperative at Isigny-sur-Mer, founded in 1931.[27] The Sainte-Mère-Église cooperative had been created to demonstrate that local traditions and quality could go hand in hand with technological and commercial innovation. At the turn of the century, it had been considered one of Europe's most modern butter-producing dairies.[28] In keeping with its founding principles, therefore, it is only logical that the united dairy cooperative should today be behind an innovation designed to bridge the gap between tradition and innovation: the robot ladle molder.

The term "robot" has been most effective in making the invention a media success, but it has little to do with reality. In fact, the machine is nothing like a ladle-wielding android mimicking the movements of the old-fashioned molders and is no more than a prosaic machine for manipulating curd automatically. The original movement of the human ladle-molder is now performed by a machine with twenty arms. Here is a description from a technician, one who would appear to be somewhat underwhelmed by the amazing device:

> The curd manipulator takes twenty ladles of curd from a vat and deposits them with precision in a recipient containing twenty Camembert molds; it does this once every fifty minutes. The work unit is therefore an arm with twenty ladles that can draw curd from a vat automatically and can assume five different positions to ensure the regular volume and uptake achieved by hand-molding.[29]

The robot passes over the molds six times in succession, each time pouring the contents of its twenty ladles into twenty receiving molds. During the forty-five-minute interval between each pass, a large part of the whey flows out. The machine's inventors consider the robot molder a triumph: it is dependable, hygienic, and economical with regard to material, and it enhances productivity. Its principal merit, however, and no small achievement for a machine, is to have been accorded the approval of the Commission des Appellations d'Origine: in other words, the cheeses it produces have the right to bear the traditional label because they have been ladle-molded.

This device can greatly increase productivity while still following the written rules governing the AOC. There has never been a shortage of persnickety and hidebound critics. They have quite rightly pointed out that half of the automated ladle is equipped with blades that slice through the curd and that, therefore, tradition is not being fully respected. However, this is not the worst infringement of the rules. The more serious threat is posed by the industrialization of the production of Camembert allowed to bear the AOC label. Besnier has installed automated machines in its factories at Saint-Maclou and Orbec to mass-produce AOC Camemberts, with the label, which are being sold at prices markedly lower than competing brands. Today, the AOC no longer indicates a distinction between Camemberts produced "in the old-fashioned way" (i.e., by hand) and those turned out by a robot.

Although it developed automated ladle-molding, the Isigny-Sainte-Mère united dairy cooperative has been careful in distributing AOC Camembert. Prior to the recognition of an *appellation d'origine controllée* for Norman Camembert, it had managed to unite the majority of dairy-and-cheese producers under its "Médaillon" brand, which is regarded as traditional Camembert even though it is neither made of raw milk nor ladle-molded. Nevertheless, it is currently the highest-priced Camembert on the market, and specialized cheese merchants consider it the most prestigious. "Médaillon" Camembert is made of "thermalized" milk; that is, milk that has been heated to a temperature just short of pasteurization. The molding is done by machine after the curd has been broken up. The care taken in fabrication, the knowledgeable use of fermentation bacilli, and the aging process explain why this cheese has a taste and an appearance so pleasing to cheese lovers. Its success is also the result of an intelligent and clever marketing policy.

The AOC subsidiaries of the Besnier group have also adopted the robot molder and are sold in supermarket chains. While the Isigny cooperative has invested heavily in its thermalized Camembert, these two brands rely on the AOC. By setting written rules, the AOC did not erect any effective protective barrier favoring the old-fashioned producer; instead, it opened the door to the industrialization of traditional production. Faced with this invasion by modern technology into the traditionalist domain, the upholders of the old-fashioned ways have banded together in their disapproval and determined to recognize only manual production as truly traditional. The controversy raises the whole question of tradition: is there a tradition in Camembert production, and if so, what are its basic principles?

Although AOC Camembert does seem legitimately able to lay claim to tradition when compared to industrial Camembert, that claim is not undisputed. Some cheese lovers are quick to invoke the "true" tradition when weighing in against Camemberts that are the result of an "automated" *origine controllée.* Such is the position of Henri Waroquier, former head of the dairy mill at Carel:

> Save for its origin, what is traditional about a Camembert whose milk comes from Dutch Holstein cows fed on imported cattle cakes and corn silage . . . and whose broken curd is ladle-molded by robots? In point of fact, it is a matter of knowing whether the *appellation d'origine controllée* label has been pasted on a true regional product or on some notion of such a product, which is really not quite the same thing at all.[30]

Of course the AOC does not guarantee any undisputable conformity with tradition, but in what precise recipe or knowledge does the true tradition reside? The method of making Camembert was not codified until relatively late, and some processes were never strictly set forth and have changed over the course of time. As for the taste, who knows what it might once have been? It is impossible to compare the taste of today's AOC Camemberts with that of the Camemberts of yore. Lacking any well-defined and fixed criteria, or any trustworthy record, there is only the memory of a taste, subjective and personal. This "Proustian memory" is quite different from any indisputable record that might allow for comparisons. If we are to believe the testimony of Professor Germain Mocquot, now deceased, a man with great expertise in soft-centered cheeses and one who had known and enjoyed the Camemberts of the 1930s, the taste of Camembert made of raw milk and ladled into the mold by hand had indeed changed over the intervening fifty years.[31] Nostalgia aside, it is certain that the environment and the production methods have both changed considerably. The length of time required to create a Camembert in the nineteenth century varied from nine to ten weeks, compared to the three to four it takes today. The length of curdling time has dwindled from four to five hours in the beginning to an hour or an hour and a half today. We can therefore wonder what reference to "tradition" really means.

In attempting to recreate tradition by fidelity to the recipes of yesteryear, we can end up losing sight of it altogether. If we are to judge by conformity to the nineteenth-century ways of doing things, then there is no doubt that the authentic Camembert tradition has disappeared forever. However, tradition is not always strict adherence to ancient recipes, nor is it the faithful reproduction of physical and chemical characteristics. It is not, nor can it be, an unchanging way of doing something in a world that is forever in flux. Desirous of preserving past practices when the modern world demands constant change, tradition is faced with the need to adapt to new economic and social conditions. The safeguarding of a tradition thus requires a constant effort to adapt the legacy of the past. The history of Camembert teaches us that from the very beginning the cheese was noted for its modernity. Weighing it down with the shackles of a group of set recipes on behalf of some narrow notion of tradition is thus counter to its very nature. Today, the Camembert tradition is more an attempt to avoid the absolute control of industrial standards than some absolute respect for a mythical past. A living tradition is not something frozen for all time, not something perfectly defined or hemmed in by immutable rules. We must take what we have and attempt to make it, in all its diversity, into something alive and vibrant.

Milk and Connections

Just to be perfectly clear, let us admit that there is no such thing as a wholly traditional Camembert. The truth is that some makers draw inspiration from tradition and attempt to work in its spirit. Their main concern is not to respect some unwritten recipes. Their main goal is to maintain a network of personal relationships among all of the parties involved to various degrees in turning out the product—dairymen, cheese makers, those involved in the aging process, and so on. When all else is in flux, the preservation of those connections is what ensures the survival of some part of the tradition. The picture I am presenting is not a very bucolic one and does not perhaps correspond in every way to actual practice. It is more an expression of the ideal that the last surviving small-scale cheese producers hope to maintain than of the reality to which they are subject. It is easy to define industrial Camembert by saying that its particular quality resides in nothing having been left to chance. On the other hand, traditional Camembert loves secrecy and mistrusts precise description.

The first prerequisite for achieving a successful Camembert is to have good-quality milk, milk from the region and produced by purebred Norman cattle, fed principally on the abundant grasses growing in natural pastureland or on hay. The milk, collected and processed under sanitary conditions, is put into containers and kept cool prior to being collected by the cheese factory, whose trucks make the rounds twice a day.[32] It is better if the collection area is restricted, with no dairy farm more than a dozen or so kilometers (about 7.5 miles) from the cheese factory. This limitation accentuates the local characteristics and quality of the milk. In fact, just as with wine, milk does have vintages and regional characteristics, and one of the best is the milk of Isigny, which has earned an AOC seal for that label's butter and cream. Camembert from the Auge does not taste the same as Camembert from the Isigny pasturelands. As Henri Le Bouc, former head of the Pierre-Lanquetot cheese factory at Orbec, has said, "Cheeses are like wines. There is the same difference between Isigny Camembert and a Camembert from the Auge as there is between a Bordeaux wine and one from Burgundy."[33] Like wine experts, cheese lovers can tell where a Camembert has come from by the taste. As one dairy manager said, "It is true, I can recognize the origin of a raw-milk Camembert with my eyes closed."[34]

Another condition that, although not indispensable, is often decisive, is that the owner of the cheese factory be a native of the region, a man who has known all of his suppliers personally and for a long time.[35] He should know their skills and abilities and should not hesitate to visit their stables and, if possible, get to know their cows.[36] As for the cheese maker, he selects his milk supplier above all on the basis of trust and respect.[37] The best milk suppliers, who provide the best-quality milk, are generally specialists in cattle breeding, and their herd is the result of a long process of selection and constant attention.

How do personal relationships, close connections, and trust produce good traditional cheeses? Some basic production principles must of course be respected: raw milk from Norman cattle, lactic maturation, manual ladle-molding without breaking the curd, proper salting, and so on. All of that, however, is possible only with stable relationships that are small in scale and marked by reciprocal respect. The changes presently taking place—for example, the abandonment of the practice of collecting milk in cans—mean making constant adaptations whose success depends more than ever on the close ties between the different persons concerned.

All of the care involved in Camembert would be in vain if, after production, the fragile cheese were to be abandoned to distributors not practiced in the art of maturation. It takes very little—storage in a place that is too cold or too warm—to affect maturation negatively and interrupt the aging process, creating a defective consistency, a runny cheese with a hard center. Here, too, the quality of the interaction between wholesalers and retailers is of prime importance in ultimate customer satisfaction. The way in which the various links in the chain are joined will lead to a good transfer of information and continued surveillance. Because raw-milk Camembert is such an unstable and fickle product, direct contact among those involved is absolutely indispensable.

In recent years, advertisements for Camembert have begun to appear on television, and several brands have attempted to create an image for themselves via this medium. However, the producers of traditional Camembert not only lack the means needed for this kind of publicity but deliberately eschew marketing and communication via modern media. As the owner of a small cheese factory has said, renown based on the quality of the product is enough to win customers and keep them faithful: "Our brand is like that. It has enabled us to forgo any advertising budget so far. . . . We have no one doing marketing."[38] The technical manager of another cheese factory said the same. For him, advertising is not necessary because the quality of the product is enough to sell it: "We do no advertising. Raw-milk Camembert is either good or it isn't. Growth is largely based on the quality of our product."[39] Where traditional products are concerned, the consumer's devotion to a brand name is created not by some advertising campaign but out of a personal relationship with his cheese merchant and trust built up by years of purchasing the same brands.

Because of its price, which is two or three times more than that of the industrial, pasteurized version, traditional Camembert is a luxury product today. However, at some 15 euros (US $12 at time of translation) per kilogram (2.2 pounds), it is a luxury that is still within the reach of the majority of cheese lovers. This price level is comparable to the prices for the new kinds of cheeses that are finding favor with lower-income buyers. Indeed, social discrimination is less the effect of price than of distribution method. Specialized dairy and cheese shops are generally to be found in middle-class neighborhoods. Although traditional Camembert is not all that accessible to lower-income buyers, that is principally because it is not often found in the places where they purchase food. Further, members of the postwar urban generations, who have known nothing but industrial cheeses, have lost their taste for strong cheeses. Raw-milk, ladle-molded Camembert is therefore the domain of enlightened cheese lovers who are able to buy in specialized dairy and cheese shops or in the regions where the cheeses are produced.

Industrialization has led to the emergence of a kind of tradition that did not exist prior to the 1950s. The hankering for tradition increases as industry becomes more widespread. However, the opposition between the two is not total. Cheese makers who hew to tradition must inevitably make some accommodation with the industrial system. On the other hand, the large industrialists seek to maintain ties with tradition. The prestige of industrial Camembert rests on tradition. Although considerably different, it retains the aura of the Camembert of yesteryear; lacking its distinctive taste, it continues to embody its sense and significance. Its shape, its label, and its overall appearance all tend to make it an object evocative of a flavorful and savory world. We can understand why, if this avatar is to prevail, the myth must remain present, not only in the images and legends evoked on the labels, but also in the production of Camemberts in the old-fashioned way and in the fervor of the cheese lovers who keep the cult alive. Thus, the survival of traditional references is an essential element in the success of industrial Camembert. The industrial producers are fully aware of this, as evidenced by the following admission made by one of them:

> It is to be hoped that some old and small-scale establishments that still work with the ladle will continue to exist and remain in operation, because in a way the image of Camembert is enhanced by such products.[40]

Such remarks would be completely incomprehensible to a Dutch or Danish cheese maker, both of whom ignore references to tradition and rely on competition and marketing tools to make their products known. In France, things are different, and tradition is necessary to sell industrial cheeses. Even newly developed cheeses have to claim a place in the cheese tradition.[41]

In the fields of cheese, wine, or any other area with a tradition, France is particularly sensitive, and the French are always ready to get fired up over them. They want to move toward modernity without violating any of their national heritage or abandoning tradition. Any challenge to that, even the most insignificant, can produce astonishing reactions, as was recently witnessed by the response to a suggested spelling reform.

As for Camembert, it has the happy privilege of offering both tradition and modernity, thus more than satisfying the national yearnings. However, its task is made more difficult by its having to excel in both areas: winning new export markets by being competitive while satisfying the demanding palates of gourmet consumers. Clearly, the problem is greater in the traditional sphere, even though this is the point on which the future turns. For if traditional Camembert were ever to disappear completely, it is highly probable that the sales of industrial Camembert, deprived of that point of reference, would rapidly begin to fall.

Chapter 6 | THE IMAGE OF CAMEMBERT

Without its label, Camembert would not be what it is. For the consumer, the two elements—the label and the contents—are inseparable when it comes to making a choice. The cheese and its label exist as a unit; they are one and the same thing. Apart from the cheese, however, the label also has its own value to the collector. Yet it remains a Camembert label even when unstuck from its box and has meaning only with reference to the cheese. Created to attract the eye and draw attention to the cheese, it has played a role in creating and spreading the myth of which it is a part. As the expression and statement of the monarch of French cheeses, the label has for over a century stood as a witness to its history.

FROM LABEL TO TYROSEME

We do not know exactly when the first labels made their appearance. In spite of all my research efforts, I have been unable to put a date to this important event in Camembert's checkered history. The Fermiers Normands company maintained that it was the first to have used the round wooden box and label for its "Jort-Corneville" brand. Léonce Abaye of the Tremblay cheese factory claimed that he had come up with the first illustrated label. Since the event is not included in any list of great inventions and since it was not reported in the newspapers, we will have to be content with speculation. One thing is sure: Marie Harel at least had no hand in the invention of a round label affixed to the lid of a round wooden box. According to the investigations by the Institut National de la Propriété Industrielle (the National Institute of Industrial Properties, or INPI), where food brand names are registered by the owners for protection, the first round label dates from 1891,[1] very shortly after the invention of the box itself.

Prior to that date, some makers had affixed a label on the sheet of paper in which they wrapped their cheeses. The earliest such label registered with INPI dates from 1867: "It is a 2 × 6 cm [0.75 × 2.5 inches] label of green, red, or yellow paper bearing the inscription 'Fromage de Camembert,' above a simple design representing a pair of medals."[2]

At the time, the best Camemberts were presented on a straw mat and wrapped in a paper bearing the producer's name, a guarantee of quality for the consumer, who was thereby made aware of its provenance. One did not buy just any Camembert; one bought a Camembert produced by one of the known makers. Some unscrupulous merchants would attempt to sell lower-quality Camemberts as the products of a reputable firm and would appropriate wrapping paper bearing such names. We have already read in chapter 2 about the method that Cyrille Paynel's Parisian distributor had used to defraud him, offering a reimbursement for returned wrappings and then utilizing them to wrap inferior cheeses to be sold at the same price, and the steps Paynel took to restore the integrity of his product.

The box lent Camembert a protection that enabled it to travel safely, but it also deprived the purchaser of a direct inspection. The consumer was confused by the boxes that concealed the merchandise he wanted and was put off by the box itself, which reminded him of the ones that used to be used for certain pharmaceutical products. The two factors worked against the cheese, whose producers prided themselves on its natural origin. The unfortunate impression created had to be rectified, and the hesitant customer needed reassurance about the origin of the cheeses being offered him. This was achieved by gluing an informative label on the box top. The first labels were white and identical to the interior wrapping paper that bore the maker's name. This was far too austere. To indicate that the contents of the box had nothing to do with any kind of pharmaceutical product, some makers began to add an illustration evocative of the Norman countryside. In the beginning, many of the labels did not bear names. Retailers would receive a supply of labels and stick them onto the Camemberts they had in stock. A blank space was provided in which they wrote the name of the maker—and sometimes their own. The system led to confusion, since clients paid more attention to the picture than to the name. It also abetted fraud, since retailers could write in any name they wanted. Some merely inscribed their own, ignoring that of the producer. At this juncture, most producers took away the retailers' right to affix the label and began to do it themselves. A resolution adopted in July 1909 by the Syndicat des Fabricants du Véritable Camembert de Normandie (SFVCN) obliged its members to stop delivering unlabeled Camemberts: "Syndicate members unanimously undertake henceforth not to sell Camembert in plain white boxes or to require that merchants enter the name of the producer on the label themselves." [3]

Labels did not immediately come into widespread use. Some makers continued to sell their cheeses on straw mats or in boxes without any sign of origin. Even today, some retail cheese sellers affix their own labels instead of the label of the maker. They justify this on the basis of the fact that they themselves have aged the cheese in their own cellars. Their appropriation of a cheese that they have not made but merely aged may lend them prestige, but it is rarely acceptable to the makers. The Norman cheese makers who sought an *appellation d'origine* obviously viewed an indication of the cheese's maker and its place of origin as an absolute necessity.

It did not take long for the label to become a decisive element in the selling of Camembert, and every maker soon began to use it. It is difficult for us today, surrounded as we are by advertising, to realize the appeal it then exerted on the consumer. In the days when it came into use, illustrated advertisements were just coming into vogue. Aside from the religious picture, the label was one of the rare colored images to enter the modest home.[4] It was hardly surprising, therefore, that it played a large part in the choice of a cheese and that it even came to be more important than the product itself.

Labels, which are intended to be both informative and decorative, did not always fulfill both of those needs. Some sought to educate the customer and emphasized the maker's name, the place of origin, and the cheese's quality with a low-key illustration that gave some realistic notion of its manufacture and the village where it had been produced. Others, however, opted for the decorative and depicted scenes that had nothing to do with the cheese but were intended solely to catch the eye. Whichever path they took, every label did convey one thing: the message was coming from the countryside and was intended for the city. Thus, the makers found an original means of expression by which they could introduce themselves to the urban market for which their products were intended. They did not tell the consumer how to use Camembert; instead, they advanced an additional meaning that emphasized the fact that this was no ordinary product but rather a special foodstuff, one that contained within it a bit of the countryside for those living far from it, an article that enabled the consumer to acquire some of the vitality of rural life and to maintain contact with it.

What did the labels depict? There seems to be a limitless range of themes. While some stuck to the realm of cheese or country life, showing fields, cattle, peasant women, or dairymaids, many turned to contemporary politics, fashion, or technological progress. No area was excluded *a priori*. Some themes were timeless, and illustrators often drew upon them, whereas others were linked to a precise event. A few recurred constantly: the countryside, women, progress, tradition, nobility, war heroes, heads of state, and other famous historical figures.

Often, the healthy abundance of a generous nature was evoked. This theme often linked a female figure with a field or a farm and its animals. One label, a magnificent illustration of this genre, was created by the aptly named André Fromage at Saint-Michel-de-Livet.[5] It depicted a full-figured Norman farmwoman holding a Camembert. Cattle grazed in a field nearby, and in the distance was a small village. Abundance is suggested by the dominant colors: the green of the field and touches of red and gold alongside the white of the woman's headdress and apron, which evokes the purity of milk and the cleanliness of the production process. The female figure, whether a peasant brimming with good health or a more discreet allegorical personage, is the dominant element, affirming her essential role in the dairy and everything involved in the handling of milk. Her message is one of purity, of life, of abundance. When she is not a farmwoman, she may represent La République, Victory, a Sower, or Abundance.

The label can be repetitious, replete with illustrations of a single idea: the profusion of nature's bounty, the content's authenticity. It can bring together two different elements as a metaphor (the Norman farmwoman and generous Nature), or it can link two dissimilar worlds, like industry and agriculture, or tradition and progress. Many labels depict the cheese factory itself, with a bird's-eye view of its various buildings and the farmhouse itself, set in a rural landscape. The label of the Alfred Marie cheese factory at Montpinçon shows a factory in the background, its tall chimney stack emitting a plume of smoke, and in the foreground a field in which a herd of Norman cattle are grazing. A factory chimney and a milk cow on the same label—how better to suggest the union of industry and agriculture that has produced the cheese contained inside?

The picture of the factory is always connected, more or less overtly, to some rural element, generally a cow. In contrast, many of these countless country scenes have no industrial connotations. Many labels depict only the rural world, a farmer's wife, cows, or apple trees. Tradition is symbolized by folklore images: Norman women in traditional costume, farmers in the local smock. Norman tradition is an important theme for many brands, whereas others opt for progress, but tradition and modernity are often telescoped together. One label shows in the foreground a Norman woman in traditional costume carrying a wicker basket of eggs and gazing into the sky to watch an airplane flying overhead. The brand name "Trait d'Union," (which means "hyphen") makes the meaning clear. Camembert is what connects the two aspects of France, traditional and modern; it provides a link between agriculture and industry.

The label also plays a part in supporting the myth itself, particularly when it refers to national themes or when it makes use of such well-known characters as Jeanne d'Arc, Napoleon, or Georges Clemenceau, who, with Maréchal Joffre, Philippe Pétain, and Josephine Baker, was one of the few notables to be depicted on a Camembert label while still alive. Maréchal Joffre, a war hero, appeared on a label in 1918 venturing a pun on his name: "J'offre le meilleur" ("I provide the best").[6] Camembert has a tendency to draw upon history, either by employing figures from a mythical past or by glorifying real persons and events. A long list could be drawn up of labels evoking current affairs: in 1909, "The Russophile"; in that same year, "Entente Cordiale"; in 1915, "Victory" (albeit a bit premature); and in 1920, "The Argonne *Poilu*" and "Heroes," which depicted the American parachutist who got himself hooked on the steeple of the church at Sainte-Mère-Église during the Allied landing on D-Day.

The cheese factories' growing demand for labels meant prosperity for some of the print shops that specialized in them.[7] Some printers suggested and created the designs for labels themselves when cheese makers were unable to come up with one. Some hired clever illustrators, but the drawing was often the work of the cheese maker himself.

The style of the label, which varied as greatly as the theme, also evolved over time. The most beautiful labels date from 1910 to 1930, the golden age of the Augeron cheese industry. Some labels from that period show a real artistic sense, both graphic and compositional. Not only did the illustrators have a great deal of imagination, but the printing and lithographic technique were often of very high quality, sometimes requiring up to seven or eight pulls.

In the 1960s, the influence of marketing led to an impoverishment of illustration, which became banal, and offset printing began to replace lithography. The label style emphasized the difference between ordinary cheeses and those of the highest quality from well-known firms. When the label is replete with different colors, objects, animals, or characters, when it is laden with signs, the brand name obviously becomes less visible. It fades into the background; it is no longer the important information to be conveyed. Such a label says nothing about the cheese it represents but attempts to divert attention or at the very least to distract consumers and keep them from being overly demanding about the box's contents. The labels of famous brands, on the other hand, those with reputation and prestige, emphasize the firm name and have few signs and pictures. The labels of such brands are like the lids to jewel boxes: they must be worthy of the noble product they describe. They will depict the producer's property or dairy (Lebourgeois Camembert) or a fine dairy cow (Lepetit Camembert), or they will consist of symbols—a ducal coronet, heraldic lions (Lanquetot Camembert)—or show the medals awarded at world's fairs and other competitions (Lepetit Camembert). The best-known Norman cheese makers naturally emphasize brand name and region, but they also use anecdotal labels—secular versions of "holy pictures" like the Happy Farmer—to sell their second-quality products, cheeses that the profession has referred to since the First World War as *éclopé,* or wounded. Non-Norman producers prefer to rely on images of the Nation, to represent timeless rural scenes, or to draw upon contemporary historical events for their illustrations.

The label is what is left of a Camembert after it has been consumed. Countless Camembert lovers, looking at the empty box, have been unable to bring themselves to throw it away without having first removed the label! Camembert labels bring a touch of color and fantasy into an image-hungry world, and it is hard to burn them in the fireplace when the empty box serves as tinder. Thus, the label lives on, stuck on the kitchen wall or decorating a notebook. Schoolchildren, inveterate collectors of all kinds of things, trade them. The earliest collections must have begun in that way. Some producers also collected their competitors' labels as sources of inspiration. In May 1914, the new craze was described in an article in the *Bulletin de Vieux Papier.* The phenomenon has since grown astonishingly. To give some intellectual weight to their hobby (as though that were necessary), collectors have come up with the pedantic term "tyroseme" to describe the Camembert label ("tyro" = cheese in Greek; "seme" = sign), and they refer to themselves as tyrosemiophiles. In 1951, the most avid collectors founded a Société de Tyrosémiophilie; in late 1960, the Club Tyrosémiophile de l'Ouest (Western Tyrosemiophile Club) was created, leading to the appearance of the Club Tyrosémiophile de France in 1969.[8] The latter organization publishes a quarterly bulletin and, despite the decline in their quality, continues to exchange labels. Some members have impressive collections of several thousand labels.

These collections, the fruits of the passion of a handful of collectors, are Camembert's family album. They recount, in images, its hundred-year history and attest to the role it has played in the history of France. Looking through them, we are made aware of the extent to which the history of this cheese is linked to that of the nation whose causes it has espoused. Were we to retain but a single image among all that have decorated Camembert box tops for over a century, the sumptuous label of "Camembert de la République," dating from 1904, which represents a majestic female sower in a Phrygian cap, would unquestionably stand as the most powerful illustration of the cheese's identification with France.

THE UNITED STATES AND CAMEMBERT

New York is a gothic Roquefort, San Francisco makes me
think of a novel in Camembert.

SALVADOR DALI

It took Salvador Dali's surreal imagination to link Camembert and the
United States, two worlds one would have thought forever foreign, so different do they seem. In fact, for a long time now, raw-milk cheeses have
been banned in the United States, to the vast displeasure of their makers.
Norman cheese makers, victims of this alimentary ostracism, have inveighed against the New World's holding its nose when confronted with
their redolent product as an act of gastronomical barbarism. And it all began with a passionate love affair. Before it began to ban Camembert, the
United States was in love with it. Before they were forced to castigate
America's lack of culture, Camembert makers had been enraptured by the
American public's appetite for their cheese, seeing the American market
as a new El Dorado. For those locally prominent Normans, a local nobility rooted in their soil, selling in the United States was proof that it was
possible to conquer the land of modernity without abandoning any of
their age-old traditions. It gave them new confidence in the future. They
saw it as a guarantee that their world and their knowledge could survive
in the industrial society they saw as inevitable.

Fifty years later, their confidence having been misplaced, their early af-
fection has turned to repulsion. Only a few die-hards in the United States
are willing to brave the ban and expose themselves to the supposed dire
health risk entailed in consuming raw-milk Camembert. As for the Normans, they feel betrayed by the country that had once welcomed their
cheese so warmly.

The Camembert myth owes a great deal to the United States. I have
told of Joseph Knirim's pilgrimage to pay homage to Marie Harel. Without that event, the Heroine of the Auge would never have had her statue,
and her name would have remained unknown. Knirim, a New York physician, crossed the Atlantic to pay his respects at the tomb of a Norman
farmer's wife. That unexpected deed caught the imagination, and from
the shock of that event, the myth was born. Knirim had not added any-

thing new to create the myth; he had not made up the story of Marie Harel and her descendants. But it took that spark from the torch of the Statue of Liberty to transform a fairly mundane tale into a myth. Having received a New York blessing, Camembert immediately acquired a label of modernity and gained international stature. A product of tradition, it was hailed by the land of big industry and productivity, and it was thus able to claim to symbolize the ability of rural France to move resolutely into the modern world.

Knirim's story is too good not to arouse some skepticism. I myself have wondered whether it was not invented out of whole cloth by the Norman cheese makers to promote their products. It is indeed hard to understand how at that period a New York physician could have heard about the origins of Camembert and the name of its purported inventor. In fact, Knirim was not the first American citizen to have shown an interest in the Norman cheese. Several scientific articles on the cheese had already been published in the United States.

The United States had been importing Norman Camembert from Le Havre since the late nineteenth century. Ships' stewards stocked it in their refrigerators and, upon their arrival in New York, would sell what had not been eaten during the voyage.[9] To meet a growing demand, exporters then appealed to the shipping companies:

> American companies used twice a week to pick up at Le Havre French products, in particular Camembert cheeses, for transport to Southampton or Liverpool, where they would be put into cold storage pending the sailing of transatlantic vessels that would bring them to the two Americas. It was not unusual to see ships loading 60,000 and more Camemberts at Le Havre.[10]

In those days, it took fifteen days for a Camembert to reach the American continent—who knows in what condition. Nevertheless, the Americans were not put off, and their consumption continued to grow. Between 1895 and 1905, American imports of cheese grew from $417,000 to nearly $3 million.[11] For the most part, these were cheeses from Switzerland and Italy. However, imports of French cheeses also increased. In 1895, they represented $140,000. The growth in demand was created by European immigrants, especially the Italians, who held onto their dietary traditions, but it was also due to the gastronomical experiences of Americans who had traveled in Europe. Faced with this growth in imports, the American government decided to finance research into developing local cheese production. There were already some local makers of Brie and Camembert, but consumers were not satisfied with their quality. Swiss immigrants had established Brie and Camembert dairies in Orange County, New York, and they brought over workers from Norman cheese factories in the hopes that their expertise would enable them to equal the French cheeses. One of these dairies was run by Normans from Isigny. After having attempted to make Camembert without achieving any satisfactory results, in 1880 they turned to making a new kind of soft-centered cheese, with a shorter aging period, which they called Isigny. This cheese gained a certain reputation on the East Coast of the United States, and some competitors began to imitate it.[12]

With few exceptions, the Americans produced pressed cheeses similar to cheddar. However, a few dairies did make soft-centered cheeses, most of which were American adaptations of Limburger.[13] A very few produced Brie, but it was an American Brie and little aged, and needless to say it had nothing to do with French Brie. Several kinds of cheese called "Camembert" were available, but as American specialists might say, "The real thing comes from France." In 1905, the status of American Camembert was not particularly impressive:

> It had been successfully produced by only one large Eastern factory, a few others had produced a cheese called Camembert, but it could not stand up to the imported variety.[14]

Several scientists, however, were very interested in Camembert, and hoped to aid in its production. Around 1905, a mycologist named Dr. Charles Thom was one of the first to study the Camembert *Penicillium,* under the aegis of the U.S. Department of Agriculture. Thom was convinced that, with the help of science, it would be possible to make true Camembert in the United States. He amassed impressive documentation and was familiar with the work of French microbiologists in the field. He was in touch with several of them, and with a certain Epstein, a Czech specialist in soft-centered cheeses. At a laboratory located in Storrs, Connecticut, Thom, who was interested in cheese flora, worked with two bacteriologists named Conn and Stocking, a chemist named Bosworth, and a cheese maker called Theodore Issajef. Their work advanced knowledge in surface flora, the bacteria that grows on the crust of the cheese. Thom and his colleagues possessed excellent theoretical knowledge of cheese-making techniques, but they did not know all of the production secrets. They complained that "the method of production is kept secret and no source of information available."[15] Confronted with that wall of secrecy, they thought that they could unravel the mystery of Norman Camemberts by subjecting them to laboratory analyses. They had their colleague, Georges Roger, send them cheeses from France. In 1905, at the end of their preliminary series of investigations, they were convinced that they were on the right track and that they had managed to come up with rational technical means of production that would enable the United States to equal France in Camembert production. If they are to be believed, the cheeses produced at the Storrs laboratory were "appreciated by connoisseurs and could stand up against the best imported cheeses."[16]

In 1908, Thom and his colleagues were euphoric: "Although large quantities of Camembert are still being imported from France, its production has been initiated on a commercial scale here in our own country with considerable success."[17] A year later, however, Thom was forced to report the failure of most of the local facilities: "Several dairies have attempted to produce Camembert, copying the French environment and equipment. Without success."[18]

The majority of American cheese factories then abandoned Camembert production. Thom attributed the failure to climatic conditions. He noted that in the United States, the time when weather conditions most resembled those of Normandy's Camembert season lasted no more than an average of six weeks. According to him, the San Francisco area, whose climate most resembled that of Normandy, would be best suited to Camembert production. However, he did not abandon the project, but instead suggested a different approach. Instead of copying French methods, he suggested putting the new technology of air-conditioning to work. One of his ideas was to seal Camemberts in cans. Finally, he pointed to what was to be the future major direction for cheese production throughout the world, namely, standardized production.[19] However, in the meantime, the United States abandoned its attempt to compete with the Norman cheese makers, who received the news with some relief.

Temporarily unproductive work in the laboratory had nevertheless paved the way for the future industrialization of cheese manufacture in the United States. The prospect opened up by the scientists, who were not hampered by any local tradition, was not one that involved a slavish imitation of Norman production methods but rather the development of processes that would allow them to achieve a similar result on an industrial scale. Thus, the American scientists experimented with adding lactic bacteria to milk in order to obtain a uniform result not subject to the unpredictable variations that affected small-scale traditional cheese factories. They worked free from any thought of "region" and in the belief that Camembert, like any cheese, could be produced anywhere in the world so long as one had quality milk and replaced traditional, empirical methods with planning and scientific knowledge. Cheddar production furnished them with a model. This traditional English cheese, which had originated in Somerset, was already being produced in the United States on a large scale.

Furthermore, the work being done under Thom's leadership was broadening scientific knowledge about Camembert's surface mold. Thom and his colleagues found two different varieties of *Penicillium,* one of which turned green and another that remained white. They called the first *Penicillium camemberti,* a name that was to prevail for some time. The other, which they called *Penicillium candidum,* they found to have a different texture. Thom's work was attentively followed in France and had considerable repercussions in scientific circles, which, for the most part, shared his view on the unreality of reliance on region or milk provenance. Several articles mentioned his work, and his name would be forever linked to *Penicillium camemberti.* This bluish mold, which had once covered all Camemberts, has disappeared today, replaced by *Penicillium candidum.* However, it is still remembered thanks to a few American research scientists and their passion for Camembert.

The Auge dairymen were probably unaware of the work of the American scientists and the links that had been formed between French and American laboratories. Their sole concern was the success of their product across the Atlantic. They would have done well to pay more attention, for what was being developed in the laboratories of the United States, where their own Camemberts were under examination, was the Camembert of the future: standardized, pasteurized, and mass-produced.

Had Knirim read the work of Thom and his colleagues? We do not know, but he could have had indirect knowledge of it from articles in the popular press and have heard of the role attributed to Marie Harel, who was mentioned in most of the specialized papers. His interest may have been whetted by reading an article that appeared in 1911, pleading for a greater consumption of cheese and praising its digestibility.[20]

After its popularity peaked early in the last century, Camembert's fortunes in the United States varied. Local production was abandoned shortly after Thom's work was completed. It resumed in the 1940s on a large scale and included pasteurization. The Normans, finally awake to the fact that the Americans' idea of cheese was not the same as their own, denounced the industrial character of the American product, which put output above taste:

> The important thing for the cheese maker [in the United States] is not to provide the consumer with a tasty product with a delicate flavor, like our Brie or our Camembert, but to come up with a standardized product, insipid in taste, without aroma, always the same and always perfect in appearance. All to be achieved at the lowest cost in mass-production factories, relying on advertising to whet demand.[21]

On 14 June 1944, the Allied air forces accidentally bombed Vimoutiers. The town center was almost totally destroyed, and two hundred civilians were killed. The statue of Marie Harel, erected thanks to Joseph Knirim, was decapitated. To make amends, in 1947, the Americans created an "Aid to Vimoutiers" committee to collect funds for the town's reconstruction. William A. Foster, chairman of the Borden company, one of the United States' largest cheese manufacturers, wrote to the mayor of Vimoutiers offering to restore the statue. Borden employees volunteered to pay for the statue's restoration or replacement. The mayor of Vimoutiers accepted the offer, and in 1950 he received from the mayor of Van Wert, Ohio, the town where the Borden factory was located, a letter announcing that "the funds that have been collected in our region to reconstruct the statue of your famous citizeness Marie Harel are on their way." Borden employees had chipped in and collected $2,000. On 18 August 1950, C. E. Eckburg, then chairman of the company, handed over the money to the French Consul in Chicago, Roger Labry, at a luncheon at the Whitehall Inn in Van Wert. It was turned over to M. Bosworth, an American architect and chairman of "Aid to Vimoutiers." The design proposal that was chosen by competition was to represent a young Norman peasant woman in traditional costume carrying a Camembert. Finished in 1953, the statue was not erected until three years later. The final version depicts a young farm girl in native garb in such a clumsy pose that one cannot imagine her having invented anything at all.

In the meantime, the Normans, almost as though they had set out to realize the Americans' stereotype of village chauvinism and the difficult French character, were engaged in public wrangling. At first, the statue was to have been unveiled on Easter Sunday 1953, but the ceremony could not take place owing to a veritable village civil war. To begin with, the local businessmen were at loggerheads, some "uptown" and some "downtown," each faction determined to have Marie Harel to themselves. The mayor threatened to resign, the village priest tried to preach reconciliation. The ceremony was finally held during the course of a commercial fair held to celebrate the union of Marie Harel and the Duc de Bourgogne,[22] in other words, the union of Normandy cheeses and the great wines of Burgundy. The symbolic marriage was accompanied by floods of liquid refreshment—no one was quite sure whether the abundance was designed to smooth over past differences or to heal still-open wounds. Dr. Pierre Couinaud, who served briefly as minister of health, presided over the festivities.

However, Normandy's cheese makers were unwilling to allow their American competitors to pay for Marie Harel's new statue, and they voiced their opposition. Nor were they happy about the inscription that the Borden company wanted to add to the statue's base, to wit: "To Marie Harel. This statue was the gift of the Borden Ohio Camembert Factory." That was going way too far! The implication that an American industrial company also produced Camembert was unbearable in the heartland of true Camembert.

The Normans' displeasure was increased by the fact that their own cheeses were no longer allowed to enter the United States. A new American regulation banned the importation of raw-milk Norman Camembert. The U.S. empire was determined to protect itself against all unhealthy emanations from Europe, from communist agents to bacteria, and especially from the fearsome "red yeast"[23] that bred on Camembert's crust. In 1951, the Food and Drug Administration banned the importation of all cheeses that were nonpasteurized or aged for less than sixty days. Franco-American relations, previously cordial, albeit tinged with suspicion, worsened. The Normans could not countenance the Americans' impudence in daring to call their soft-centered cheese "Camembert" and in banning their own authentic product on some crazy pretext. Maurice Lanquetot, the former chairman of the SFVCN, felt the rigor of the new American regulation when customs officials in New York tossed his raw-milk Camemberts overboard.

Eventually, the Borden company modified the text of the inscription. To calm Norman feelings, the American cheese makers deleted all references to Camembert and simply proposed the following: "This statue is offered by 400 men and women making cheese in Van Wert (Ohio)." Yet the feelings of the Norman cheese makers were not completely soothed. They could not stand the idea that Marie Harel's statue was being restored by an industrial cheese company that was fifty times larger than the largest concern in Normandy. The mayor of Vimoutiers prudently put the statue in storage and waited two years before unveiling it.

Finally, on 4 October 1954, Vimoutiers got a look at the new statue. The chairman of the SFVCN chose to boycott the ceremony, but many other cheese makers did attend. In the presence of the United States ambassador, the mayor of Vimoutiers, and local elected officials, the chairman of the Borden company made a speech prior to unveiling the statue. He began by recalling the links between Van Wert and Marie Harel, links that the Norman cheese makers preferred to ignore: "Today, the thoughts of the people of Van Wert are on you. Indeed, at this very moment a ceremony is being held in Ohio to unveil the original statue of Marie Harel." And it was true: on that very day the inhabitants of Van Wert were unveiling the model of the Vimoutiers statue, which had been placed at the entrance of the Borden company, thus underlining its distant connection to the Norman farmer's wife.

Foster called the invention of Camembert "one of the greatest gastronomical feats of our time," and he noted that "the reputation of this wonderful cheese has spread to every civilized country." He concluded by expressing a wish: "May the presence of this statue in your charming little town remind you of the friendship of your American admirers!"

Notwithstanding that hope, the lack of understanding between Normans and Americans began to seem permanent. Raw-milk Camembert continued to be banned in the United States, while the Norman cheese makers continued to deny the use of the name "Camembert" to the factory-produced and pasteurized copies being turned out on American soil. Nevertheless, the industrialization of Camembert production in the United States turned out to prefigure what would happen in Normandy itself, and in a very few years. And the conversion of the largest Norman cheese factories to pasteurization was to enable exportation to the United States to pick up again on a modest scale.

There is, however, one deep-rooted misunderstanding that still persists between the small Norman cheese makers and the United States of America. During the course of my conversations with them, I heard them say on many occasions that the Americans were the victims of their abuse of pasteurized foods. They do not deny that raw-milk Camembert contains germs, but they regard that defect as a virtue. In a world teeming with bacteria, they believe that it is a mistake to try to avoid them entirely. They believe that the ingestion of Camembert will strengthen the body by making it accustomed to bacteria that it will inevitably encounter at some point. One retired cheese maker told me the following:

> Paul Buquet, who was a great cheese maker, told me, "When we used to milk by hand, sure, there was some splattering and dirt, but there were lactic bacilli as well, and cheese making went on successfully." His words were a bit simplistic, but they reveal the excesses we engage in today. Today, the Americans do not eat anything that is not pasteurized, but they no longer have any intestinal flora either. We have intestinal flora; we have to give it something to work on.

The argument sums up the whole Norman view of vaccination. The absence of intestinal flora as a result of an asepticized diet will weaken the poor Americans, whereas the Normans, used to a diet that is natural and robust, will be able to withstand anything. This popular common sense, rudimentary as it may be, is not without some basis in fact. Every traveler has had the unfortunate experience of finding out that he cannot ingest every local specialty with impunity.

Today, the large Camembert producers have adopted the American methods denounced by the Auge cheese makers. They no longer merely export cheese, they are buying American firms. Bridel, for example, purchased a Wisconsin cheese factory in 1987.

The tumultuous history of the relationship between the United States and Camembert is a reflection of Franco-American relations: a mixture of passionate mutual interest, reciprocal exchanges, and incomprehension. Americans made Normandy aware of its cheese-making identity by welcoming its produce and paying homage to Marie Harel. But the United States, as an industrial power, is interested in the past for what it can learn from it, not because it wants to preserve it. The Normans believed that the United States was honoring their traditions and did not understand that what attracted them was their inventiveness and commercial expertise, not the subtle aromas of their cheeses. Their somnolence during the 1930s, due to their prosperity and to their firm belief in their own superiority, cost the Norman cheese makers dearly. By the time they woke up, American production methods, especially when adopted by their French competitors, swept them away in a few short years.

THE CAMEMBERT CONDITION

Every cheese appeals to the senses. Because of their consistency and their aroma, the soft cheeses have more sensual appeal than others, and Camembert is outstanding in this area as well. It is not that it has any special qualities or that its consistency and aroma are more unique than those of other soft cheeses. However, it does have a special place in our imaginations, and we therefore feel more strongly about it. Proof of this can be seen every time we watch a cheese lover in the process of shopping for a good Camembert. It all begins at the cheese display. Among all of the boxes stacked there, several have labels that stand out. Thus, the first contact is visual, and the labels serve to illustrate the wide range of choices. The regular customer looks them over to see whether a favorite brand is present and whether any new brand has appeared on the scene. The vivid colors of the labels in a section in which the principal product colors are pale tones, yellows and grays, make the Camembert label stand out. However, the label is nothing but a thing to catch the eye, and who knows what it conceals? Thus, it is risky to base one's choice on appearance alone. Everyone knows that the label does not make the Camembert.

Selecting a Camembert is an adventure whose outcome remains uncertain up to the very last moment. For most other cheeses, choice is a matter of brand name, but when it comes to Camembert there is enormous uncertainty. The cheese can be completely different depending on its aging time, the season of the year, and the hazards and chance involved in its fabrication. No two Camemberts are alike, and determining which one will best suit one's taste is a demanding art. There are no agreed canons and standards of perfection. We all have our own appreciation of Camembert and do not need an expert to tell us what we like. Some like their cheese barely aged; others will opt for the oldest. The indecisive amateur will remove the box lid and attempt to pierce the secret of the cheese, which does not reveal itself at first glance. There is an attempt to discern the color of the crust through the slightly opaque waxed-paper wrapping. Is it whitish, does it have an ivory tinge, are there reddish-orange spots? According to that inspection, the consumer will try to guess its stage of development, for its maturity is said to be reflected in the color of the crust. That, however, is still not enough, since a good-looking cheese can conceal an unfortunate, dried-out interior. Visual inspection is not enough; touch must be brought into play.

There are many methods of testing the consistency of Camembert, all of them indicative of the buyer's temperament. Some go at it boldly, almost brutally, pressing their finger firmly and directly in the center of the cheese. Others prefer to take the cheese out of its box and hold it between their thumb and forefinger, exerting a mild pressure. This is the best way to gauge the cheese's interior consistency. If it does not yield properly to pressure, the soft center has probably not been sufficiently aged. If, however, the fingers meet with little or no resistance, one should immediately be suspicious; unless one is perversely fond of runny cheeses, it is best to steer clear of an unduly soft center. Those in search of simpler pleasures prefer cheeses with a supple and mellow consistency.

After having tested several Camemberts, sometimes just for the pleasure of it, the buyer will make a selection and carry off the cheese—that is, if the client does not go away empty-handed, having finally given up in the face of such second-rate produce. Unfortunately, few cheese merchants still allow the customer to touch-test the cheeses. They generally prefer to forbid the practice, which is hard on the cheese. Indeed, many Camemberts have met a premature end by being pierced with a sharp fingernail on an unduly brutal finger! The cheese merchant therefore reserves the privilege of testing the cheeses and selecting one that will suit the customer. Many consumers are frustrated by this ban, and some have given up buying in cheese shops and have turned to the open shelves of the supermarket, where they can indulge their passion freely. Of course, if the shop is crowded, one can sometimes manage to test a Camembert oneself at the cheese store, and if one is a regular customer, the owner may even afford an opportunity to feel a few.

In supermarkets, the absence of vendors allows consumers to choose for themselves from a large variety of brands. Many will perform the touch test, but many others select their Camemberts solely by price or brand without even opening the box. My own lengthy observations in supermarkets indicate that approximately 60 percent of consumers pick their Camembert without testing it. True, industrial Camemberts are less subject to variation, their stability is greater, and the time that they remain on the shelf for sale tends to be better controlled, so that nowadays the consumer can be more certain about the character of the cheese he or she is buying. The inclusion of optimum-use dating on the box has also reduced uncertainty. However, the relief of uncertainty has also meant a loss in pleasure, for it is an enormous pleasure to have managed to select a delicious cheese all by oneself!

As everyone knows, Camembert has a strong aroma, and the odor varies according to the length of time it has been aged. Subtle in the beginning, it grows stronger by the day and is an indicator of the cheese's degree of maturity. It is not easy to sniff a cheese in a cheese shop; it is frowned on, as if it were somehow immodest. You can sniff a melon, but not a Camembert. Of course, the two smells are not the same. Camembert's aroma is of another kind; one might even call it a stink. If one did not know the source, the smell of Camembert would be considered unpleasant, reminiscent of suspicious physical emanations, a disgusting, intimate smell. The expression *"Ça sent le Camembert!"* ("It stinks of Camembert!") is part of everyday language in France and often indicates the disagreeable odor of unwashed feet. Travel on the metro or in a train compartment with a Camembert in your bag, and you will soon notice an uneasy and inquiring expression on the faces of your fellow travelers, some of whom will give you an indignant or surprised glance and eventually move away. They obviously believe that you yourself are the cause of some unpleasant body odor or a sufferer from a poor digestion. Yet should you offer the same person a taste of the Camembert that is actually guilty of producing the suspect smell, he or she would most likely be delighted to share it with you.

Thus, Camembert's powerful aroma is no impediment to its consumption — quite the contrary. Why is it that such strong-smelling cheeses are tasted with such delight? Saying that it is because the taste is agreeable, despite the odor, is not a satisfactory answer. For taste and smell are uniquely linked. When we taste a cheese, we do not eradicate its smell, which remains present and is a part of our pleasure. And is it really that surprising? Actually, Camembert is liked *because* it smells. Disgust for putrid odors is neither universal, natural, nor absolute. It is the result of our education. The small child is attracted by its own excrement and will readily handle and play with it. One of the first educational no-nos, and one of the strongest, deals with that attraction, which is strictly and vehemently reprimanded. The child must be made to understand that everything that has a strong excremental odor is filthy, disgusting, and taboo. Any infraction of this ban will anger its parents. Thus, from our earliest childhood we are trained to avoid anything that is at all reminiscent of such odors. Eating cheeses enables us to get around this prohibition and to take a permissible pleasure in something that smells bad. Eating Camembert is an opportunity to transgress without breaking the law, to partake in forbidden pleasure. And, as we all know, any transgression does entail a certain amount of pleasure.

If the smell of Camembert abets rather than weakens the appetite, it is because it evokes other bodily odors. In France, a whole repertoire of suggestive remarks is at hand when a Camembert is eaten among friends. "It smells like a negligent little girl," is probably the most common, if not the most elegant. It is indecent — indeed unfitting — to talk about it, but it does smell, and no one can deny it. We live in a period when great pains are taken to avoid or conceal such smells, and one does one's best not to emit them. What showers and soap are unable to do away with, deodorant and cologne manage to conceal with more acceptable smells. However, the repression of such effluvia only makes our quest for them in other forms more determined. Freud linked the repression of the sense of smell to the civilizing process. According to him, in adopting an upright stance, man lost a great part of the olfactory capacities he had once used, especially in finding a sexual partner. However, although the sense of smell no longer plays an acknowledged role in amorous selection, and although bodily odors are eradicated as much as possible, there is still something left. The smells emitted during sexual congress may provoke disgust or excitement, but they rarely create indifference.

In the intimacy of the home, the acrid smell of an unwrapped Camembert is a prelude to its consumption, the first element involved in tasting it. The delicacy of a raw-milk Camembert does not withstand refrigeration, and if one is averse to smells, it is advisable to eat it at once. Its odorous presence becomes more marked once it is removed from its box and its waxed-paper wrapping. Consumption is the moment of truth. The cheese aficionado will now know whether the right choice was made or whether appearances were misleading. Appetite whetted by the cheese's appearance and smell, the cheese lover removes the last bit of wrapper and at last contemplates the downy surface. The knife is plunged in, starting in the center, and a slice is cut out. Before being raised to the lips, the consistency and color of the interior are examined. The ideal Camembert is completely "done": its soft center is homogenous and the color of yellowed ivory, sometimes with a vein of white in the center that is soft to the touch. There are many ways of eating it, from the most civilized—on a plate with knife and fork to remove the crust—to the most sensual, with the fingers, without removing the crust. It should offer the slightest resistance as it is bitten into and its aroma is released, with a slightly salty and subtly acrid taste.

To eat a Camembert means not only to ingest it but to appreciate it with every sense. The sight first, then the first caressing touch, then the perception of its inner aroma, are all preludes either to pleasure or distaste, and finally, consumption, accompanied either by delight or by disappointment.

In many ways, the mysterious realm of cheeses and that of sex share a common border. First of all, there is milk itself, a liquid whose production is ultimately the result of copulation. Traditionally, with the exception of shepherds, cheeses are made by females. After all, they have a natural familiarity with that nourishing substance. Milking cows, skimming milk, and making butter and cheese are all traditional female activities. Unique among foodstuffs, the production of cheese is a physical act. Milking itself is done by hand. The milkmaid squeezes vigorously on the cow's udder with both hands, directing the warm milk into a receptacle held between her legs. This intimate physical contact continues throughout the process. After the clotting period, the curd is tested with the back of the hand or a finger is inserted into it to ascertain whether it is ready for molding. The principal stages of the process—turning, salting, and packing—also require direct hand contact. To appreciate this physical aspect, one need only watch the head cheese maker as he moves through the drying room, lifting a Camembert on the rack and passing his hand over the white, downy surface of the cheese. He caresses the cheese and delicately feels it before replacing it. Unfortunately, modern technology and an obsession with hygiene have deprived industrial Camemberts of this repeated contact.

The soft cheeses undergo amazing changes. A liquid, milk, is mixed with another liquid, rennet, and their union forms a solid. The passage from liquid to solid has been used as a metaphor for fecundation by Western civilizations seeking a theory to explain the mechanics of procreation. In his *Generation of Animals,* Aristotle found an analogy between the action of male semen on female blood and that of rennet on milk. Indeed, like blood, milk coagulates naturally. The Bible also employs this metaphor. Several ancient writers, among them Pliny the Elder, Galen, and Clement of Alexandria, came up with the same notion. For the latter,

> In the beginning, the embryo . . . resembles milk that has just begun to clot; and no cheese maker would begin to mold such milk before it had clotted completely: in like manner, creation does the same with the human being.
>
> *The Instructor* 1.6

Popular folk literature in France, which was the only kind available to the people during the Ancien Régime, apart from the Bible, popularized this analogy. This explanation of the action of the sperm attributed contraceptive powers to certain plant extracts or herbs, such as nettle juice, that could halt or prevent coagulation.[24] The parallel between the mixing of rennet and milk and the mingling of sexual fluids is also embodied in an old saying: To say that a woman had "let herself turn to cheese" meant that she had strayed sexually.[25] According to the myth, Camembert owes its existence to the joint action of a woman and a priest. It is difficult not to view that as a symbolic expression of this need to bring two complementary elements together. The woman provides the milk, and as for the priest, his contribution can be interpreted in several ways according to which facet of his character one wishes to emphasize. He can be no more than a propitiator, because of his consecration, or more prosaically, he can represent virility.

After clotting, changes occur according to some mysterious dynamic. One cannot help but think of changes in the human body. More than any other cheese, Camembert seems to have a life of its own, one that is hard to control. Its substance, at first fragile and flaccid, becomes more solid and more consistent and grows a downy crust that changes color. The initial solidification then undergoes an inverse metamorphosis, a progressive softening that sometimes becomes almost liquid. There is something almost uncanny and mysterious about the whole process that makes us think of organic mysteries and transformations. The cheese's ultimate oozing stage when it is completely aged evokes other emissions, both male and female, menstrual or spermatic, according to one's tastes and fantasies. Some, for whatever reason, enjoy removing the runny center of an overly ripe Camembert by cutting it out obscenely with a knife.

The way one talks about Camembert and the ribaldry that sometimes accompanies its consumption attest to the cheese's evocative power. Its aroma is obviously the element that gives rise to the greatest number of comments and jokes, but its consistency and runny quality are not far behind. Here, men who are unable to speak simply and openly about their sexuality allow their imaginations full rein. They compare a good Camembert to a desirable woman. Georges Bisson, who owned a cheese factory early in the last century, used to say that the crust of a good Camembert should be almost transparent so as to reveal its flesh, like a veil on the face of a pretty woman. For partisans of old-fashioned Camembert, there is no good cheese without some blemish. Pierre Androuet, a well-known cheese maker who spoke admirably about cheeses and the pleasure they provide, liked to say that one could not have a good Camembert unless a bit of manure or cow dung had fallen into the milk. Knowing the care with which cheese makers treat the milk to be used to produce Camemberts, his words surprise us, yet he is merely voicing a fantasy according to which there must be some blemish or flaw in order for milk, a liquid of purity, to turn into a strong-smelling and strong-tasting cheese. His words also reveal that in Camembert we seek the strong odors of the countryside and nature, and that in our imaginations Camembert is indeed linked to dirt and excrement.

For years, fermented cheeses, which are the ones with strong odors, have incurred the disapproval of the medical profession and been disdained by the wealthy. The Italian historian Piero Camporesi devoted a chapter of his book, *L'Officine des Sens (The Pharmacy of the Senses)* to these curious outbursts against cheeses.[26] The fiercest of them was emitted by a seventeenth-century German physician, Johan Petrus Lotichius. Cheese is condemned in language that makes reference to both the excremental and the sexual. He describes it as "milk's turd," "curds from the lower body parts," and "a coitus of the worst kinds of matter." He inveighs against what he calls a "pestilential, coagulated ball." Cheese is described as putrefying dead matter, teeming with worms. Lotichius seems to consider cheese as almost the product of sorcery: "Some young women prepare varieties in which they mix coriander, caraway, thyme, and other such herbs."

For the medical profession, cheese was inevitably harmful; its smell alone should warn away anyone of any refinement. Such violent disapproval was so outrageous that it tells us that cheese consumption did indeed extend beyond the lower classes and that purportedly "respectable" people appreciated its gaminess. Was it a practice that was disapproved of and thus inadmissible, one indulged in by debauched aristocrats drawn to base and vulgar turpitude, or was it a vice that was widely shared but kept hidden? We do not know. The actions of Joseph Knirim, the New York physician, to promote the consumption of Camembert were a clear sign of the reversal of the medical profession's attitude to cheese, which, after centuries of infamy, finally came to be regarded as a healthy and commendable foodstuff.

Strong cheeses have not only aroused the anathema of doctors, they have also provoked violent revulsion in the refined and the sensitive, as illustrated by the edifying life of the French saint Marguerite Marie Alacoque. This holy nun sought out the most severe expiatory means by which to mortify her flesh and could not imagine any more violent suffering than the eating of cheese. The very thought of it nearly made her faint. However, so powerful was her love of God that she was bound and determined to undergo the trial, despite the warnings of her Mother Superior. After having put it off for years, she finally made up her mind to make the sacrifice and, after having nearly given up several times and having spent an entire night in prayer, she managed it. For this pure soul, eating a revolting substance like cheese, laden as it was with every worldly turpitude, was the supreme sacrifice, a descent into the slime of the world. Her disgust for cheese, which obsessed her—she thought about it for years on end—was equaled only by her disgust for her own body, which she mortified.

Camembert, a living substance produced by an animal organism, constantly reminds us of the body, of sensual pleasure, of sexual fulfillment, and of all that is forbidden in it. Now that it is a foodstuff approved by dieticians, who are our new directors of conscience, we can consume it with a clear mind. Today, we can all enjoy a brief and delicious moment of transgression with a piece of Camembert. However, other threats loom on the horizon. The countries of northern Europe and the United States, on behalf of so-called "safer food," want to impose universal pasteurization and ban the consumption of "untreated"—in other words, raw-milk—cheese. Hygiene is only a pretext, since the new alimentary bans are principally aimed at soft cheeses, the ones that have the strongest smell, and do not pay much attention to other products that are far more receptive to pathogenic bacteria. Hidden puritanism is thus reentering through the back door in the form of provisions purportedly aimed at alimentary hygiene. Now that it has been banished from the bedroom, the moral order is trying to get at us at the dining table.

Chapter 7 | PERMANENCE OF THE MYTH

In 1991, Camembert celebrated its bicentenary. From all appearances, France's national cheese is doing well, and the myth surrounding it is still flourishing. Indeed, the event created considerable attention and was widely celebrated. A great many articles were published, and the press naively reported a number of amazing stories about the cheese's invention and its early career, thereby contributing even further to the enrichment and diversity of that already legendary saga. The outburst of attention was a good indication of the durability of the myth itself, to which we all pay homage and which continues to inspire deference. Of course, there is no counting the many bitter remarks of the gastronomes who continue to complain about the mediocre quality of much of today's Camembert, and they only make us more receptive to the praise lavished on the real thing. No iconoclast has yet gone so far as to spoil the image of the national cheese.

Beset by perils on all sides, our national Camembert therefore appears to be holding its own, and its success seems to remain high. In 1984, 45 percent of the French named it as one of their favorite cheeses, putting it ahead of Roquefort.[1] According to market studies, 60 percent of French households consume it, and they like it enough to eat nearly two per week. In total, nearly two million Camemberts are eaten each day in France, a quantity that represents some 190,000 tons. It accounts for 17 percent of the overall cheese market,[2] the far greater part. A study by the Société Française d'Enquêtes par Sondage, the largest French market research company, also indicates that it is the cheese with the highest recognition factor. Seventy-eight percent of the French are able to identify it when it appears on a cheese platter, whereas only 60 percent recognize Gruyère and only 51 percent recognize Roquefort.[3] If we are to go by these figures, therefore, Camembert is hardly a myth; it has earned its place on the French table.

However, we do detect some signs of weakness and the presence of some disturbing threats. After years of increase, Camembert consumption has fallen slightly since 1986. The small traditional cheese makers are disappearing one by one, while standardization is posing a threat to the cheese's identity. It is not wholly unreasonable to imagine that in a decade or so we may find nothing but industrial Camembert, whether pasteurized or raw-milk, ladle-molded or produced by machine. The threat is a real one. The end of regionally produced Camembert made the old-fashioned way would, after all, be the logical epilogue to the disappearance of the rural world. Is Camembert not fated to experience the same changes that have touched the French countryside and led to the disappearance of its rural population? The Auge itself, the cradle of Camembert, is in decline, and some of its pastures are now lying fallow. Why should the cheese outlive the world that produced it? However, its disappearance is not inevitable; there are still grounds for hope. To begin with, the demand for traditional cheeses is steadily increasing. When even the present-day cheese makers disappear without leaving heirs, it is not inconceivable that new ones will appear on the scene, eager to revive and produce the raw-milk, ladle-molded Camembert that the gourmets demand. However, although there is some hope, and although regional Camembert still has chances of survival, we must nevertheless face the fact that an era has indeed come to an end.

Particular and finicky cheese lovers often express their discontent with the current product, maintaining—like the famous Pierre Androuet, a French specialist in cheeses—that it is all over, that Camembert will never be Camembert again. This refrain is nothing new; it has been heard for almost as long as the cheese has been in existence. As early as 1894, Victor-Eugène Ardouin-Dumazet was maintaining that the golden age of true Camembert was over. The famous geographer spoke out against the large-scale production of Camembert outside the borders of Normandy:

> We have more manufactured products than those that are farm-produced. . . .
> We must take a stand in favor of a radical change in our economic habits
> lest we continue to see a gradually diminishing number of Camemberts wor-
> thy of the name.[4]

In fact, the situation that Ardouin-Dumazet was denouncing at the end of the nineteenth century was caused by the increase in the number of cheese factories, which had in turn been caused by the rapid growth in demand for the cheese. The good and the bad were already being lumped together under the appellation "Camembert." This situation only served to heighten the complaints of cheese lovers, who have always inveighed against the present and yearned for some mythic golden age. However, in fact, the Camembert appellation was never a guarantee of quality. There has always been a Camembert for the middle classes and one for the working classes, both bearing the same name, one of them a perfectly aged traditional product, the other a cheap imitation, a Camembert for special occasions and a Camembert for every day. As a result, there has always been a wide range of prices. There are few other consumer products so available to so many sizes of pocketbook, from the cheapest morsel that makes a tramp's meal to the specially aged and cellar-cured Camembert of one's own local cheesemonger that one hardly dares to sniff when it appears on the cheese trolleys in great restaurants. The diversity is almost dizzying, but it also has its advantages. It means that everyone, whatever their taste or means, can eat Camembert and, in so doing, take part in the same celebration along with every other French person. It also reflects the diversity of the country itself, in all its contradictions. In particular, it helps us to interpret the conflict-filled relationship between tradition and modernity, with its balance of opposition and complementarity.

Thanks to its disconcertingly multifaceted nature, Camembert can embrace every opinion and embody all of France's worries, as well as all of its sources of pride. Like its very substance, it is enormously malleable. Every time a discussion of Camembert arises, whether in conversation or in print, the French nation is also the subject. Every one of the important questions of our age can be found reflected in this cheese, and each of its misfortunes can be interpreted with reference to the nation's fate. As an avatar of the national sensibility, Camembert takes on the country's concerns and communicates them in its own language. Whatever France's preoccupations may be—the threat of Japanese competition, European integration, the end of the rural world—they all find in Camembert a ready mirror and a specific form of expression. If we look back at some of the great questions that concern us at this turn of the century, we note that Camembert is also somehow involved, just as it was in the past, whether it was the First World War or the question of industrialization.

The French are obsessed by the thought that their regional products might be refused entry to a country, and they are fearful that the globalization process may force them to abandon a part of their national patrimony. The establishment of the single European market, with common hygienic standards, has revived those fears and reawakened the trauma caused by the closing of the American border. Will Camembert be allowed to travel, or will it become a victim of the rigorous northern European obsession with hygiene? In recent years, it has become a test of France's progress in alimentary hygiene. Every time a Camembert factory is either built or modernized, its backers make the point that it is in conformity with European standards and emphasize the strict hygienic controls they have set up. To use the current professional jargon, Camembert has moved into the "ultraclean" era. Yet, although the hygiene challenge has been met, has it not been at the cost of some loss of character? To put it another way: is it possible to achieve impeccable hygiene without ceasing to be French? Such is the dilemma confronting raw-milk Camembert. Hygienic rigor and gourmet quality have long been viewed as incompatible. One can either have a Camembert that is bacteria-free but tasteless, or one can savor a full-flavored cheese whose bacterial content would send the health inspectors into shock. For raw-milk Camembert, the question is still pending: will it be possible to abide by the regulations and also preserve its incomparable taste? Concern over whether the Norman cheese makers will manage to achieve this is part of France's fears of a loss of identity within the European framework. Debates over the Maastricht Treaty often make reference to the threats that the European standards pose to traditional French cheeses, and to Camembert in particular. In the opinion of the treaty's opponents, France—like Camembert—is being forced to abandon its identity as the price of its integration into the European Economic Community.

Japan, which is feared for its technological and competitive skills, has given rise to astonishing fantasies. Some alarmist articles have maintained that the Japanese are preparing to invade France with their own Camemberts, a danger that is most likely quite imaginary. Although some Japanese firms have indeed begun to make a local "Camembert," the country's milk supply is far too limited for it to envisage any exportation. Yet the notion that Camembert too might become a target for Japanese businesses reveals the degree to which the French today fear Japan's commercial heft. Although symbolized by Camembert, it is the country itself that feels threatened by a Japanese takeover.

And the threats also come from within. As we have seen, the French have always been concerned by domestic change, fearful that the nation, by changing, will lose its identity and its rich tradition. The struggle between pasteurized and raw-milk Camembert illustrates the constant battle being waged in France between tradition and modernity. On the one hand, we have Eternal France, proud of its rich gastronomical heritage, secure within its borders, bathed in the scents of its elegant perfumes and the more earthy odors of its farm products, both delighting the senses of the refined. On the other hand, we have cutting-edge industry, high-tech and ultraclean Camembert, and the world of the bar code. That somewhat caricatural contrast is nonetheless a good illustration of the balancing act being performed in France by its modern technology, always a megabyte behind that of Japan, and its luxury craftsmen. It reveals a deep concern and a dream: the dream of having both worlds, of being able to carry off a difficult and elegant acrobatic feat without falling.

For more than two centuries, Camembert has been a concrete symbol of national cohesiveness and especially of the bond between the country's rural and urban citizens. The disappearance of the farming class, like European integration, must inevitably have an effect on the future of Camembert and on its myth. Indeed, both phenomena directly affect France's identity. What will France, an old rural country, be like without its farmers? What will its personality be within a Europe that has been made uniform? In what way can Camembert now manage to embody the idea of a vanished rural population? Does it still truly have a role to play in French society, aside from being merely something to eat? A survivor of a bygone era and a vanished world, the cheese stands as a witness to history, a messenger from the past to remind the French of their peasant origins. However, its future should not be confined to symbolizing the country's rural past. Laden with a prestigious history, a witness to the Republic's greatest hours and to all of the changes that have occurred in French society over the past two centuries, Camembert can remain a national landmark, a French point of reference, only if it can retain its diversity and manage to withstand the current pressures that are being exerted to standardize it.

NOTES

PREFACE. OPENING THE BOX

1. Georges Colomb, alias Christophe, born in 1856 in Lure (Haute-Saône), was also the creator of *La Famille Fenouillard* and *Savant Cosinus. Le Sapeur Camember* appeared in *Le Petit Français Illustré,* a newspaper for schoolchildren, from January 1890 to September 1896.

CHAPTER 1. A MYTH IS BORN

1. The details of this unbelievable scene have been supplied by Auguste Gavin himself. After having become mayor of Vimoutiers, he recounted the episode in 1956 in a speech he made at the unveiling of the second statue of Marie Harel, erected to replace the first, which had been destroyed in the bombings in 1944. (Maurice Cardon, *Bulletin du Club Tyrosémiophile de France* 51 [July 1973]: 9–13.)
2. Xavier Rousseau, *Le Camembert* (Argentan, France: Imprimerie des Trois Cantons, 1927), 7.
3. Roger Veisseyre, *Technologie du Lait,* 3d ed. (Paris: La Maison Rustique, 1979).
4. Jean-Robert Pitte, "Le Pays aux 365 Fromages," *L'Histoire* 85 (1985): 24–31.
5. Patrick Coyle, *The World Encyclopedia of Food* (London: Francis Pinter, 1982), 124.

6. Quoted by Alfred Sauvy in *Histoire Économique de la France entre les Deux Guerres,* vol. 2 (Paris: Fayard, 1984), 9.

7. From 1926–30, the birth rate was only 1.12 percent.

8. *Le Gaulois* (13 April 1928).

CHAPTER 2. MARIE HAREL
AND HER DESCENDANTS

1. Jean de La Varende, *En Parcourant la Normandie* (Monaco: Les Flots Bleus, 1953), 93.

2. Thomas Corneille, *Dictionnaire Universel Géographique et Historique,* vol. 3 (Paris: Chez Jean-Baptiste Coignard, 1708), 739.

3. Charles Jobey, *Histoire d'Orbec* (1778), 632.

4. Ibid.

5. Ibid.

6. Jean Boullard, *Vimoutiers* (Vimoutiers, France: 1937).

7. Gérard Roger, *Marie Harel, "Inventeur" du Fromage de Camembert, de la Légende à l'Histoire* (Vimoutiers, France: Société Historique de Vimoutiers, 1976).

8. Jules Morière, "De l'Industrie Fromagère dans le Département du Calvados," in *L'Annuaire Normand* (1859): 100.

9. Courmaceul manuscript, 1791.

10. *L'Écho des Clochers de Camembert et des Champeaux* (1947).

11. Henri Pellerin, "Deux Prêtre Réfractaires Cachés à Camembert à l'Époque de la Révolution," *Le Pays d'Auge* (December 1962): 19–24.

12. Pomereau de la Bretèche, *Mémoire sur la Généralité d'Alençon* (1698).

13. Dumoulin, *La Géographie ou description générale du royaume de France divisé en ses généralités* (Amsterdam, 1762–67). Exmes, the principal village of the canton, located in the southern point of the Auge.

14. Dumoulin, *La Géographie ou Description Générale du Royaume de France Divisé en Ses Généralités* (Amsterdam: 1762–67).

15. Edmond Garnier, *L'Agriculture dans le Département de la Seine et le Marché Parisien du Point de Vue du Ravitaillement Alimentaire* (Poitiers, France: 1939).

16. Arthur Young, *Travels in France during the Years 1787, 1788, 1789* (London: George Bell and Sons, 1889), 116.

17. Jean-Robert Pitte, "Le Pays aux 365 Fromages," *L'Histoire* 85 (1985): 28.

18. *L'Annuaire Normand* (1865): 248.

19. Roger, *Marie Harel*, 18.

20. *Le Moniteur Universel*, no. 222 (10 August 1863).

21. *L'Annuaire Normand* (1851).

22. From a manuscript notebook by Cyrille Paynel, 1873. This notebook was edited in 1997 by Archives Départementales du Calvados at Caen under the title *Carnet de Cyrille Paynel un Éleveur-Fromager du Pays d'Auge*.

23. Ibid.

24. Ibid.

25. Ibid.

26. Jules Morière, "De l'Industrie Fromagère dans le Département du Calvados," in *L'Annuaire Normand* (1878): 88–89.

27. Communal monograph, Archives du Calvados, Br. 9353.

28. Bernard Garnier, "Paris et les Fromages Frais au XIXe Siècle," in *Histoire et Géographie des Fromages* (Caen, France: Centre de Publication a l'Université de Caen, 1987), 123–34.

29. *L'Annuaire Normand* (1877): 460.

30. *L'Annuaire Normand* (1852).

31. Ibid.

32. Armand-Florent Pouriau, *Laiterie, Art de Traiter le Lait, de Fabriquer le Beurre, et les Principaux Fromages Français et Ètrangers* (Paris: Librairie Audot, 1872).

33. Armand-Florent Pouriau, *La Laiterie* (Paris: Audot, Lebroc et Cie., 1881).

34. Ibid., 481.

35. Ibid., 461.

36. Ibid.

37. Bernard Garnier, "Paris et les Fromages Frais."

38. Victor-Eugène Ardouin-Dumazet, *Voyages en France,* 6th series (Paris: Berger-Levrault, 1894), 139.

39. Ibid.

40. Pouriau, *La Laiterie,* 469.

41. Morière, "De l'Industrie Fromagère" (1878): 88–89.

42. Ibid.

43. Vincent Houdet, *Laiterie, Beurrerie, Fromagerie* (Paris: Encyclopédie des Connaissances Agricoles, Hachette, 1907), 90.

44. Louis Bochet, *Manuel Pratique de l'Industrie Laitière* (Paris: Frisch, 1895), 532–42.

45. Morière, "De l'Industrie Fromagère" (1878): 90.

46. E. Ferville, *L'Industrie Laitière, le Lait, le Beurre, le Fromage* (Paris: J.-B. Ballière et Fils, 1888), 232.

47. Morière, "De l'Industrie Fromagère" (1878): 91.

48. Morière, "De l'Industrie Fromagère" (1878).

49. Pouriau, *La Laiterie,* 475.

50. Jules Morière, *Le Département du Calvados à l"Exposition Universelle de 1867* (Caen, France: A. Hardel, 1869), 89.

CHAPTER 3. CAMEMBERT GOES NATIONAL

1. Vincent Houdet, *Rapport sur la Fabrication des Fromages à Pâte Molle (Camembert et Brie)* (Paris: Imprimerie Nationale, 1896).

2. François Mackiewicz, *Fromages et Fromagers de Normandie* (Le Puy-en-Velay, France: Christine Bonneton, 1983).

3. Jean Boullard, *Vimoutiers* (Vimoutiers, France: 1937).

4. Philippe Jacob, *Bulletin du Club Tyrosémiophile de France* 106 (January 1991): 12–15.

5. Houdet, *Rapport.*

6. *Annales de l'Institut Pasteur,* 1904.

7. *L'Industrie Laitière* (1926): 104–7.

8. Maurice Desfleurs, *Contribution à la Connaissance du Genre* Penicillium. *Application à la Fabrication des Fromages à Pâte Molle, et Notamment du Camembert* (Caen, France: Faculté des Sciences, 1966), 1.

9. Léon Lindet, *Évolution des Industries Qui Transforment les Produits Agricoles* (Paris: Librairie de l'Enseignement Technique, 1920), 35.

10. Émile Louïse, *L'Annuaire Normand* (1901): 129.

11. Pierre Mazé, "Les Microbes dans l'Industrie Fromagère," *Annales de l'Institut Pasteur* (1905), 388–89.

12. Vincent Houdet, *Laiterie, Beurrerie, Fromagerie* (Paris: Encyclopédie des Connaissances Agricoles, Hachette, 1924), 96.

13. Desfleurs, *Contribution à la Connaissance du Genre* Penicillium.

14. Maurice Beau and Charles Bourgain, *La Science Fromagère,* vol. 2 (Paris: J.-B. Ballière et Fils, 1927), 69.

15. Beau and Bourgain, *La Science Fromagère,* vol. 2, 62.

16. V. Le Fort, "La Fromagerie de Saint-Maclou," *La Revue Illustrée du Calvados* (January 2–5, 1914).

17. Beau and Bourgain, *La Science Fromagère,* vol. 2, 532.

18. In chapter 5, I recount the ups and downs of the struggle to get the *appellation d'origine.*

19. General Assembly of 13 May 1911, Archives of the SFVCN.

20. Archives of the SFVCN, March 1921.

21. Archives of the SFVCN, April 1921.

22. Meeting of 18 November 1922, Archives of the SFVCN.

23. General Assembly of 31 July 1909, Archives of the SFVCN.

24. General Assembly of 1 April 1922, Archives of the SFVCN.

25. General Assembly of 21 April 1923, Archives of the SFVCN.

26. General Assembly of 21 April 1923, Archives of the SFVCN.

27. Archives of the SFVCN, 1931.

28. General Assembly of 27 September 1924, Archives of the SFVCN.

29. General Assembly, 1913, Archives of the SFVCN.

30. General Assembly of 25 April 1925, Archives of the SFVCN.

31. Archives of the SFVCN, January 1921.

32. Ibid.

33. Meeting of 28 October 1928, Archives of the SFVCN.

34. General Assembly of 31 July 1909, Archives of the SFVCN.

35. In 1920, twenty-eight of nearly one hundred syndicate members were locally elected officials (Archives of the SFVCN, 1920).

36. Jean-Jacques Becker, *La France en Guerre, 1914–1918* (Brussels: Complexe, 1988), 22–23.

37. Quoted in Michel Augé-Laribé, *La Politique Agricole de la France, 1880–1940* (Paris: PUF, 1950), 308.

38. *Le Monde,* 10 November 1988.

39. Archives of the SFVCN, 1916.

40. Ibid.

41. General Assembly of 22 December 1917, Archives of the SFVCN.

42. Paul Cazin, *L'Humaniste à la Guerre* (Paris: Plon, 1920).

43. Archives of the Land Armed Forces, 1916.

44. Archives of the SFVCN, October 1915.

45. *Le Matin,* 31 October 1916.

46. Meeting of 11 May 1918, Archives of the SFVCN.

47. Meeting of 21 September 1918, Archives of the SFVCN.

48. Each army's central depot had a double purpose: supplying the division cooperatives and facilitating the supply of food to company messes (Archives of the Land Armed Forces, 1916).

49. Archives of the SFVCN.

50. General Assembly of 8 December 1917, Archives of the SFVCN.

51. Meeting of 15 December 1917, Archives of the SFVCN.

52. Meeting of 17 January 1916, Archives of the SFVCN.

53. Letter from Paul Vignioboul to the prefect of Calvados dated 16 October 1915.

54. Interview with Paul Vignioboul, *Le Matin,* 31 October 1916.

55. *L'Effort du Ravitaillement Français Pendant la Guerre et pour la Paix 1914–1920* (Paris: Librairie Félix Alcan, n.d.).

56. Antoine Schiekevitch, *Enquête sur la Situation des Industries dans le Département du Calvados,* vol. 1 (Caen, France: Henri Delesques, 1918), 157.

57. Schiekevitch, *Enquête,* 82–85.

58. Françoise Thébaud, *La Femme au Temps de la Guerre de 14* (Paris: Stock/Laurence Pernoud, 1986), 156–57.

59. Jacques Meyer, *La Vie Quotidienne des Soldats Pendant la Grande Guerre* (Paris: Hachette, 1966), 175.

60. Schiekevitch, *Enquête,* 158.

61. Governmental decree of 12 July 1919.

62. Meeting of 21 January 1922, Archives of the SFVCN.

CHAPTER 4. THE REIGN OF THE GREAT FAMILIES

1. General Assembly of 30 April 1927, Archives of the SFVCN.

2. *L'Annuaire Normand* (1892): 93–94.

3. V. LeFort, "La Fromagerie de Saint-Maclou," *La Revue Illustrée du Calvados* (January 1914): 2–5.

4. Marc Justafre, "L'Étude Prosopographique du Groupe Socio-professionel des Fromagers de Boissey Depuis le XVIIIe Siècle" (master's thesis, University of Caen, 1987).

5. Le Fort, "La Fromagerie," 3.

6. In 1914, there were 311 cheese dairies in Normandy, 167 of which were in the Auge, not to mention the region's private farm production.

7. In 1888, Jean-Marie Lavalou, the future manager of the Bourg-Saint-Léonard cheese factory, described the Le Tremblay cheese factory as it had existed at the conclusion of his training period. In 1926, René Rollet, the son of the then-manager, based his thesis in agriculture on it.

8. We know about the Quesnot cheese factory in Calvados thanks to a thesis in agriculture of 1924 by Jean de Neuville, the manager's brother.

9. Ministére de l'Agriculture, Office de Renseignements Agricoles. *Enquête sur l'Industrie Laitière de 1903* (Paris: Imprimerie Nationale, 1903), 43.

10. Ibid., 71.

11. Geneviève Busnel, interview by author, Caen, France, 5 May 1985.

12. Ibid.

13. General Assembly of 12 July 1930, Archives of the SFVCN.

14. Archives of the SFVCN, 22 May 1910.

15. LeFort, "La Fromagerie," 4.

16. Ibid.

17. Jean Neuville, "Une Fromagerie de Camembert au Pays d'Auge" (thesis, Caen, France, 1924).

18. Ibid., 67.

19. Meeting of 23 January 1921, Archives of the SFVCN.

20. General Assembly of 25 April 1925, Archives of the SFVCN.

21. General Assembly of 12 July 1930, Archives of the SFVCN.

22. *Revue Laitière Française* (October 1985): 32.

23. Pierre Boisard and Marie-Thérèse Letablier, "Liens Locaux de Production et Standards Industriels—Le Cas du Camembert," in *Dossier de Recherche* 15 (Paris: Centre d'Étude et de l'Emploi, 1986), 50.

24. François Mackiewicz, *Fromages et Fromagers de Normandie* (Le Puy-en-Velay, France: Christine Bonneton, 1983), 72.

25. Ibid.

26. Geneviève Busnel, interview by author, Caen, France, 5 May 1985.

27. Ibid.

28. Meeting of 28 February 1914, Archives of the SFVCN.

29. Meeting of 25 April 1925, Archives of the SFVCN.

30. Meeting of 8 May 1937, Archives of the SFVCN.

31. Meeting of 14 January 1939, Archives of the SFVCN.

32. Alfred Gallier, *Le Calvados* (Caen, France: Henri Delesques, 1909).

33. Geneviève Busnel, interview by author, Caen, France, 5 May 1985.

34. Interview with a cheese factory manager by the author, Saint-Pierre sur Dives, France, 1988.

35. Jules Morière, *Le Département du Calvados à l'Exposition Universelle de Paris* (Caen, France: 1986), 11–12.

1. In 1952, there were still forty-three Camembert factories in Calvados (M. Mauger, "Les Industries de Transformation du Lait dans le Calvados," [thesis, University of Caen, 1954], 74).

2. General Assembly of 13 February 1943, Archives of the SFVCN.

3. Marcel Monteran, *Monographie et Fabrication du Fromage de Camembert* (Paris: Veuve Lebroc, Maison Rustique, 1908), 38–40.

4. General Assembly of 13 February 1943, Archives of the SFVCN.

5. Governmental decree of 26 October 1953.

6. Antoine Blondin, *Rivarol* 1 (18 January 1951). This sarcastic quotation was passed on to me by Henry Rousso.

7. The Française Frisonne Pie Noir (French Fresian Black and White), a breed of dairy cattle, is the result of crossbreeding with stock from the Netherlands and is prevalent throughout Europe.

8. The manager of the Besnier factory at Domfront, *Ouest-France,* 26 August 1982.

9. Pierre Boisard and Marie-Thérèse Letablier, "Liens Locaux de Production et Standards Industriels—Le Cas du Camembert," in *Dossier de Recherche,* 15 (Paris: Centre d'Étude et de l'Emploi, 1986), 103.

10. *Revue de l'Industrie Agro-alimentaire* (1988): 28.

11. *Revue de l'Industrie Agro-alimentaire* 358 (2 December 1985): 46–47.

12. Boisard and Letablier, "Liens Locaux de Production et Standards Industriels," 107.

13. *Ouest-France,* 27 August 1982.

14. *Ouest-France,* 26 August 1982.

15. *Ouest-France,* 26 August 1982.

16. In 1992, Bongrain SA, a large corporation with many subsidiaries dealing with foodstuffs, signed a partnership with the ULN. The deal led to the creation of a partnership, the Compagnie Laitière Européenne.

17. Meeting of 23 May 1909, Archives of the SFVCN.

18. Meeting of 10 December 1910, Archives of the SFVCN.

19. Archives of the SFVCN.

20. *Journal des Halles et Marchés,* 18 August 1910.

21. Francis Marre, *Le Problème Juridique du Camembert* (Paris: Editions Scientifiques Françaises, 1914).

22. Marre, *Problème Juridique,* 5.

23. *Journal Officiel* (2 September 1983): 2699.

24. Ibid.

25. Among the many labels that invoke tradition and are perceived as being traditional, that of the cooperative dairy union in Isigny-Sainte-Mère stands out particularly. In addition to it, there are a few farm producers who produce a few dozen Camemberts per day, albeit unlabeled, for local markets.

26. The decree of 26 October 1953 specifies that Camembert is a soft-centered cheese produced by natural draining, with a unified curd and in the shape of a flat cylinder 10.5 to 11 centimeters (4 to 4.25 inches) in diameter, made solely of rennet-curdled cows' milk, lightly salted, having a surface mold, and with a minimum 40-percent fat content and a total dry content weight of not less than 110 grams (3.8 ounces). A new decree, with stricter specifications, is being investigated.

27. Philippe Jacob, *Les Grandes Heures des Laitiers en Normandie* (Luneray, France: Éditions Bertout, 1991).

28. V. LeFort, "Septieme Congrès de l'Industrie Laitière à Bayeux," *La Revue Illustrée du Calvados* 10 (1913): 142–47.

29. *La Voie Lactée* 202 (27 January 1986): 12.

30. *Revue Laitière Française* 478 (October 1978): 76.

31. Germain Mocquot, "Fromages d'Hier et d'Aujourd'hui," *Culture Technique* 16 (1986): 246–51.

32. This is the ideal, although no cheese factory still collects milk in cans; they all use tank trucks, and suppliers have been provided refrigerated tanks.

33. François Morel, "Camembert Pierre Lanquetot, une Réputation à Défendre," *La Technique Laitière* 998 (1985): 56–59.

34. Michel Waroquier, *Ouest-France,* 27 August 1982.

35. Michel Waroquier, former manager of the Carel cheese factory, is, to our knowledge, the only non-Norman producer of traditional Camembert. Hailing from the northern part of France, he does not hide the fact that he has had trouble gaining acceptance from his peers, even though he married a Norman woman who was the daughter of a cheese maker.

36. Today, most dairies delegate these essential approaches to suppliers to hired "cultural relations agents," who are technicians entrusted with advising the milk suppliers.

37. A retired cheese maker told us in an interview that suppliers preferred to sell their milk to her father-in-law, who owned a small cheese factory, rather than to Nestlé. "You know, in the country, as a general rule, and certainly in those days, we fairly loathed those people, those industrial wheeler-dealers."

38. Boisard and Letablier, "Liens Locaux de Production et Standards Industriels," 44.

39. Ibid.

40. Boisard and Letablier, "Liens Locaux de Production et Standards Industriels," 62.

41. Such is the case, for example, with the Pavé d'Affinois cheese produced by the Guilloteau cheese factory. However, this new cheese, despite its countrified name, is made according to a completely new process known as ultrafiltration.

CHAPTER 6. THE IMAGE OF CAMEMBERT

1. Bernard Primaux, "L'Institut National de la Propriété Industrielle et les Étiquettes de Fromages," *Bulletin du C.T.F.,* no. 96 (1987): 18.

2. Ibid., 12.

3. General Assembly of 31 July 1909, Archives of the SFVCN.

4. Jean-Pierre Lanares, *Le Bon Roy Camembert* (Paris: Éditions Bréa, 1982).

5. Jean Froc, Michel Vivier, and Marie-Noéle Vivier, *Un Siècle d'Activité Fromagère en Pays Augeron* (Saint-Pierre-sur-Dives, France:

Conservatoire des Techniques Fromagères Traditionnelles de Normandie, 1985), 13.

6. Primaux, "Étiquettes de Fromages," 14.

7. This was particularly true for the Malherbe print shop at Caen, Grange at Paris, Jombart at Lille, and Garnaud at Angoulême.

8. *Bulletin du C.T.F.,* no. 97 (1988).

9. Antoine Schiekevitch, *Enquête sur la Situation des Industries dans le Département du Calvados,* vol. 1 (Caen, France: Henri Delesques, 1918), 161.

10. Ibid.

11. United States Department of Agriculture, Bureau of Animal Industry, *Varieties of Cheese, Descriptions and Analyses,* by C. F. Doane and Herbert William Lawson (Washington: Government Printing Office, 1896).

12. United States Department of Agriculture, Bureau of Animal Industry, *The Cheese Industry of the State of New York,* by B. D. Gilbert (Washington: Government Printing Office, 1896).

13. This cheese takes its name from the Belgian province of Limbourg, where it originated. It is in the shape of a squared parallelepiped and is a soft cheese with a washed crust, brick-red in color. It can be compared to Maroilles (Pierre Androuet, *Guide du Fromage* [Paris: Stock, 1971], 364).

14. United States Department of Agriculture, Bureau of Animal Industry, *The Camembert Type of Soft Cheese in the USA,* by Herbert William Conn, Charles Thom, et al., bulletin no. 71 (Washington: Government Printing Office, 1905).

15. Ibid., 15.

16. Ibid.

17. United States Department of Agriculture, Bureau of Animal Industry, *Proteolytic Changes in the Ripening of Camembert Cheese,* by Arthur W. Dox, bulletin no. 109 (Washington: Government Printing Office, 1909).

18. United States Department of Agriculture, Bureau of Animal Industry, *Camembert Cheese Problems in the United States,* by Charles

Thom, bulletin no. 115 (Washington: Government Printing Office, 1909), 10.

19. Ibid.

20. United States Department of Agriculture, Bureau of Animal Industry, *The Digestibility of Cheese*, by C. F. Doane, circular no. 115 (Washington: Government Printing Office, 1911).

21. Labet, "État Économique Actuel de la Production Fromagère en France," *Industrie Laitière* 36 (1949): 149–55.

22. Gérard Roger, *Marie Harel, "Inventeur" du Fromage de Camembert, de la Légende à l'Histoire* (Vimoutiers, France: Société Historique de Vimoutiers, 1976), 11.

23. The name given the bacterium *Brevibacterium linens*, which is responsible for the reddish tinge of the crust.

24. Nicole Belmont, "L'Enfant et le Fromage," *L'Homme* 105, XXVIII (1) (January–March 1988): 13–28.

25. Léo Moulin, *Les Liturgies de la Table* (Paris: Albin-Michel, 1989), 313.

26. Piero Camporesi, *L'Officine des Sens: Une Anthologie Baroque* (Paris: Hachette, 1989). The first chapter, "Le Fromage Maudit" ("Accursed Cheese"), 7–37, is devoted to the repulsion cheese can exert.

CHAPTER 7. PERMANENCE OF THE MYTH

1. Poll taken by the Société Française d'Enquêtes par Sondage (*Cuisine et Vins de France*, 400 [September 1984]: 23).

2. Marlène Delesse, "Camembert. Des Marchés en Crise," *Revue Laitière Française* 471 (1988): 17–20.

3. *Le Crémier-Fromager* (November 1990): 6.

4. Victor-Eugène Ardouin-Dumazet, *Voyages en France*, 6th series (Paris: Berger-Levrault, 1894), 139–40.

Association Latière Français (French Dairy Association), 35

Association Normande, 35, 44, 45, 53, 158

Auge region: as AOC delimitation, 179–80; Brie method in, 7, 10; cattle grazing economy of, 39–40; cheese specialties of, 36, 37–38, 41; gender complementarity in, 46; location/topography of, 36–37; milk's status in, 82–83; rural decline of, 222

Augeron graziers, 39–40, 41–42, 46

automatic molding machine, 185, 187–90

automobile manufacturing, 20

bacteriophages, 169

Baker, Josephine, 200

banquets, 100, 138

Bard, Jean (Dr. Boulard), 27, 30

Barel-Lanos, Mme, 57

Beaumoncel farm (Camembert village), 4, 28; Harel's marriage at, 32; recusant priest at, 7, 33; research on residents of, 30–31

Béchet, Michel, 173

Bernières-d-'Ailly cheese factory, 122

Besnier, André, 172

Besnier, Michel, 172, 184

Besnier firm (Domfront), 122, 157, 158, 171; AOC label for, 186; cheese factory takeovers by, 173–74; label identity of, 172–73; ladle-molding method of, 189

Bienfaite cheese factory, 96

birth control ban, 19

Bisson, Désiré, 123

Bisson, Georges, 123, 218

Bisson cheese factory, 109, 123, 174

Blondel, M., 71–72

Blondin, Antoine, 165

Bois-d'Amont, 71

Boisseau, Bernard, 77

Boissey community, 52, 53

Bondes cheese, 41

Bondons cheese, 41, 80

Bonvoust, Charles-Jean, 33

Borden company (Van Wert, Ohio), 208–9, 210

Bosworth (a chemist), 205–6

Bosworth, M. (an architect), 208–9

Boulard, Dr. (pseud. Jean Bard), 27, 30

Bourdon, Abbé, 33

Bourdon cheese factory, 174

boutonnière (buttonhole test), 62

boxes: and cheese quality, 132; negatives of, 197; origins of, 70–72; Syndicate's regulation of, 97, 198

box factories, 72

Braud brothers, 89

Bray region, 36, 38, 41

Bréguet airplane, 21

Bridel firm, 114, 119, 120, 172, 174, 212

Brie cheese, 7, 10, 52, 77, 181, 205

broad mix milk, 168–69

Bulletin de Vieux Papier, 202

Buquet, Paul, 211

Buquet cheese factory, 174

Buquet-Serey dynasty, 126

Busnel, Geneviève, 134, 136, 146–47

Busnel cheese factory, 134, 146–47

buttonhole test (boutonnière), 62

Caen (Calvados region), 34

Calmesnil, M. de, 30

Calvados region: Camembert production in, 51–52, 114; first Camembert factory in, 34; lace-making industry of, 158–59; milk prices in, 97

Camembert cheese: advertising for, 90–92; and AOC label, 16–17, 88, 184–86, 236n26; aroma of, 214–16; bicentennial celebration of, 221; boxes for, 70–72, 97, 132, 197, 198; color of, 72–74, 79–81; consistency of, 213–14; consumption statistics on, 221–22; definition of, 57, 177–79, 186; delimitation problems of, 179–82, 183; diverse quality of, 223; as family product, 34–35, 117–18; fat content of, 88–89; Harel family's claims to, 54, 57; historical dating of, 26–28; Joseph Knirim on, 3; milk used for, 29, 65, 192; monument to inventor of, 1–2, 4–5, 17, 18; as national symbol, 6, 22–23, 135–36, 223–24; pasteurization of, 160–64, 165–66, 184; price of, 193–94; profitability of, 45; railroad's contribution to, 42–44, 50; rival producers of, 54–56, 57–59, 85–87; sales of (1886–1894), 52; sales of (1984–2000), 187 fig.; sexual/forbidden images of, 216–20; with Syndicate seal, 89–90, 183–84; traditional ideals of, 191–93, 194–95, 200, 237nn35–37; U.S. ban on, 203, 209–10; U.S. import of, 204–5; U.S. research on, 205–6; war's linkage to, 108, 112–13, 115; wartime label of, 101–2; wartime provision of, 103–7, 232n48. *See also* AOC Camembert; industrial Camembert

Camembert cheese production: climate effects on, 133, 206; curdling phase of, 61–62, 65–66; difficulties of, 53–54, 60–61; industrialized methods of, 170–72, 187–89; Norman innovations in, 67–68, 119, 121, 133–34, 150–51; outside of France, 176–77; packaging phase of, 132–33; of pasteurized product, 163–64, 165–66; rooms used for, 132; sexual imagery of, 216–18; traditional principles of, 191–93, 236n32, 237n35; tradition controversy of, 190–91; U.S. studies on, 205–6; women's role in, 46; working conditions during, 143. *See also* Norman cheese factories; Norman cheese makers

Camembert de la République label, 202

Camembert labels: appearance/style of, 201, 212; on Besnier Camembert, 172–73; with cheese maker's name, 87, 118; collections of, 202; during First World War, 101–2; on imitation Camembert, 57, 87; on Le Tremblay Camembert, 132–33; origins of, 196–98; with raw-milk distinction, 184–85; on second-quality products, 202; themes of, 199–201; on ULN Camembert, 175. See also *appellation d'origine contrôlée*

Camembert myth: color component of, 73–74; as historical-legendary mix, 13–14; of national consecration, 11–12; priest's role in, 8–10; railroad's role in, 42–43; scholarly investigation of, 26–27; summary of, 7; U.S. ties to, 203–4; Vimou-

43; wartime bidding proposal to, 110–11

Le Tremblay cheese factories: Camembert label of, 196–97; master cheese maker at, 142; memoir on, 233n7; milk collection at, 130, 131; packaging process at, 132–33; profits of, 134; steam innovations at, 133–34; unique status of, 124–25; working hours at, 145

Leveau, M., 71

L'Hoëst, Eugène, 23–24

Liercy-Lévy cheese factory, 56

Lille market (Flanders), 51

Limburger cheese, 205, 238n13

limestone *(fleurines)*, 178

Livarot cheese, 7, 14, 37, 181; Camembert yields versus, 50, 52; curdling of, 65; first use of name, 38; historical dating of, 27–28; milk used in, 29; traditional production of, 53

Lotichius, Johan Petrus, 219

Louïse, Émile, 77–78, 79

Louis XVIII, 41

Lutin cheese factory, 174

Maastricht Treaty, 224–25

Mackiewicz, François, 133, 138–39

Le Mait (journal), 151

Maroilles cheese, 65

Marre, Francis, 182

marriages, 125–26

Matignon Accords (1936), 145

Le Matin (newspaper), 105

Mazé, Pierre, 75, 77, 78, 122, 162, 182

Médaillon Camembert brand, 189

Méline, Jules, 129

Mesnil, Maurice, 77

milk: AOC 1983 rules on, 185; Camembert's type of, 29, 65; complex nature of, 161–62, 169–70; curdling of, 61–62, 65–66, 67–68; excremental image of, 219; fat content of, 88–89; fixed price on, 97; geographic origin of, 179, 192, 236n32; germ controversy over, 203, 209–10, 211, 224; industrial production of, 167–69, 235n7; pasteurization of, 160–62, 163–64, 184; profitable use of, 45; respected status of, 82–83; sexual images of, 216–18, 219; steam heating of, 133–34; testing of, at factory, 84, 142; thermalized, 189; U.S. experiments with, 207; wartime shortage of, 93, 106, 107, 110–12. *See also* dairy cows; dairy farmers; milk collection

Milk (journal), 151

milk collection: AOC 1983 rules for, 185; by Besnier firm, 173–74; at Calvados factories, 129–30; competitiveness of, 92–97; female process of, 216–17; hours of, 142; from local source, 179, 192, 236n32; transport methods of, 84, 131; trust component of, 82–83. *See also* dairy cows; dairy farmers; milk

milkmen (milk collectors), 142

Millerand, Alexandre, 1–2, 12, 22

Mocquot, Germain, 190

mold: color component of, 75–79; found in Normandy, 75; taste effects of, 79; U.S. research on, 207; and whiteness conversion, 80–81

molding process: in AOC 1983 decree, 185; automated method of,

molding process (continued)
187–89, 190; description of, 62–
63; pasteurization's impact on, 164,
165; types of molds for, 67; working conditions during, 143
Le Moniteur Universel (newspaper),
43–44
Monteran, Marcel, 162
Montier, Mme, 55
Morice, Marie-Louise, 34, 83–84,
129
Morière, Jules, 60, 66, 178; on cheese
income, 51–52; cheese industry
role of, 35, 44, 45; on Marie Harel,
32; on lace-making industry, 158–
59; on rennet, 67
Moulin de Carel cheese factory,
174
Munster cheese, 65

Napoleon I, 14, 200
Napoleon III: factual account of,
43–44; mythical encounter with,
4, 7, 10–11, 43; national consecra-
tion role of, 11–12
National Institute of Agronomy,
75
National Institute of Industrial Prop-
erties (Institut National de la
Propriété Industrielle), 197
Nestlé company, 96, 103
Neufchâtel cheese, 37, 41, 65
Neuville, Jean de, 129, 233n8
newspapers: advertising in, 92; on
monument to Harel, 18, 23; on
Napoleon III's visit, 43–44; Vig-
nioboul's interview in, 105
Nord département, 57
Norman cheese factories: building
layout of, 132; dairy farms linked

to, 130, 136–37; disaffected workers of, 146, 147–48; early locations
of, 51–52; family assistance programs of, 139–40; as family business, 117–18, 125–27, 137–38, 152,
155–56; hiring practices of, 98,
141–42; labels' depiction of, 200;
milk collection methods of, 84,
131, 142; nationalized product of,
112–13, 115; number of, in 1914,
233n6; outside competition with,
54–55, 57–58, 85–86, 87, 113–15,
177; packaging process at, 132–33;
Pasteur Institute's use of, 74–75;
pasteurization's impact on, 160–
61, 166, 174; as takeover candidates, 173–74; technological innovations in, 67–68, 119, 121, 133–34,
150–51; wartime label of, 101–2;
wartime labor shortages of, 102,
108–9; wartime provisioning by,
103, 104–7; whiteness conversion
in, 80–81; working conditions/
hours at, 143–45, 155. *See also*
cheese factory workers; Norman
cheese makers
Norman cheese makers: advertising
by, 90–92, 193; agricultural domain of, 149–50, 153–54; author's
conversations with, 148–49; commercial success of, 134–35, 148,
154; dairy farmer's bond with, 82–
83, 154, 192, 237nn36,37; delimitation proposal by, 179–82; employees' relations with, 98, 137–38,
140–41; on fat content, 88–89;
goodwill banquets of, 100; government's relations with, 99–100,
154–55; and Harel statue controversy, 209, 210; hygiene dilemma

of, 211, 224–25; industrialization rejected by, 156–58, 159; marital ties of, 126–27; in milk disputes, 92–97, 110, 111–12; native origins of, 192, 237n35; as new social category, 149; reputation's importance to, 87; Syndicate seal for, 89–90, 183–84; on U.S. Camembert, 208. *See also* Norman cheese factories; Syndicat des Fabricants du Véritable Camembert de Normandie

Normandy: Camembert's origins in, 16–17; Camembert Syndicate of, 59, 85–86; cheese-making regions of, 36; cheeses of, 37–38; Joseph Knirim's homage to, 4; mold in, 75; Napoleon III's visit to, 43–44; problematic delimitation of, 179–82, 183; transition to cheese making in, 44–46. *See also* Auge region

Nothdurft, Willi, 102–3

odor of Camembert, 214–16

L'Officine des Sens (*The Pharmacy of the Senses,* Camporesi), 219

Orbec, Madeleine d', 125

Orbec casein factory, 103

Orbiquet cheese factory, 119

Orne sector (the Auge), 51, 52, 97

packaging process: boxes used in, 70–72; of sorting/labeling, 132–33

Parent, Pierre, 33

Paris: beef cattle sales in, 39–40; cheese tarif plan of, 87; railroad access to, 11–12, 42–43. *See also* Les Halles

Paris-Granville railway line, 42–43

Pasteur, Louis, 74

Pasteur Institute, 74, 80; mold studies by, 75–79

pasteurization: Camembert's resistance to, 162–64; cheese-maker victims of, 166, 174; of Norman Camembert, 184; productivity impact of, 164, 165–66; purposes of, 161–62; standardization effects of, 160–61; universal threat of, 220, 222, 224–25; U.S. dependency on, 209–10, 211. *See also* industrial Camembert

Pavé d' Affinois cheese, 237n41

Paynel, Cyrille (Marie Harel's grandson), 32, 44, 60, 81; beef cattle of, 47; on bookkeeping records, 45; Camembert yields of, 52; cheese dairy of, 46–47, 48–50; on fertilization methods, 48; genealogy of, 34; on Lille market, 51; on middlemen, 50, 197; myth's perpetuation by, 35; production methods of, 62–64, 67

Paynel, Thomas (Marie Harel's son-in-law), 7, 34

Paynel, Victor (Marie Harel's grandson), 67; genealogy of, 34; Napoleon III's encounter with, 4, 7, 10–11, 43

peasantry. *See* countryside

Penicillium: album, 76–77, 78–80; *camemberti,* 79, 80, 207; *candidum,* 76, 77, 78–80, 81, 170, 207; *glaucum,* 79–80

Perrier, Charlotte (Marie Harel's stepmother), 31

Perrier, Jean, 31

Perrier, Sieur, 30

Pétain, Philippe, 200

United States (continued)
to, 204–5; industrialized production in, 206–8, 212; raw-milk ban in, 203, 209–10, 211; statue's restoration by, 208–9, 210

U.S. Food and Drug Administation, 209–10

Vallée cheese factory, 174
Veisseyre, Roger, 14
vendors, 64, 213–14
Viger, Albert, 144
Vignioboul, M. Paul, 93; on labor shortages, 108; on milk preparation, 61; on milk shortage, 110; on noncompetition, 94; on wartime provisioning, 105, 106, 107
La Villette meat market (Paris), 47
Villette meat market (Paris), 47
Vimoutiers (Normandy): Camembert museum at, 29; cheese market at, 29, 32; Harel's dedication at, 1–2, 18; myth's exploitation by,

15–16, 25, 31; priest lynching at, 33; reconstructed statue at, 208–9, 210

Viviani, René, 102

Waroquier, Henri, 190
Waroquier, Michel, 237n35
Western Tyrosemiophile Club (Club Tyrosémiophile de l'Ouest), 202
Wilhelm, Kaiser, 101
women: with cheese-making secrets, 56; cow milking by, 216–17; dairy products role of, 40, 46, 53; family dynasties of, 117–18, 119, 120–21; labels' depiction of, 199–200; in lace-making industry, 158–59; packaging duties of, 132–33; urban exodus of, 146; wartime labor role of, 102, 108–9
World War I. *See* First World War
World War II, 101, 164–65

Young, Arthur, 40

Compositor: G&S Typesetters, Inc.
Text: 11/14 Adobe Garamond
Display: Gill Sans Book
Printer and binder: Maple-Vail Manufacturing Group